Monday, Oct...

'Hamlet' and other Shake

'Hamlet' and other Shakespearean essays

L. C. KNIGHTS

CAMBRIDGE UNIVERSITY PRESS

Cambridge London Melbourne

Published by the Syndics of the Cambridge University Press
The Pitt Building, Trumpington Street, Cambridge CB2 1RP
Bentley House, 200 Euston Road, London NW1 2DB
296 Beaconsfield Parade, Middle Park, Melbourne 3206, Australia

This collection © L. C. Knights 1979
'An Approach to *Hamlet*' was first published by Chatto & Windus
(1960). 'Personality and Politics in Julius Caesar' was first pub-
lished in the Shakespeare Quatercentenary number of *Anglica*
(Japan). '*Timon of Athens*' was first published in *The Morality of
Art* ed. D. W. Jefferson (Routledge & Kegan Paul, 1969). 'The
Tempest' was first published in *Shakespeare's Last Plays* ed. Richard
Tobias (Ohio University Press, 1975). 'Shakespeare's Politics' was
first published in the *Proceedings of the British Academy*, vol. 43.
'The Thought of Shakespeare' was first published in *The Hidden
Harmony* (The Odyssey Press Inc., N.Y., 1966). 'Shakespeare's
Tragedies and the Question of Moral Judgment' was first pub-
lished in *Shenandoah: The Washington and Lee University Review*, XIX,
3, 1968. 'The Question of character in Shakespeare' was first
published in *More Talking of Shakespeare*, ed. John Garrett (Long-
man, 1959). 'Historical Scholarship and the Interpretation of
Shakespeare' was first published in the *Sewanee Review* 63 (Spring
1955). '*King Lear* as Metaphor' was first published in *Myth and
Symbol*, ed. Bernice Slote (Bison Books, University of Nebraska
Press, 1963). 'How Many Children Had Lady Macbeth' was first
published by Gordon Fraser: The Minority Press (Cambridge,
1933). '"Integration" in *The Winter's Tale*' and 'Shakespeare and
History' were first published in the *Sewanee Review* 84 (Fall 1976)
and 86 (Summer 1978): copyright 1976 and 1978 by the University
of the South; reprinted by permission of the editor.

First published 1979

Printed and bound in Great Britain
by W & J Mackay Limited, Chatham

ISBN 0 521 22784 4 hard covers
ISBN 0 521 29642 0 paperback

Contents

Preface

The republication of essays on Shakespeare, selected from work done over a period of forty-five years, is only justified to the extent that they can still prompt fresh understanding and enjoyment: they succeed or fail by that primary criterion of all literary criticism. They do not offer an approach to Shakespeare claiming any sort of primacy over a variety of other approaches. They do not, in fact, offer a systematic approach at all, nor anything that could be subsumed in a system. All the same, I should claim that behind all of them are certain beliefs, or critical attitudes, that I take this opportunity to make briefly explicit.

An idea that I keep coming back to in my own reading is that the continuing life of masterworks of the imagination is a continually changing life, for the life in question only exists in the quickened apprehension of different people in different times and circumstances: not a startlingly original idea, though it has not yet I think, had the recognition and clarification it deserves. What it means, among other things, is that the critic's job is to prompt his readers to see what, *for them*, is genuinely 'there': that is why he works, so far as possible, in terms of what can be pointed to as functions and aspects of a work's central drive, of—in Coleridgean terms—its living and life-producing 'idea'. Naturally he can only do this if he has something of his own to say; but he does his best to avoid what Martin Buber calls 'the gesture of interference'. The studies of individual plays included here (with the exception of the earliest of them all, on *Macbeth*, which has the dogmatism of a youthful convert, and is commented on in another essay) were conceived and carried out in this spirit.

In the second place, the imaginative vitality of great literature— even though, when engaged with it, we may be directly conscious only of that—is part of the whole life of the mind. So any genuinely responsive reading of Shakespeare, as of any other great author, necessarily—and perhaps indispensably—fertilizes other fields of thought, about history, social and political life, even about the nature of 'thought' and the way we make our personal affirmations. Some of the essays are directly concerned with these more general matters, which also find their way into the more circumscribed critical essays.

Each essay can be read as a single excursion into its subject. But I should like to think that some readers will make cross-references and connexions, both for the fuller development of a point made in passing and sometimes (since the essays were, after all, written over a considerable period of time) for correction and readjustment. Thus, 'Shakespeare and the Question of Moral Judgment' adds something to the conclusion of 'An Approach to *Hamlet*', though certainly without cancelling that conclusion; and in the essay on *The Tempest*, I relate specific—or 'practical'—criticism to the ways in which we reach out for meaning and significance. There is one essay, an attempt to define the limitations of the historical approach to Shakespeare, that calls out for development. Certain paragraphs offer a first shot at defining the problems covered by my phrase about the continually changing life of a work of art—at defining, say, what Mandelstam meant when, remarking that 'Dante's contemporaneity is inexhaustible, measureless and unending', he called the cantos of the *Divine Comedy* 'missiles for capturing the future'. Professor John Lawlor's critique of this essay (*Sewanee Review*, LXIV, 2, Spring, 1956) notably challenged and expanded my then conception of 'historical scholarship', without, I think, diminishing the importance of the point I have chosen to comment on here: it is a matter to which, in a different context, I hope to return.

All the essays started life as lectures. Most of them appeared in *Explorations* (1946), *Further Explorations* (1965) and *Explorations 3* (1976), all of which were published by Chatto & Windus, as was *An Approach to 'Hamlet'* (1960). I should like to acknowledge the help of publishers with whom my connexion goes back so far in easing the way of the present reprint. Two of the essays here, not previously collected, appeared in the *Sewanee Review*: '"Integration" in *The Winter's Tale*' (originally a lecture to the Scientific Section of the British Psychoanalytical Society) in the issue for Fall, 1976 (LXXXIV, 4), and 'Shakespeare and History' (originally a public lecture at the Queen's University, Belfast) in that for Summer, 1978 (LXXXVI, 2). I am deeply grateful to the University of the South, the publishers of this admirable journal, and to its Editor,

Professor George Core, for permission to reprint. I also owe a special debt to my editor at the Cambridge University Press, Miss Diane Speakman.

Finally, I apologize for a small amount of repetition (as distinct from cross-reference) that it was impossible to eliminate.

L.C.K.

Cambridge, 1978

PREFACE

...

I

An Approach to *Hamlet*

*H*AMLET is, I suppose, that play of Shakespeare's about which there is most disagreement. There is no need for me to remind you of the bewildering variety of different things that have been said both about the Prince of Denmark and his play; it is enough to remark that more has been written about *Hamlet* than about any other of Shakespeare's plays, and that if, in the twentieth century, *Hamlet* has yielded to *King Lear* the distinction of being the play in which the age most finds itself, there is still no lack of widely differing interpretations of the former piece. Indeed I once decided that if ever I should write or talk about *Hamlet* at any length—a task that I have shirked up to now—I should use as my title 'Through the Looking-Glass', so clear is it that, more than with any other play, critics are in danger of finding reflected what they bring with them to the task of interpretation, so difficult is it, once you are in the play, to be sure of the right direction. And it is not many months since a writer in the *Listener* remarked that 'every fresh critic who sets out to define the intentions of the author of *Hamlet* ends up in his own particular dead-end in queer street'. So the hazards are, it seems, considerable.

Let me, therefore, call attention to my title, which is not 'An Interpretation of *Hamlet*' but 'An Approach to *Hamlet*'. Interpretation is of course involved; but

what I want to emphasize is, first, that the interpretation is tentative—a kind of thinking aloud which I
hope will be found useful by other people; and,
secondly, that I propose to set the play in relation to
other plays of Shakespeare, to try to see it in a particular perspective, rather than to attempt a detailed
commentary.

Hamlet belongs to the year 1600 or to the early
months of 1601. It thus comes near the beginning of a
period when Shakespeare was much concerned with
the relationship between the mind, the whole reflective
personality, and the world with which it engages.
Particularly he seems to have been preoccupied with
distortions in men's way of looking at the world; and
the plays in which this preoccupation is active raise,
in various ways, the problem of the relation of 'knowledge' to the knower, to what a man is, to the true or
distorted imagination. What I wish to do in this first
lecture is to bring some of these plays together, not in
strict chronological order, nor indeed in any strictly
systematic way, but simply to elicit what—for all their
difference—they have in common, and to see if their
linked preoccupations may not form a context for the
play towards which, in the remaining three lectures,
our attention will be mainly directed.

There is no need for me to tell you that Shakespeare,
from time to time, showed a very considerable preoccupation with man's subjection to illusion, 'the
seeming truth which cunning times put on To entrap
the wisest' (*M. of V*. III. ii. 100-101); it was a preoccupation that noticeably deepened in the period
immediately preceding the great tragedies. Now the

question posed by the undoubted power of illusion branches in two directions, towards the deceiver, and towards the deceived. Shakespeare, like many another writer, was certainly interested in the deceiver, especially the one who does not merely assume a deliberate disguise, like Iago, but is false in subtler ways, like Cressida, or deceives himself as well as others, like Angelo—of whom the Duke said, 'Hence shall we see, If power change purpose, what our seemers be'. But his main interest seems to have centred on the deceived, and a question that he asks with some insistence is how men come to make false or distorted judgments about other persons or about the world at large—what it is in their own natures that makes them capable of being deceived. This preoccupation seems to be present in two of the middle comedies. At all events, in *Much Ado about Nothing* (1598) the credence given to the slanderer may well be intended, as Mr. James Smith has suggested, to precipitate a judgment on the society represented by Claudio and Don Pedro (*Scrutiny*, XIII, 4, 1946). And I would tentatively suggest that *All's Well that Ends Well*—that unsatisfactory play (1602-3)—only makes sense when it is seen as a kind of morality play in which Bertram is for long unable to recognize his true good in Helena.

Both *Troilus and Cressida* (c. 1602) and *Othello* (1603) pursue the problem at a much deeper level. *Troilus and Cressida* is far too complex a play to be dealt with briefly, and here a few words must suffice. I have tried to show elsewhere[1] how both Greeks and Trojans are presented as subjected to time and appearance—the Greeks, because they stand for public life and an impersonal 'reason', divorced from feeling and intuitive intelligence; the Trojans, their complementary opposites, because their way of life is based on a passionate and wilful assertion of the untutored self. The play, as I said, is complex. For our present purposes it is enough to note how Shakespeare presents Troilus, not simply as the victim of Cressida's unfaithfulness but as, to some extent, self-deceived. The way in which he meets experience is both presented and, I think, criticized in the poetry that is given him to speak—the poetry through which his attitude to life is defined. Of this, Mr D. A. Traversi, in an essay published twenty years ago (*Scrutiny*, VII, 3, 1938) gave a classic account. In the imagery of the love poetry, there is, he says, 'a poignant thinness', which conveys simultaneously 'an impression of intense feeling and an underlying lack of content'. Of a characteristic passage he remarked: 'The emotions are intense enough, but only in the palate and the senses; they scarcely involve any full personality in the speaker'. And Traversi further pointed out that the expression of Troilus's 'idealism' through the imagery of taste underlines its unsubstantiality and its subjection to time. It is, we may say, the over-active element of subjective fantasy in Troilus's passion that gives to his love poetry its hurried, fevered note, with a suggestion of trying to realize something essentially unrealizable; it is his intense subjectivism that commits him to a world of time and appearance. At the risk of

[1] In *Some Shakespearean Themes*, Chapter IV.

4

drawing an over-simple moral from a complicated play, I would put the matter thus: if both Troilus and the Greeks are shown as 'fools of time', this is not because there is something hostile to men's hopes and aspirations in the very nature of things, so that 'checks and disasters' necessarily 'grow in the veins of actions highest reared'; it is because of some failure at deep levels of the personality, which can be called indifferently a failure of reason or of the imagination. If this is right it marks an interesting connexion with *Othello*, where attention centres on those elements in Othello's mind and feelings, his attitudes towards himself, that make him so vulnerable to Iago.

On *Othello* there are two brilliant essays—one by Wilson Knight, in *The Wheel of Fire*, and one by F. R. Leavis, in *The Common Pursuit*; to both of them I am very much indebted, and I wish to mention them before going on to suggest how the play develops the theme—the relationship between self and world—that is our present concern.

Othello, we may say, defines the peculiar weakness and vulnerability—the capacity for being deceived—of a particular attitude to life. That attitude is defined and made present to our imaginations through a mode of speech. Othello's character is given us not only by what he says but by the way he says it, within the accepted conventions of poetic drama,[1] and I must ask

---

[1] This is an obvious instance of what Mr Arthur Sewell, in his most helpful book, *Character and Society in Shakespeare*, calls 'the distillation of personality into style'.

you to call that style to mind before I go on to make the observation that will link this play with those others with which I wish to associate it. Almost any of Othello's utterances when he is truly himself will serve. Take for example his reply to Iago's excited account of how Brabantio is incensed against him:

> Let him do his spite:
> My services, which I have done the signiory,
> Shall out-tongue his complaints. 'Tis yet to know—
> Which, when I know that boasting is an honour,
> I shall promulgate—I fetch my life and being
> From men of royal siege, and my demerits
> May speak unbonneted to as proud a fortune
> As this that I have reached.

Consciousness of worth is expressed in every line, not only in explicit statement but in tone and movement; and the lofty tone is emphasized by phrases that are the opposite of common or idiomatic. A moment later we have,

> But that I love the gentle Desdemona,
> I would not my unhoused free condition
> Put into circumscription and confine
> For the sea's worth . . .

—where there is suggested for the first time Othello's nostalgic feeling for the life of action, 'the pride, pomp, and circumstance of glorious war'. Our impression is made up of a sense of calm and assured dignity, of something a little exotic, and of Othello's conscious-ness of worth—'My parts, my title and my perfect [fully prepared] soul'.

6

This is the Othello whom we see in the next scene, when, with grave deliberation, he makes his defence against Brabantio before the Venetian Senate:

> Most potent, grave, and reverend signiors,
> My very noble and approved good masters. . . .

How different this is, in tone and manner, from the quick, nervous phrasing of Macbeth! Of course Othello goes on to tell us something about himself which would be important however he told it: he has been a soldier all his life,

> And little of this great world can I speak,
> More than pertains to feats of broil and battle . . .

but the manner is equally important. 'Pertains' brings out the unidiomatic quality; the phrasing is 'monumental'. At the same time there is a suggestion of poetry in the way Othello sees himself:

> For since these arms of mine had seven years pith,
> Till now some nine moons wasted, they have used
> Their dearest action in the tented field.

A romantic glamour is thrown over the kind of life Othello has lived, and over himself as someone eminently suited to lead that kind of life. The romantic note is developed when he goes on to tell of his wooing:

> Wherein I spake of most disastrous chances,
> Of moving accidents by flood and field,
> Of hair-breadth scapes i' the imminent deadly breach,
> Of being taken by the insolent foe,
> And sold to slavery, of my redemption thence,
> And portance in my travel's history . . .

7

'Imminent', 'redemption', 'portance'—all have a latinized or foreign flavour, just as the Cannibals—the Anthropophagi—who come in a moment later, are obviously exotic. And with this goes an unconscious egotism:

> She loved me for the dangers I had pass'd,
> And I loved her that she did pity them.

It is also important to realize that what Wilson Knight calls 'the Othello music', the Othello idiom, is one that does not engage very closely with actuality. Value is insistently attributed to what is remote, or to that world of simplified action where Othello was, so to speak, at home—the world so far removed from that Cyprus where he is called on to meet the new experience of getting to know the wife who loved him.

Now it is precisely this Othello who succumbs—and succumbs so promptly—to Iago in the temptation scene. This is in essentials the point that Leavis makes so well in the essay to which I have referred. The speed with which Iago successfully develops his attack Leavis explains in terms of something self-centred and self-regarding in Othello's love—something that prevents him from seeing Desdemona fully as a complete person. What Iago can exploit is not only Othello's romantic naïvety, his ignorance of all but the world of external affairs, but Othello's consciousness of his own worth—'I would not have your free and noble nature Out of self bounty be abused'. On the tremendous and awful vow that Othello makes when he finally commits himself to revenge—

8

> Like to the Pontic sea,
> Whose icy current and compulsive course
> Ne'er feels retiring ebb . . .
> Even so my bloody thoughts, with violent pace,
> Shall ne'er look back . . .

Leavis comments: 'At this climax of the play, as he sets himself irrevocably in his vindictive resolution, he reassumes formally his heroic self-dramatization—reassumes the Othello of "the big wars that make ambition virtue". The part of this conscious nobility, this noble egotism, this self-pride that was justified by experience irrelevant to the present trials and stresses, is thus underlined. Othello's self-idealization, his promptness to jealousy and his blindness are shown in their essential relation.'

It is for reasons such as these that Othello is vulnerable to Iago—that Iago who is so much less than a fully drawn 'character' whose motives we are invited to examine, and so much more than a mere 'necessary piece of dramatic mechanism'. What we have to notice here is that Iago's mode of speech is at the opposite pole from Othello's. It is idiomatic, whereas Othello's is rhetorical; it is realistic, drawing readily on the commonplace and everyday, whereas Othello's is exotic; and it conveys a persistent animus.[1] Iago's vocabulary, his idiom, imagery and allusions, come from a world in which the common is the commonplace: cumulatively, the suggestion is of a world not only without glamour but without ideals, the world of conventional jokes about women—'to make fools laugh i' the alehouse',

[1] Leavis speaks of Iago's 'deflating, unbeglamouring, brutally realistic mode of speech'.

as Desdemona says. There is of course nothing wrong with common idiom as such. The point is that Iago uses it to deflate: there is almost invariably animus either against the object to which he applies his comparisons, or against the subject from which his comparisons and references are drawn. Iago's world is one in which things and people are manipulated, a world completely without values; and his manner of speech gives expression to a view of life that attributes reality to nothing but the senses and the will: 'Virtue! a fig! 'tis in ourselves that we are thus or thus.' Taking notice of these things we may say with Wilson Knight that Iago is 'the spirit of denial, wholly negative', adding also that it is precisely this coarse, reductive cynicism against which an egocentric romanticism is so defenceless. Iago, as Maud Bodkin says, is 'the shadow-side of Othello'.[1] What the play gives in the temptation scene and later is something like possession —possession by foul imaginings. This too is reflected in Othello's language when it becomes as coarse and brutal as Iago's.

Let me now draw these reflections to a point where they may be seen to fit into the general argument. Grace Stuart, in her book *Narcissus: a Psychological Study of Self-Love*, speaks of Othello as a Narcissist who tries to make of the woman with whom he fell in love a mirror for his idealized self, or for those qualities in himself that he found most acceptable, and it is clear that it is, fundamentally, a failure to love that makes the tragedy. But besides this, the moral centre of the play, there is what may be called the metaphysical

[1] *Archetypal Patterns of Poetry*, Chapter V.

centre, and although the two are inseparable they may be distinguished. At the height of his perplexity Othello twice refers to Iago's ability to know:

> This honest creature doubtless
> Sees and knows more, much more, than he unfolds.

> This fellow's of exceeding honesty,
> And knows all qualities, with a learned spirit,
> Of human dealings . . .

The question at the heart of the play is, in the moral world, the world of human relationships, what can we know? The answer is, we know only what our habitual categories and modes of thought—formed by our whole disposition—allow us to know. Iago (witness his idiom and habitual turn of phrase) lives in the world of the knowing wink: his categories are reductive ('nothing but'). Now there are aspects of the world that these categories, to some extent, fit: some women are as Iago describes them, and Roderigo is a fool—though even here his animus and perverse satisfaction in seeing the worst severely limit his knowledge. Where the categories are worse than useless Iago can only know a travesty: 'The Moor is of a free and open nature. . . . And will as tenderly be led by the nose as asses are': that is all Iago knows about an open nature. But Othello's categories, also, are not framed to give him true knowledge about human life. His romantic self-dramatization leaves him at the mercy of the 'knowing' man, or of that demon of cynicism that masks itself as disillusioned knowledge. To know it is necessary to love—to love with that outgoing generosity of spirit for which this play constantly finds the word 'free'. Othello 'is of a free and open nature'; that is, he has the potentiality of freedom; but, as the play shows him, he is not fundamentally free, and the tragedy traces his deepening entanglement in illusion. What Othello represents—and this is where the play comes home to each one of us—is a particularly exalted conception of the self, a picture of 'me' as 'I' should like to appear— and as to some extent I may appear—but which, because it *is* a picture, is necessarily static, a fixed posture. This posture, moreover, is the opposite to a ready responsiveness to life as it comes to meet me: it is self-dramatizing and self-regarding, and to that extent it is a barrier against the knowledge that would bring freedom.

We can now go on to a final consideration. In the plays we have just glanced at the wrong judgments are completely wrong. In *Julius Caesar* (1599), which came shortly before *Hamlet*, and in *Timon of Athens*, which I think (though there is much scholarly opinion against me) came shortly before *King Lear*, the interest shifts to the distorting intrusion of subjective elements, even when the facts of the case as presented are such as go a long way to justify Brutus's or Timon's view of the world.

Since time is not unlimited, and since I want to keep the main lines of my argument clear, I shall say little about *Julius Caesar*. There are, I think, three main points to be made. (i) The political situation—the situation created by Caesar's rise to power—is complex; and although there is clearly some truth in the unfavourable view of Caesar, the situation as a whole does not allow of a simple judgment. (ii) Brutus does so simplify: he concentrates on a selection of the facts before him in the interests of an abstract view of 'the general good':

> It must be by his death: and for my part,
> I know no personal cause to spurn at him,
> But for the general . . .

(iii) In this way Brutus does not only involve himself in a web of specious argument (as in the soliloquy from which I have just quoted), he constructs an unreal world: and because this world—the world where his decisions are formed—does not correspond with the real world—the world where acts have necessary consequences—his actions are disastrous. In other words, Brutus deceives himself because, like other characters in this play, he tries to make the public world, the political world, completely independent of the world of living men known in direct personal relationships. There is no time to develop this, but I think there is no doubt at all that the play consistently emphasizes both the 'public'/'private' contrast that I have just mentioned, and the lack of correspondence between Brutus's imaginings and the reality.

> O! that we then could come by Caesar's spirit,
> And not dismember Caesar. But, alas!
> Caesar must bleed for it. And, gentle friends,
> Let's kill him boldly, but not wrathfully;
> Let's carve him as a dish fit for the gods,
> Not hew him as a carcass fit for hounds.

That is not how political murders are carried out, as the play takes care to remind us later:

>   . . . when your vile daggers
> Hack'd one another in the sides of Caesar:
> You show'd your teeth like apes, and fawn'd like
>   hounds . . .
> Whilst damned Casca, like a cur behind,
> Struck Caesar on the neck.

The incongruity between intention and effect is ironically underlined in the excited proclamation after the murder—

> And, waving our red weapons o'er our heads,
> Let's all cry 'Peace, freedom, and liberty!'

—for the upshot of course is neither peace nor republican liberty, and the whole play may be taken as a comment on the words of Cicero,

> But men may construe things after their fashion,
> Clean from the purpose of the things themselves.

Julius Caesar, in short, is not a play where we are required to take sides for or against Caesar; it is a powerful study of one of the sources of illusion in public life; particularly it is a study of the distortion of a complex actuality by an abstracting, simplifying habit of mind, working in the interests, not of life, but of 'reasons of state'.

Timon of Athens is a play of many problems, and the one towards which I want to direct your attention in such time as remains is the largest of them, for it concerns the nature of Timon's misanthropy. Put simply, it is that the speeches of disgust and vituperation addressed to mankind at large are extraordinarily powerful, yet at the same time distorted and excessive, and the problem is to know how we are to take them. It does not seem to me adequate to regard them as expressing the disillusioned revulsion of a noble nature. Nor, with the superb artistic control of *King Lear* in mind, does it seem profitable to consider the view, once popular, that Shakespeare is here indulging a merely personal, unbalanced rage. When, betrayed by his false friends, Timon has turned his back on Athens, why does his denunciation take the particular form it does? More especially, why is his first long soliloquy, after the mock banquet, 'without the walls of Athens' (IV. i), so full of sexual nausea, for which nothing so far in the play has prepared us?

> Let me look back upon thee. O thou wall,
> That girdest in those wolves, dive in the earth,
> And fence not Athens! Matrons turn incontinent!
> Obedience fail in children! Slaves and fools,
> Pluck the grave wrinkled senate from the bench,
> And minister in their steads! To general filths
> Convert, o' the instant, green virginity!
> Do't in your parents' eyes! Bankrupts, hold fast;
> Rather than render back, out with your knives,
> And cut your trusters' throats! Bound servants,
>   steal!
> Large-handed robbers your grave masters are,
> And pill by law. Maid, to thy master's bed!
> Thy mistress is o' the brothel. Son of sixteen,

> Pluck the lined crutch from thy old limping sire,
> With it beat out his brains! Piety, and fear,
> Religion to the gods, peace, justice, truth,
> Domestic awe, night-rest, and neighbourhood,
> Instruction, manners, mysteries, and trades,
> Degrees, observances, customs, and laws,
> Decline to your confounding contraries,
> And yet confusion live!

Now it is true that Timon has reason to be bitterly disillusioned and angry; the Senate is usuring—so we have been led to suppose—the Lords of Athens are monsters of meanness, 'friendship' and 'society' have been found false. But what are matrons, maids, and sons doing here? and why are they exhorted to drown themselves in an anarchy compounded of incontinence and impiety? It can of course be said that for Timon, as for others, once 'the bonds of heaven' are 'loos'd' in any particular instance there seems nothing to prevent a general dissolution of all 'sanctimonies' (the concluding lines of my quotation seem to justify this use of the terminology of *Troilus and Cressida*). In fact, however, the play has shown nothing to justify this wholesale indictment, resting as it does on the assumption of general evil, and making more of 'lust and liberty', with their accompanying diseases, than of the betrayal of friendship, which we have in fact observed.

For an explanation we have to wait until Timon's next outburst in IV, iii.[1] This scene—'Enter Timon from the cave'—opens with a superb indictment that,

[1] The intervening scene is given to the loyal Steward, Flavius, and the servants, and its general effect is to restore Timon to a more favourable light ('so noble a master,' 'kind lord'), whilst still leaving us with a question about his 'goodness' and 'bounty'.

unlike the previous soliloquy, has the whole force of the play, of what has been demonstrated in the play, behind it, the first seventeen lines being concerned almost exclusively with the difference that mere material goods can make to a man's standing.

> Who dares, who dares,
> In purity of manhood stand upright,
> And say, 'This man's a flatterer'? if one be,
> So are they all; for every grise of fortune
> Is smooth'd by that below: the learned pate
> Ducks to the golden fool . . .

Then, before the theme of money's power is taken up again, comes once more the comprehensive misanthropy:

> all is oblique;
> There's nothing level in our cursed natures
> But direct villany. Therefore, be abhorr'd
> All feasts, societies, and throngs of men!
> His semblable, yea, himself, Timon disdains:
> Destruction fang mankind!

'His semblable, yea, himself, Timon disdains.' This, it seems to me, forms the climax of the play, casting a retrospective light over the opening scenes, where Timon was shown at the height of his fortunes. If there had been any doubt of how we should take them (and there shouldn't, really, have been any), none remains. The purpose of Timon's so much emphasized 'bounty' was to buy a flattering picture of himself. 'You see, my lord, how ample you're beloved'—remarks such as this are the 'sacrificial whisperings' rained in his ear. And the stage directions confirm the impression of an

inordinate thirst for approval: Timon's first approach
is heralded with 'trumpets'; at the 'great banquet'
with 'loud music' of the play's second scene, 'they all
stand ceremoniously looking on Timon'[1]; and during
the masque, 'the Lords rise from table, with much
adoring of Timon'. There is indeed, as Apemantus
remarks, much 'serving of becks and jutting-out of
bums'. And it is not only Apemantus, the professional
cynic, who reveals these feasts as 'pomps and vain-
glories', nor a mere Senator who sees them as 'raging
waste'. To the trustworthy Flavius it is a 'flow of riot',

> When all our offices have been oppress'd
> With riotous feeders, when our vaults have wept
> With drunken spilth of wine, when every room
> Hath blaz'd with lights and bray'd with minstrelsy.

When, again in Flavius' words, 'the means are gone
that buy this praise', the flattering picture—like the
one the painter brought for sale—is gone too. Morally,
as well as materially, there is nothing that Timon can
take from Athens,

> —Nothing I'll bear from thee
> But nakedness, thou detestable town!

—indeed a datum of the play is that *this* society has
nothing to offer.[2] It is as completely unaccommodated
man that Timon is forced to look within, and, finding
himself hateful ('yea, himself, Timon disdains'), what
he finds within he projects onto the world at large.

---

[1] This stage direction was, I find, added by Johnson; but the
action seems to be indicated by the text.

[2] See J. C. Maxwell's Introduction to the New Cambridge edition
of the play.

Hence the sweeping and inclusive disgust of the first soliloquy outside the walls of Athens. The attempt to buy assurance has failed, and the instinctive movement is flight, from the self as much as from society, leading inevitably to death. Apemantus, for all his exaggerated cynicism, is allowed to say some true things, and we feel that in his exchanges with Timon in IV, iii he makes a 'placing' comment: 'The middle of humanity thou never knewest, but the extremity of both ends. . . . An thou hadst hated meddlers sooner, thou should'st have loved thyself better now'. Timon has taken on the Apemantus role—indeed, as has been said, 'Apemantus is what Timon becomes'[1]—and the first thing we are told about Apemantus is that he is one 'that few things loves better Than to abhor himself'.

The question that we find ourselves pondering, therefore, as we read this play, is—In what ways is a statement, true in itself, like Timon's account of his false friends, vitiated by a failure of integrity in the person making it? In other words, the question concerning the validity of Timon's judgment of society is subordinate to the question—How did Timon come to feel like this? How does a man reach such extremes of hatred and rejection? And the conclusion to which the play leads us is that although Timon, in his denunciation of Athens, of mankind, may say some true

[1] 'Apemantus is what Timon becomes. . . . Even in the first three acts, though Apemantus and Timon are opposites, they are oddly drawn towards each other, as if they found a peculiar importance in each other's company. . . . They are, as it were, two aspects of a single self, the extremes between which the personality of a human being can alternate.' Geoffrey Bush, *Shakespeare and the Natural Condition*, p. 62.

things, he speaks from an attitude that is itself flawed. Since the purpose of his bounty seems to have been, at least in part, to purchase a flattering picture of himself, the misanthropy that results when the picture is destroyed is in effect a violent expression of self-dislike; and this is true even though the world of the play presents plenty of matter for denunciation.[1]

Similar considerations are, I believe, relevant to *Hamlet*. For the world with which Hamlet has to deal is indeed evil, and the play shows convincingly what may be called the logic of corruption; but the emotions and attitudes that Hamlet brings to bear when he confronts that world are themselves the subject of a radical questioning.

[1] After completing this section I found some support for my view of *Timon* in an interesting essay by Andor Gomme, in *Essays in Criticism*, IX, 2, April 1959.

I WISH to start this lecture by drawing your attention to Professor H. D. F. Kitto's *Form and Meaning in Drama*. It would be almost an impertinence for me to praise it, but I may say that even for a Greekless reader it is a fascinating experience to see how a scholar who is also a critic sets about his task of eliciting the moral centre and the unifying pattern of plays by Aeschylus and Sophocles. Now in this book Professor Kitto has a long chapter on *Hamlet* that can be read with profit by any student of Shakespeare, and I want to use that chapter—both by way of agreement and of disagreement—as a means of introducing my own reflections on the play.

The great Greek tragedies, Professor Kitto insists, are 'religious drama'—'a form of drama in which the real focus is not the Tragic Hero', as conceived for example by Aristotle, 'but the divine background' (p. 231). Our attention is certainly demanded for the figures on the stage, but it does not stop there; it goes beyond them to a philosophic conception of the general laws that govern human life, and it is these laws that, with varying degrees of naturalism or of departure from it, the action is designed to demonstrate. We do not say of the characters, How life-like they are! We say, Yes this is indeed the way things happen in the moral world. Now Hamlet also is 'religious drama', of which the artistic unity is lost 'if we try to make the Tragic Hero the focus' (pp. 244-5). The theme is evil, its contagion, and its inevitable self-destruction—'evil breeding evil, and leading to ruin' (p. 324). In the final scene 'we are made to feel that Providence is working in the events; an eternal Law is being exemplified: "There is a special providence in the fall of a sparrow." . . . What is taking place is something like the working-out of Dikê'—or Law (p. 327). As for Hamlet himself, what paralyses him is an overwhelming sense of evil not only in Claudius or his mother but in almost the whole world constituted by the court of Denmark: his is 'a real paralysing despair in the face of a life that has suddenly lost its meaning' (p. 290). Weeds—the 'things rank and gross' in Denmark's unweeded garden—

> weeds can choke flowers. These weeds have choked Ophelia, and at last they choke Hamlet, because he could not do the coarse work of eradicating them. First, his comprehensive awareness of evil, reversing every habit of his mind, left him prostrate in anguish and apathy; then, the desire for vengeance being aroused, he missed everything by trying to encompass too much; finally, pursuing honour when it was nearly too late, he found it, but only in his own death. So finely poised, so brittle a nature as Hamlet's, is especially vulnerable to the destructive power of evil (pp. 327-8).

Now I feel sure that Professor Kitto is right about the nature of Hamlet's paralysis; but I also think that his development of the idea of the 'contagion' (p. 337) suffered by Hamlet is not a full or adequate answer to the questions raised by the play. Is it enough to say that Hamlet 'feels himself being inexorably dragged down . . . to actions which, being free, he would condemn'—such as the murder of Rosencrantz and Guildenstern? (p. 320). Is it enough to say that 'Hamlet's "madness" was but the reflection of the evil with which he found himself surrounded, of which Claudius was the most prolific source' (p. 327)? Can we in short sum up the play as Kitto does towards the end of his essay?

> In *Hamlet*, Shakespeare draws a complete character, not for the comparatively barren purpose of 'creating' a Hamlet for our admiration, but in order to show how he, like the others, is inevitably engulfed by the evil that has been set in motion, and how he himself becomes the cause of further ruin. The conception which unites these eight persons in one coherent catastrophe may be said to be this: evil, once started on its course, will so work as to attack and overthrow impartially the good and bad; and if the dramatist makes us feel, as he does, that a Providence is ordinant in all this, that, as with the Greeks, in his way of universalizing the particular event. (p. 330).

I think this is, at best, a partial summing-up; and I also think that there is some confusion that we should try to dissipate. Evil of course can 'overthrow' the good as well as the bad, in the sense that it can torture and kill them. But to the extent that they are 'engulfed' by it, as Hamlet is said to be engulfed —and this, in context, refers not to his happiness but to his nature—to that extent they deviate from good-ness. Kitto tells us that 'in Denmark, Hamlet's fineness must necessarily suffer corruption' (p. 320). But why? I cannot feel that 'contagion' is an adequate answer. What I do feel is that the play prompts us to look much more closely at the attitudes with which Hamlet confronts his world and the gross evil in that world.

Now I want to insist that I admire Kitto's essay very much. It is, to say the least, a fine example of a salutary tendency of recent criticism to see Shakespeare's tragedies as imaginative wholes rather than as dramatic constructions designed to exhibit 'character', however fascinating. And what gives the essay its value is not only the acuteness of its specific analysis but its concern with those moral and religious issues to which the presentation of 'character' is strictly subordinate. But if Shakespearean tragedy is 'religious drama' (for we can apply this term to other plays besides *Hamlet*) in so far as it is concerned not simply to draw the portrait of an outstanding individual but to focus the fundamental laws of human life, it is, I think, religious in a different way from that defined in Kitto's account of Greek tragedy. This, we are told, shows the working out of inexorable laws. And so indeed does *Hamlet*—but with this difference: we are required not only to *watch* the august working out of the law which the dramatist's understanding of spiritual and psychological truth enables him to put before us; we are required to enter imaginatively into the spiritual and psychological states with which the given experience is confronted. And this additional dimension—the dimension of inwardness—forces us to be something other than

24

spectators. Kitto writes, 'we may say that both in the Greek trilogy (the *Oresteia*) and in Shakespeare's play the Tragic Hero, ultimately, is humanity itself; and what humanity is suffering from, in *Hamlet*, is not a specific evil, but Evil itself' (p. 335). Yes, in *Hamlet* the preoccupation *is* with Evil itself, but this is presented with a greater immediacy than Kitto's account, taken as a whole, suggests. And when we attend to this—the full imaginative effect—there is a timbre or quality that perplexes us. Our perplexities centre on Hamlet, and when we attend to them we find that Shakespeare is not simply presenting the working out of Law, Dikê, he is also—I think—questioning the perceiver.

And now, before coming directly to the play, I wonder if I may take one more bearing on it with the help of a book of a very different kind—the *De Consolatione Philosophiae* of Boethius, who, in Dante's words, unmasks the deceitful world (*il mondo fallace*) to whoso gives him good hearing, and whose thought had such profound influence throughout the Middle Ages and beyond. The *Consolation*, written in prison when Boethius was awaiting death (524 A.D.), was one of the main transmitters of pagan philosophy to the middle ages—it was translated into English by, among others, King Alfred and Chaucer—and in it may be found some of the seminal ideas of medieval thought, such as the naturalness of good, goodness as being, evil as mere negation, evil as a perverted and unnatural attempt to achieve the happiness that all men desire; for Boethius as for so many after him, ignorance and passion are the causes of wrong choice, and vice is 'a sickness of the mind'. The book is not—as, knowing the circumstances of its composition, one might perhaps expect—a plea for stoic endurance; it is a sustained and varied demonstration of how a man may find and preserve his essential nature under the impact of great adversity and great perturbation. At the heart of it is the perception that man's essential nature cannot be satisfied by anything less than that goodness which is the desired health of the soul: being, the blessedness of virtue, and happiness are one and the same.

Now all this is nobly argued and, as I said, the book had an enormous influence in the Middle Ages and beyond. It was certainly well known in Shakespeare's day; Queen Elizabeth I translated it, and the current Loeb edition is substantially based on the translation of one, I. T., which first appeared in 1609. Whether Shakespeare did in fact read it I do not know, for although there are many passages and phrases in the *Consolation* which at once call to mind passages and phrases in Shakespeare's works—mainly, as it happens, in *Hamlet* but also in *King Lear*—these may have come down simply as part of the common stock of the age. There is however nothing to forbid the supposition that he had read the *Consolation*, and I want for the moment to play with the fancy that we can see him as he comes to the end of it. As he puts it down he says, 'This is a great and noble book, a book to return to and meditate on. It tells how a man may meet and rise above adversity, And yet . . . it is "philosophy", and there are more things in heaven and earth than philosophy can take official notice of: there's the whole turbulent living consciousness out of which such philosophy as we may achieve must draw its life. If I am to write my play about a man who is really cornered, really "tormented in this sea of fortune" as Boethius puts it, I've got to give not the abstract words for all that is over against him, but the whole oppressive feel of it. . . . And there's the complication of it all for the poor playwright. For if I make my Hamlet the central consciousness of the play, and try to show how his world *feels*—how indeed it smells—to him, then his feelings, the feelings that I imagine for him, will enter into the picture of the world that my play gives. Put it another way. In the very act of describing Hamlet's world as it feels to him in his own immediate consciousness, I have to describe Hamlet, to define that consciousness. That, though I have tackled something like it before, is a very pretty problem indeed. I don't think that my young man will answer the questions that his world, my play, will force upon him, though he may perhaps in his very failure point the way to an answer . . . And there's another challenge too. This book of Boethius's—it gives us great and noble thoughts; what it doesn't give, what it isn't intended to give, is all that lies behind thought in the obscurer regions of the soul where thought begins. One day I may be able to show how real thinking in this region—the region of the great questions—depends on the feelings and the imagination. . . . I'll show a man feeling his way through, and seeing feelingly. . . .'

King Lear, however, is still some way ahead, and *Hamlet* is our present concern. Let us turn to the play.

What—if we refuse to intellectualize too much, to follow clues as in a detective story, to engage in the fascinating sport of character dissection—what is the main imaginative impact that the play makes upon us? As Professor C. S. Lewis insisted in his British Academy Lecture, *'Hamlet': the Prince or the Poem?* (1942), *Hamlet* is not about a man whose character is an enigma to be unravelled, it is about a man who suffers a certain kind of experience, and the man and the experience go together. It is not about a man who could not make up his mind, or a man with peculiarly puzzling reasons for refusing to act; it is a play about death and—to use for the moment a wide and loosely defining phrase—it is a play about corruption. When we are really living through the experience both are present to our consciousness under wide-ranging aspects: death as mere physical fact and as metaphysical terror; corruption as obtuseness, gross sensuality and deliberate contrived evil. I think this is obvious enough, but let us pause for a moment to make it vivid to our minds. And since Hamlet's consciousness, which dominates so much of the play, will shortly be the main object of our consideration, let us for a moment consider the action of the play, so far as possible, as directly presented, without reference to what Hamlet himself may say about it.

It is well known how, right at the start of each of his tragedies, Shakespeare establishes the 'atmosphere'—something that is not just a vaguely effective background but an integral part of the play's structure of meanings. In *Hamlet*, with the usual effective economy of means, we are made aware of a cold darkness that makes men 'sick at heart'. In the surrounding stillness ('not a mouse stirring') men's voices ring out sharply and with subdued apprehension. In this 'dead vast'—vacancy, void, emptiness—'and middle of the night', when Bernardo points to the 'star that's westward from the pole', and speaks of 'the bell then beating one', there is something of that sense of a surrounding non-human that reverberates from the steeples in Robert Frost's 'I will sing you One-O':

> In that grave One
> They spoke of the sun
> And moon and stars,
> Saturn and Mars . . .

In that setting—which will shortly contrast so strongly with the light and pomp and self-important complacency of King Claudius's court—we first hear of, then see, a dead man's ghost. It is of course important not to rewrite Shakespeare's plays for him but to follow his lead as closely as we may. But the emphasis here is indeed Shakespeare's. As C. S. Lewis says, 'The Hamlet formula, so to speak, is not "a man who has to avenge his father", but "a man who has been given a task by a ghost" '. And he adds that whereas in the other tragedies plenty of people are concerned with dying, 'no one thinks, in these plays, of being dead. In *Hamlet* we are kept thinking about it all the time, whether in terms of the soul's destiny or of the body's.' The dead man's ghost is the mainspring of the action, which involves, finally, eight other deaths. Of that original death the memory is indeed 'green', from the first scene, through the re-enactment of the murder by the Players, to the rhetorical question of Fortinbras at the end,

> O proud Death!
> What feast is toward in thine eternal cell . . .?

And it is quite early offered as an example of obvious and inescapable mortality: 'your father lost a father, That father lost, lost his'; it is 'as common As any the most vulgar thing to sense'; the 'common theme' 'is death of fathers', and reason

> still hath cried,
> From the first corse [ironically, Abel's] till he that
>   died to-day,
> 'This must be so'.

From this until the Play scene the theme is mainly expressed by Hamlet, but from the killing of Polonius the presence of death is very close indeed. Polonius, interred 'in hugger-mugger', is 'compounded with dust'; death shares with sex the burden of Ophelia's mad songs; there is the long elegiac description of her drowning. Above all, there is Act V, scene i—the scene with the grave-diggers. Here, as so often in Shakespeare, a dominant theme entwined in a complex action is for a short space given full and exclusive prominence.

> What is he that builds stronger than either the mason, the shipwright, or the carpenter? . . . a gravemaker; the houses that he makes last till doomsday.

To the accompaniment of snatches of song, in which love gives way to death, the Clown throws up the skulls that Hamlet comments on: politician, courtier,

lawyer, tanner, fine lady, jester, Caesar, Alexander—
not one can escape this fate. The moral is enforced
with the simplification of a *danse macabre*:

> Now get you to my lady's chamber, and tell her,
> let her paint an inch thick, to this favour she must
>   come; make her laugh at that.

On the one hand, then, is death, on the other is life
lived with a peculiarly crude vigour of self-assertion.
In the world that Hamlet confronts, men mostly, as
the phrase goes, know what they want—plenty to eat
and drink, sexual satisfaction, and power—and they
see that they get it, pursuing their limited aims with
a gross complacence, fat weeds that rot themselves in
ease on the wharf of oblivion. At this stage there is no
need to describe in detail the forms of corruption of
that Denmark in which any decent man would feel
himself in prison. There is murder, of course, but even
before we know that Claudius is a murderer, it is clear
that on his first appearance we are intended to register
something repulsive. His very first speech is a masterly
example of 'the distillation of personality into style'.

> Though yet of Hamlet our dear brother's death
> The memory be green, and that it us befitted
> To bear our hearts in grief and our whole kingdom
> To be contracted in one brow of woe,
> Yet so far hath discretion fought with nature
> That we with wisest sorrow think on him,
> Together with remembrance of ourselves . . .

That, surely, is the tone and accent of Milton's Belial;
we need know nothing of Claudius's previous activities

to react to those unctuous verse rhythms with some
such comment as 'Slimy beast!'. Neither the King's
practical efficiency in dealing with the public affairs of
his kingdom, nor his ostensible kindness towards his
nephew, can wipe out that first impression. This is the
man whose accession to the throne, and whose in-
decently hasty—and, in an Elizabethan view, incestu-
ous—marriage with his dead brother's wife has been
'freely' endorsed by the 'better wisdoms' of the
Council. In the whole Court of Denmark there is no
one, Hamlet apart, to utter a breath of criticism. How
should there be? The ethos of the place—so we
are told, or directly shown—is made up of coarse
pleasures—

> This heavy-headed revel east and west
> Makes us traduced and tax'd of other nations;
> They clepe us drunkards, and with swinish phrase
> Soil our addition;

it is made up of moral obtuseness (Polonius), syco-
phancy (Rosencrantz and Guildenstern), base and
treacherous plotting (Laertes) and—since Shakespeare
didn't introduce Osric at the climax of the tragedy for
the sake of a little harmless fun—brainless triviality.
This is the world that revolves round the middle-aged
sensuality of Claudius and Gertrude. 'Something is
rotten in the state of Denmark'; and if anyone should
be in any doubt of the completeness with which corruption permeates that state, I suggest, before his next
re-reading, a glance at Professor Kitto's chapter. 'What
humanity is suffering from, in *Hamlet*, is not a specific
evil, but Evil itself.'

Now it is well known that some other plays of this period exhibit, with an almost obsessive insistence, death and corruption—Webster's tragedies, for example. But when we have finished *The White Devil* or *The Duchess of Malfi*, we are likely to find ourselves in some perplexity concerning what it is all about. What is the point of it? When we have finished reading *Hamlet* we have at least a fair idea of what it is about. The point is not a display of accumulated horrors; it is the effect of these on a particular kind of consciousness. It is this that is the centre of interest, and the question that is so often pursued, almost, as it were, in isolation from the full imaginative effect, Why does Hamlet delay? is entirely subordinate to the wider and more inclusive question: What is the impact on Hamlet's consciousness of the world with which he has to deal? If, at this point, I may risk a bald anticipatory summary of what must be dealt with at more length, I would say this: that Hamlet, in his confrontation of this world, feels himself paralysed because an exclusive concentration on evil, or—say—something in the manner of the concentration, is itself corrupting.

> The finished man among his enemies?—
> How in the name of Heaven can he escape
> That defiling and disfigured shape
> The mirror of malicious eyes
> Casts upon his eyes until at last
> He thinks that shape must be his shape?
> And what's the good of an escape
> If honour find him in the wintry blast?

That, from Yeats's 'A Dialogue of Self and Soul', is in no sense a summing-up of *Hamlet*; but it does, I think, suggest something of the play's central concern. 'The characters', if I may quote C. S. Lewis again, 'are all watching one another, forming theories about one another, listening, contriving, full of anxiety. The world of *Hamlet* is a world where one has lost one's way. The Prince also has no doubt lost his. . . .' It is because attention is centred so continuously on this losing of the way by a character who in so many and such obvious ways is superior to those who surround him, that the play is so radical an examination of the problem of consciousness, of self-identity. That is why the line that everyone thinks of in connexion with this play—though we all quarrel about its meaning—is, 'To be, or not to be, that is the question . . .'

The climax of the first movement of the play—that is, of Act I—is Hamlet's encounter with the Ghost. It is important that we should get clear with ourselves how we are intended to take it. At first it seems that Shakespeare is careful to keep the status of the Ghost more or less neutral. The first we hear of it is Marcellus's 'What, has this thing appear'd again to-night?' As a ghost, it is of course a 'dreaded sight', a 'portentous figure', but it is also, simply, 'this apparition', 'illusion', 'this present object'. When Horatio tells Hamlet what has happened, it is 'a figure like your father' and 'the apparition'. None of this provides any very clear answer to the question that an audience is likely to ask —What sort of a ghost is this? Is it good or bad? There are however some suggestive tonings. The Ghost, though 'majestical', starts 'like a guilty thing' when the cock crows, and we are told that this is because the bird's 'lofty and shrill-sounding throat' awakes 'the god of day', but dismisses 'to his confine' 'the extravagant and erring spirit'. Both these adjectives may mean no more than wandering out of bounds or straying, but the immediately following lines suggest rather more than this.

It faded on the crowing of the cock.
Some say that ever 'gainst that season comes
Wherein our Saviour's birth is celebrated,
The bird of dawning singeth all night long;
And then, they say, no spirit dare stir abroad;
The nights are wholesome; then no planets strike,
No fairy takes, nor witch hath power to charm,
So hallow'd and so gracious is that time.

Now I cannot believe that these lines were put in for the sake of an incidental bit of 'poetry'—no more than I could believe it of the temple-haunting martlets passage in *Macbeth*, which similarly contrasts so markedly with the thick and oppressive atmosphere that permeates most of the play. Here, in the passage before us, not only is Christmas night wholesome, hallowed and gracious, because various malign influences are as powerless to act as spirits such as this are to stir abroad, the limpid freshness of the verse emphasizes an accepted Christianity ('our Saviour's birth') which, it seems in place to remark, is directly opposed to the code of revenge. Ah but, we may be told, in *Hamlet* Shakespeare is using the conventions of the revenge play, in which quite different assumptions about the duty of revenge prevail. This has always seemed to me a very rum argument indeed. Shakespeare may use various dramatic conventions—such as the foreshortening of time or the impenetrability of disguise—when they suit his purpose; but he never—what great poet could? —allows convention to shape his essential matter. I cannot believe that the poet who was going on to write *Measure for Measure* (perhaps his next play), which is about forgiveness, who was going on to create the figure of Cordelia, and to write those plays of which a main part of the burden is that 'the rarer action is in virtue than in vengeance'—I cannot believe that such a poet could temporarily waive his deepest ethical convictions for the sake of an exciting dramatic effect. It is almost like believing that Dante, for a canto or two, could change his ground and write approvingly, say, of the enemies of the Empire. If this ghost turns out to be one who clamours for revenge, then we have every reason to suppose that Shakespeare entertained some grave doubts about him.

This, however, is to anticipate. All we can say when the first scene ends is that the play has given us reason to be suspicious of the Ghost. When in scene iv it appears to Hamlet himself, his address to it still allows for alternative possibilities:

Be thou a spirit of health, or goblin damned,
Bring with thee airs from heaven, or blasts from hell,
Be thy intents wicked, or charitable . . .

but what is emphasized at the end of this same speech is that for the 'dead corse' to revisit 'the glimpses of the moon' is to make night 'hideous'; it is also

So horridly to shake our disposition
With thoughts beyond the reaches of our souls.

There follows the—surely choric—warning of Horatio:

> What if it tempt you toward the flood, my lord,
> Or to the dreadful summit of the cliff
> That beetles o'er his base into the sea,
> And there assume some other horrible form,
> Which might deprive your sovereignty of reason
> And draw you into madness? think of it;
> The very place puts toys of desperation,
> Without more motive, into every brain
> That looks so many fathoms to the sea
> And hears it roar beneath.

No one, I suppose, can read these lines without recalling the description, in *King Lear*, of that Dover cliff over which Gloucester thinks to peer with his sightless eyes—a scene which, in the parallel progress of the two old men, reminds us of how Lear too had peered into the abyss that opened up within, for 'the mind, mind has mountains; cliffs of fall Frightful, sheer, no-man-fathomed'. Edgar, evoking the scene, declares, 'I'll look no more, Lest my brain turn', and Horatio—

> The very place puts toys of desperation,
> Without more motive, into every brain. . . .

'Desperation', moreover, like 'desperate' a few lines later ('He waxes desperate with imagination'), is a far stronger word than, say, 'recklessness' (it is related to 'despair'), and I think we may say that the speech as a whole gives us an unambiguous clue: the Ghost is tempting Hamlet to gaze with fascinated horror at an abyss of evil.

Now the evil is real enough: that also has been established in Act I, and there is certainly nothing

unnatural in the violence of Hamlet's recoil from it—
'O! that this too too sullied flesh would melt. . . .' The
question is how Hamlet will deal with this world—
deal with it not only in action, but *within himself*. The
Ghost's demand, when the two are finally confronted
alone, is for an exclusive concentration on it, and it is
to that demand that Hamlet gives himself up.

> Remember thee?
> Yea, from the table of my memory
> I'll wipe away all trivial fond records,
> All saws of books, all forms, all pressures past,
> That youth and observation copied there;
> And thy commandment all alone shall live
> Within the book and volume of my brain,
> Unmix'd with baser matter.

There is a terrible significance in that repeated 'all', for
what it means is that Hamlet does not merely see the
evil about him, does not merely react to it with loathing and rejection, he allows his vision to activate
something within himself—say, if you like, his own
feeling of corruption—and so to produce that state of
near paralysis that so perplexes him.

LECTURE 3

T HE point of view that I am putting forward is that what we have in *Hamlet*—as in *Othello* and, less successfully, in *Timon*—is the exploration and implicit criticism of a particular state of mind or consciousness. It is an extremely complex state of mind, in which reason and emotion, attitudes towards the self and towards other persons and the world at large, are revealed both directly and through a series of encounters; and our business is to see how the different ingredients (so to speak) are related in such a way that a particular judgment or assessment of experience is precipitated. Since that remark sounds formal and moralistic let me add two qualifying statements. The first is that what we have to do with is not a state of mind that can be adequately described in terms of abstract reason. As J. I. M. Stewart has said, in *Character and Motive in Shakespeare*:

> It is . . . necessary to recognise that the poetic drama, like myth, is part-based upon an awareness, largely intuitive, of the recesses of human passion and motive. . . . Of just what Shakespeare brings from beyond this portal [of the depths of the mind], and how, we often can achieve little conceptual grasp; and often therefore the logical and unkindled mind finds difficulties which it labels as faults and attributes to the depravity of Shakespeare's audience

39

or what it wills. But what the intellect finds arbitrary the imagination may accept and respond to, for when we read imaginatively or poetically we share the dramatist's penetration for a while and deep is calling to deep.

That, I think, is well said. Hamlet's state of mind, the Hamlet consciousness, is revealed not only at the level of formulable motive, but in its obscure depths; and it is revealed through the poetry. In the second place, the judgment of which I spoke is not a matter of formal approval or condemnation of a dramatic figure conceived as a real person. No doubt it is partly that; but essentially it is part of an imaginative apprehension of life in which, with the whole force of our personality ('judgment ever awake and steady self-possession combined with enthusiasm and feeling profound or vehement'), we try to see fundamental aspects of human life in their true status and relationships. And what we judge, in this sense, is not someone 'out there', but potentialities of our own being.

In the particular complex of feelings and attitudes that constitute the Hamlet consciousness it is not easy to separate causes and effects, but I think that most people would agree that what is emphasized from the opening scenes is a movement of recoil and disgust of a peculiar intensity. Whether this negative emotion is, as T. S. Eliot once claimed, 'in excess of the facts as they appear' is a question that may be waived for the moment. What is indisputable is that for the greater part of the play it is stronger than any counterbalancing movements of positive and outgoing life. And the determining moment, when this imbalance is accepted as a kind of compulsion is, as we saw in the last lecture, the encounter with the Ghost. When Hamlet swears to 'remember'—with such ominous repetition of the word—he commits himself to a passion that has all the exclusiveness of an infatuation.

> Remember thee?
> Ay, thou poor ghost, while memory holds a seat
> In this distracted globe. Remember thee?
> Yea, from the table of my memory
> I'll wipe away all trivial fond records,
> All saws of books, all forms, all pressures past,
> That youth and observation copied there;
> And thy commandment all alone shall live
> Within the book and volume of my brain,
> Unmix'd with baser matter.

There is, I remarked, a terrible significance in that *all*. Now Hamlet's exclusive concentration upon things rank and gross and his consequent recoil from life as a whole determine his attitude to death, which also is purely one of negation. Some contrasts may help us here. When T. S. Eliot's *Little Gidding* was first published a notable review of that poem, by D. W. Harding, appeared in *Scrutiny* (XI, 3, 1943). Speaking of the way in which a sense of spiritual values can reveal a significant pattern in a life which must otherwise appear meaningless and fragmentary, Harding remarked of the closing sections of the poem:

> One effect of this view of time and experience is to rob the moment of death of any over-significance we may have given it. For the humanist of Section II life trails off just because it can't manage to endure. For

the man convinced of spiritual values life is a coherent pattern in which the ending has its due place and, because it is part of a pattern, itself leads into the beginning. An over-strong terror of death is often one expression of the fear of living, for death is one of the life-processes that seem too terrifying to be borne. In examining one means of becoming reconciled to death, Mr. Eliot can show us life, too, made bearable, unfrightening, positively inviting: 'With the drawing of this Love and the voice of this Calling'.

'An over-strong terror of death is often one expression of the fear of living.' There is of course an instinctive recoil from dying, expressed magnificently by Shakespeare in Claudio's outburst—'Aye, but to die, and go we know not where'—in *Measure for Measure*; but we are speaking now of settled attitudes, and I think it is obvious that strong, unfrightened and affirmative attitudes to death can only exist as part of strong, unfrightened and affirmative attitudes to living. We could cite the superb closing pages of the Second Part of *The Pilgrim's Progress* (of which I remember F. R. Leavis once remarking to me that no civilization could long endure that did not incorporate in itself some comparable affirmative attitudes); but perhaps here Shakespeare is our most relevant witness, and we may recall how in *The Tempest* the sense of wonder and freshness goes with a serene acceptance of the full human condition; indeed that speech in which Prospero speaks of the transience of all things human begins,

You do look, my son, in a moved sort,
As if you were dismay'd; be cheerful, sir.

Now for Hamlet, on the other hand, death is mere negation; but at the same time he is fascinated by it, fascinated not merely by 'the dread of something after death', but by the whole process of earthly corruption, as in the long brooding on the skulls in the churchyard, culminating in the gratuitous fantasy of the progress of Alexander:

> To what base uses we may return, Horatio! Why may not imagination trace the noble dust of Alexander, till he find it stopping a bung-hole?

To which, you remember, Horatio replies, "Twere to consider too curiously, to consider so'; but Hamlet does not heed him. Certainly the facts that Hamlet dwells on here, as he had dwelt on them in connexion with the death of Polonius, are facts that have to be assimilated somehow, but it is the tone and manner that are betraying:

> —Now, Hamlet, where's Polonius?
> —At supper . . . Not where he eats, but where he is eaten; a certain convocation of politic worms are e'en at him. Your worm is your only emperor for diet; we fat all creatures else to fat us, and we fat ourselves for maggots . . .

and again:

> —Dost thou think Alexander looked o' this fashion i' the earth?
> —E'en so.
> —And smelt so? pah!

It need cause no surprise that these attitudes of fascinated revulsion combine with a regressive longing for the death that, from another point of view, appears so repulsive. We shall shortly have occasion to look at the 'To be, or not to be' soliloquy in some detail. Here I would simply call attention to the way in which it expresses this basic aspect of Hamlet's attitude to death. The speech (if I may make use of what I have written elsewhere) 'is built up on two contrasted sets of metaphors. Life, "this mortal coil", is at best something which hampers and impedes, imposing "fardels" under which we "grunt and sweat"; "the slings and arrows of outrageous fortune", "the thousand natural shocks", and "the whips and scorns of time" present it as an actively hostile force; and in "a sea of troubles" the power that it has to inflict pain is felt as continuous and irresistible like the sea. Death, on the other hand, is presented simply as a relaxing of tension and an abandonment of the struggle. The reiterated "sleep", the soothing "quietus", and the smooth and weighted "consummation", make plain why death is so ardently desired by a spirit which, whether "suffering" or "opposing", feels itself continually on the defensive against a world conceived as entirely hostile.' The essay from which I am quoting I have come to feel as decidedly fragmentary and provisional, but I see no reason to retract the conclusion that what we have here is a quality of moral relaxation, a desire to lapse *back* from the level of adult consciousness. What has to be added is that Hamlet finally accepts death in words of a peculiarly haunting quality to which we shall return; but it is from the standpoint of a life that has been largely emptied of significance.

Hamlet is a man who in the face of life and of death can make no affirmation, and it may well be that this irresolution—which goes far deeper than irresolution about the performance of a specific act—this fundamental doubt, explains the great appeal of the play in modern times. The point has been made by D. G. James in *The Dream of Learning*. Shakespeare's play, he says, 'is an image of modernity, of the soul without clear belief losing its way, and bringing itself and others to great distress and finally to disaster'; it is 'a tragedy not of excessive thought but of defeated thought', and Hamlet himself is 'a man caught in ethical and metaphysical uncertainties'. Now I am sure that Mr. James is right in emphasizing the element of scepticism in Hamlet's make-up—the weighing of alternative possibilities in such a way as to make choice between them virtually impossible; and I sympathize with his wish 'to elevate Hamlet's intellectual distresses to an equality in importance with his emotional state', for 'the strength of the emotional shock he has suffered is equalled by the weakness of his mind in the face of difficult moral and metaphysical issues. Hamlet was, after all, an intellectual.' But at the same time I feel that the play incites us to a closer examination of the intimate and complex relationship of thought and feeling, of intellectual bafflement and certain aspects of the emotional life; in the play before us the dominant emotions are activated by certain specific shocks but they cannot be attributed solely to these.

In an essay called *Hamlet and Don Quixote* Ivan

Turgenev took up this very question of Hamlet's scepticism, but instead of regarding it as a purely intellectual matter he related it to central attitudes of the self, to a certain moral inadequacy.

> Hamlet (he says) is, beyond all things else, analysis and egoism, scepticism personified.
>
> He lives only to himself. He is an egoist, and as such can have no faith in himself; for no man can have faith save in that which is outside self and above self.
>
> None the less Hamlet clings tenaciously to this 'I', this self in which he has no faith. It is a centre to which he constantly returns because he finds that in this world there is nothing to which he can cleave with all his soul.
>
> A sceptic, Hamlet is preoccupied with his own personality; but he ponders its strategical situation, not its duties.[1]

In other words, Hamlet is one of those in whom 'the "I" in the individual' preponderates, not 'something outside the "I", which the individual prefers to the "I" '. Now I think that this also is true, but again, taken in isolation, it does not quite do justice to the imaginative facts as we know them; for what it ignores is the pain and the passion—the genuine pain of loss and the genuine passion of revulsion against what is really evil. Max Plowman perhaps, in an essay called 'Some Values in *Hamlet*' (reprinted in *The Right to*

---

[1] I quote from the translation by Robert Nichols (London: Henderson, 1930). I was reminded of the existence of Turgenev's little known essay by the reference in Miss Rebecca West's *The Court and the Castle: the Interaction of Political and Religious Ideas in Imaginative Literature*: in the chapters on *Hamlet* Miss West has some interesting things to say about current misconceptions of the play.

46

Live) brings us nearer the mark when he speaks of Hamlet as one who has risen above the level of the merely instinctive—the level at which most of those who surround him live, and at which revenge is an obvious duty—but who has not risen to full and adequate consciousness.

> For as we come to objective consciousness, we realize that no one lives to himself: we know, in fact, that life consists in the interplay of subject and object, and that the completely isolated person can only be said to exist; for to be completely isolated is to lack intercourse with anything outside the self.

Hamlet, on the other hand, is in the intermediate state of self-consciousness, 'the most unlovable of all conditions': 'Hamlet is self-conscious man in an unconscious world'; what he suffers from is 'a fixation of self-consciousness'. The point, you see, is very close to that made by Turgenev. But there is this difference: Max Plowman sees Hamlet's state as one phase in a development that is not peculiar to any one individual; however far Hamlet goes astray he starts from a point through which everyone—or almost everyone—must pass who is to rise above the instinctive and unself-knowing to that state of genuine being for which one name is consciousness.

I think we shall not be far wrong if, in seeking to account for Hamlet's paralysis, his inability to affirm, we give special prominence to his isolation and self-consciousness. Now consciousness, as distinguished from Hamlet's self-consciousness, is dependent upon love and relationship, and the name that Blake gave to consciousness, as Max Plowman remarks in this same essay, is the Imagination. Hamlet, for all his ranging mind and his nervous susceptibility, is not in this sense imaginative; in Blakean terms he is in the power of his Spectre.

> Each Man is in his Spectre's power
> Untill the arrival of that hour,
> When his Humanity awake
> And cast his own Spectre into the Lake.

These lines occur in the Rossetti MS. Looking up other instances of 'Spectre' in the Index to the edition of the Prophetic Writings by Sloss and Wallis, I found (what I had not noticed before) that Blake also used them in *Jerusalem*: in the drawing showing Albion in despair (Plate 41) they are engraved in reverse on the stone at the feet of the seated bowed figure, his face covered by his hands; and it is not irrelevant to our present concerns to notice that the passage immediately following this illustration begins,

> Thus Albion sat, studious of others in his pale disease,
> Brooding on evil . . .

I hope you will not misunderstand me. I do not think that Shakespeare wrote *Hamlet* as an esoteric commentary on Blake's Prophetic Books, or that Hamlet's Ghost is to be identified with Blake's Spectre. It is simply that both poets had some comparable insights, and the one may be used to bring out the meaning of the other. Blake's Spectre is the rationalizing faculty, self-centred and moralistic, working in isolation from the other powers and potentialities of the mind. Unless redeemed by Los, the Imagination, in dealing with the self and with others it can only criticize and accuse, creating around itself what Wordsworth was to call 'a universe of death.'

Hamlet, 'studious of others in his pale disease, Brooding on evil,' is, in this sense, in the power of his Spectre. He is indeed, as Mr James and many others have insisted, an intellectual, a man given to reason and reflection. But what Shakespeare is bringing in question in this play is what it means to be an intellectual in any but a sterile sense, the conditions on which this capability can be indeed 'god-like'. Hamlet's intellectuality, the working of his mind, is largely at the service of attitudes of rejection and disgust that are indiscriminate in their working. Let me repeat what I have said before: the Denmark of this play is indeed an unweeded garden; there are facts enough to justify almost everything Hamlet says about this world; but what we have to take note of is not only what he says but a particular vibration in the saying. We can define this in relation to his self-disgust, his spreading sexual nausea, and his condemnation of others.

When Hamlet first reveals himself in soliloquy it is in terms of a revulsion for which the preceding court scene has in some measure prepared us.

O! that this too too sullied flesh would melt,
Thaw and resolve itself into a dew . . .

His flesh is sullied because it is the flesh of a woman who, in a matter of weeks from the death of her first husband, has married her husband's brother: 'a beast, that wants discourse of reason, Would have mourn'd longer'; she is moreover infatuated with a man who clearly has some of the qualities of the 'satyr' that Hamlet attributes to him. These are données of the case, and it need occasion no surprise when Hamlet declares that 'virtue cannot so inoculate our old stock but we shall relish of it'. This sense of being tainted is both explicable and natural, but Shakespeare is careful to show us that there is more than this involved in Hamlet's bitter judgment on himself. The disgust with the self that we must all at some time feel, for whatever cause, changes its quality when it is used to shock and damage, as Hamlet uses it to damage his dawning relationship with Ophelia.

> *Hamlet.* . . . if you be honest and fair, your honesty should admit no discourse to your beauty.
> *Ophelia.* Could beauty, my lord, have better commerce than with honesty?
> *Hamlet.* Ay, truly; for the power of beauty will sooner transform honesty from what it is to a bawd than the force of honesty can translate beauty into his likeness; this was sometime a paradox, but now the time gives it proof. I did love you once.
> *Ophelia.* Indeed, my lord, you made me believe so.
> *Hamlet.* You should not have believed me; for virtue cannot so inoculate our old stock but we shall relish of it; I loved you not.

Ophelia. I was the more deceived.

Hamlet. Get thee to a nunnery; why wouldst thou be a breeder of sinners? I am myself indifferent honest; but yet I could accuse me of such things that it were better my mother had not borne me. I am very proud, revengeful, ambitious; with more offences at my beck than I have thoughts to put them in, imagination to give them shape, or time to act them in. What should such fellows as I do crawling between heaven and earth? We are arrant knaves all; believe none of us. Go thy ways to a nunnery.

We may for the moment leave on one side the question of what Hamlet, in this and similar passages, is doing to another's consciousness—driving a wedge into it so that it too must inevitably suffer—though that Shakespeare was not indifferent to it we know from Ophelia's madness and her—apparently half-sought—death. But if we ask whether what Hamlet says or implies about himself is mature self-knowledge or, as Turgenev suggests, mere self-flagellation, I do not think that the answer can be in any doubt. 'I am very proud, revengeful, ambitious; with more offences at my beck than I have thoughts to put them in, imagination to give them shape, or time to act them in.' This, it has been said, 'sounds very terrible, but considered carefully it amounts to nothing'. What it means, it seems to me, is that Hamlet is in a state of panic recoil not only from sex but from those aggressions and self-assertive drives that sooner or later we have to come to terms with and put to constructive use. Many of Shakespeare's characters, it is true, are constrained to take stock of things within of which they are bitterly ashamed. There is, for example, Lear:

> Poor naked wretches, whereso'er you are,
> That bide the pelting of this pitiless storm,
> How shall your houseless heads and unfed sides,
> Your loop'd and window'd raggedness, defend you
> From seasons such as this? O! I have ta'en
> Too little care of this. Take physic, pomp . . .

Or there is Posthumus, in prison and awaiting death:

>   My conscience, thou art fetter'd
> More than my shanks and wrists; you good gods, give me
>   give me
> The penitent instrument to pick that bolt;
> Then, free for ever! Is't enough I am sorry?
> So children temporal fathers do appease;
> Gods are more full of mercy. Must I repent?
> I cannot do it better than in gyves,
> Desir'd more than constrained; to satisfy,
> If of my freedom 'tis the main part, take
> No stricter render of me than my all . . .
>   . . . and so, great powers,
> If you will take this audit, take this life,
> And cancel these cold bonds. O Imogen!
> I'll speak to thee in silence.

To say that there is an absolute difference of tone and intention between these self-communings and anything that Hamlet may say by way of self-condemnation is to comment on the obvious. When indeed he has anything real to repent of, his self-exculpatory manner suggests something like obliviousness to what he has done. Of the murder of Polonius:

> For this same lord,
> I do repent; but heaven hath pleased it so,
> To punish me with this, and this with me,
> That I must be their scourge and minister . . .

—to be followed shortly by 'I'll lug the guts into the
neighbour room'. Of his unseemly ranting in Ophelia's
grave with Laertes, whose father he has killed, and for
whose sister's death he is at least in part to blame:

> What I have done,
> That might your nature, honour, and exception
> Roughly awake, I here proclaim was madness.
> Was't Hamlet wrong'd Laertes? Never Hamlet;
> If Hamlet from himself be ta'en away,
> And when he's not himself does wrong Laertes,
> Then Hamlet does it not; Hamlet denies it.
> Who does it then? His madness; if't be so,
> Hamlet is of the faction that is wrong'd;
> His madness is poor Hamlet's enemy.

One can hardly resist the feeling that some of the
energy that Hamlet expends in unpacking his heart
with words might more profitably have been directed
—and with more humility—towards a stricter account-
ing of his share in the harm done to others.

It is much the same with his sexual insistence. Grant
that he is deeply wounded—as who would not be?—
by his mother's conduct:

> why, she would hang on him [her first husband]
> As if increase of appetite had grown
> By what it fed on . . .

> O, most wicked speed, to post
> With such dexterity to incestuous sheets!

> Rebellious hell,
> If thou canst mutine in a matron's bones,
> To flaming youth let virtue be as wax
> And melt in her own fire . . .

Grant this, and it still does not excuse his obscenity towards Ophelia—Ophelia whom he had said he loved, and she believed him—and it would not excuse it even if we were to accept Professor Dover Wilson's shift of a stage direction in II. ii. which makes Hamlet suspect her as a willing decoy of Claudius and Polonius. What he says to her in the 'get thee to a nunnery' scene and in the play scene can only be described in D. H. Lawrence's terms as 'doing dirt on sex'. But Hamlet was shocked by the revelation of the power of sex? Yes indeed, as an adolescent may well be horrified and frightened when the revelation of dangerous powers within comes as part of a traumatic experience. But Hamlet was not in years an adolescent; he was, as Shakespeare tells us, a man of thirty. As for his too vivid picturing of his mother's life with Claudius—

> Not this, by no means, that I bid you do;
> Let the bloat king tempt you again to bed;
> Pinch wanton on your cheek; call you his mouse;
> And let him, for a pair of reechy kisses,
> Or paddling in your neck with his damn'd fingers,
> Make you to ravel all this matter out . . .

—there is enough, here and elsewhere, to give plausibility to the psycho-analytic speculations of Dr. Ernest Jones.

I am of course aware that what Hamlet says to his mother in the Closet scene may be regarded as part of a necessary and proper attempt to break the alliance between her and the smiling murderer; but through it all runs the impure streak of the indulgence of an obsessive passion.

> Come, come, and sit you down; you shall not budge;
> You go not till I set you up a glass
> Where you may see the inmost part of you.

If with genuine, even with passionate, concern, you want to help someone in great need, someone in desperate ignorance of his true condition, do you, I wonder, say, 'This is what you are: see how ugly you look'? Well, perhaps you may; but certainly not in such a way that you seem about to make an aggressive attack. The Queen's immediate reaction, which acts as a stage direction indicating Hamlet's whole bearing, is, 'What wilt thou do? thou wilt not murder me? Help, help, ho!' Perhaps we may again invoke Lear, who as he comes to see more and more clearly the evil in the world, is also constrained to speak words of passionate denunciation: the difference, from the point of view of our present concern, is that these, like Lear's 'burning shame', have an almost impersonal intensity. Hamlet, in his denunciations, is never free of himself, never centres entirely on the matter in hand or the person before him.

Hamlet, in short, is fascinated by what he condemns. His emotions circle endlessly, but find no direction. And it is because of the impurity and indiscriminateness of his rejections that, brief moments of friendship and respite apart, he takes refuge in postures. There is a further point to be made here. I do not remember seeing the question asked, but why, on the success of the Gonzago play, does Hamlet call for the recorders?

> Ah, ha! Come, some music! come, the recorders!—
> For if the king like not the comedy,
> Why then, belike,—he likes it not, perdy.
> Come, some music!

True, Shakespeare knew that the recorders would be needed for the scene with Rosencrantz and Guildenstern, but this can hardly affect the reason imputed to Hamlet. The answer surely can only be that Hamlet intends the players to finish off the evening with a concert which Claudius will hear, thus keeping him in suspense and leaving the initiative of action to him: it will be one more *arranged scene*, and thus in line with Hamlet's habitual tendency to make everything, even what he deeply feels, into a matter of play-acting. Again and again intrinsic values, direct relations, are neglected whilst he tries out various roles before a real or imagined audience. He dramatizes his melancholy—for he insists on his suit of inky black even whilst denying its importance—just as he dramatizes his love and his fall from love and his very grief at Ophelia's death; his jests and asides imply an approving audience 'in the know' and ready to take the point; he is fascinated by the business of acting (and highly intelligent about it), and he falls naturally into figures of speech suggested by the theatre—'make mouths at the invisible event', 'Who calls me villain? breaks my pate across?' etc. Before the last scene the note of sincerity is found in few places except some of the soliloquies and the intimate exchanges with Horatio.

Now to say that Hamlet adopts histrionic, even at times melodramatic, postures is to bring into view another matter of central importance—that is, the static quality of Hamlet's consciousness. It is not for nothing that the popular conception is that this is a play about delay. Delay in the action, that is in the carrying out of Hamlet's strategy against the King, can of course be explained: he had to find out if the Ghost was telling the truth about the murder, and so on. But the fact remains that one of the most powerful imaginative effects is of a sense of paralysis. Hamlet feels, and we are made to feel, that he is 'stuck', as we say on more homely occasions.

> Sure he that made us with such large discourse,
> Looking before and after, gave us not
> That capability and god-like reason
> To fust in us unused. Now, whether it be
> Bestial oblivion, or some craven scruple
> Of thinking too precisely on the event,—
> A thought which, quarter'd, hath but one part
>   wisdom
> And ever three parts coward,—I do not know
> Why yet I live to say 'This thing's to do,'
> Sith I have cause, and will, and strength, and means
> To do't.

Hamlet is here of course referring to the specific action of revenge, and commentators have been quick to point out that in regard to outward action he is neither slow nor a coward. But there is another and more important sense in which his self-accusation here is entirely justified, in which he is indeed 'lapsed in time and passion'—that is, as Dover Wilson explains, arrested or taken prisoner ('lapsed') by circumstances and passion. Hamlet, as everyone says, is an intellectual, but he does little enough effective thinking on the moral and metaphysical problems that beset him: his god-like reason is clogged and impeded by the emotions of disgust, revulsion and self-contempt that bring him back, again and again, to the isolation of his obsession. Effective thinking, in the regions that most concern Hamlet, implies a capacity for self-forgetfulness and a capacity for true relationship.

With this, I think, we reach the heart of the play. If, as I said earlier in these lectures, in the world of the play there is, on the one hand death, on the other, life lived with a peculiarly crude vigour of self-assertion, in such a world where are values to be found? If we are true to our direct impressions we must admit that *that* is Hamlet's problem, and questions concerning the authenticity of the Ghost or the means whereby Claudius may be trapped are subordinate to it. Hamlet's question, the question that he is continually asking himself, is, How can I live? What shall I do to rid myself of this numbing sense of meaninglessness brought by the knowledge of corruption? But behind this, and implicit in the play as a whole, is the question of being, of the activated consciousness. Hamlet comes close to putting this question directly in the great central soliloquy, but he glides away from it. And no wonder, for the problem is insoluble in the state of unresolved emotion in which he delivers himself of his thoughts; as Coleridge was never tired of insisting, thinking at the higher levels is an activity of the personality as a whole.

Perhaps, before attempting our final analysis, this is a matter that we may pause to consider, for it is of great importance; and I should like to quote from an admirable paper by Professor Dorothy Emmet called *Coleridge on the Growth of the Mind*:[1]

> Yet a further condition of the creative growth of the mind is moral integrity . . . Our thinking is bound up with our characters as morally responsible people. Yet Coleridge can distinguish between the kind of conscientiousness which can stultify the growth of the mind and the kind which is its condition. A strong sense of duty may be 'the effect of selfness in a mind incapable of gross self-interest. I mean the decrease of hope and joy, the soul in its round and round flight forming narrower circles, till at every gyre its wings beat against the *personal self.*' *The decrease of hope and joy*: in writing of Pitt, Coleridge remarked that 'his sincerity had no living root of affection'; and again, that 'the searcher after truth must love and be beloved'. For the creative power of the mind depends in the last resort on a deep underlying state which Coleridge calls Joy. Here the *locus classicus* is the *Dejection Ode*.

As Professor Emmet indicates, Coleridge's central concern is with the interrelation of all our faculties, with the need, as he puts it elsewhere, 'to keep alive the heart in the head', for 'deep thinking is attainable only by a man of deep feeling, and . . . all truth is a species of

---

[1] *Bulletin of the John Rylands Library*, Vol. 34, No. 2, March, 1952; reprinted (1967) in *Coleridge*, ed. Kathleen Coburn (Twentieth Century Views).

revelation'. Among the objects that he ascribes to himself in *The Friend* is 'to make the reason spread light over our feelings, to make our feelings, with their vital warmth, actualize our reason'; for, as he goes on to remark, '. . . in the moral being lies the source of the intellectual. The first step to knowledge, or rather the first condition of all insight into truth, is to dare commune with our very and permanent self'.[1] What all these quotations indicate is that in matters of essential concern, 'knowledge' is not simply deduction from experiment or the end of a logical process, it is a function of being, for *Quantum sumus scimus*, as we are, so we know.

[1] *Biographia Literaria* (ed. Shawcross), Vol. I, p. 98; letter to Poole, March 23, 1801; *The Friend*, General Introduction, Essays XV and XVI.

THERE is, perhaps, no well-known passage in Shakespeare that has been found so perplexing as that in which Hamlet communes with himself between the preparation of the play to catch the conscience of the king and its performance—'To be, or not to be, that is the question . . .' It can perplex for various reasons, one of them being the variety of different explanations of crucial phrases that can reasonably be made. (In the Furness Variorum edition the text completely disappears for a couple of pages whilst a footnote marshals conflicting interpretations of the opening and general tenor; at a rough estimate the 34 lines of the soliloquy have some 440 lines of small-type commentary.) Another reason is that the speech is almost too well-known for its features to be seen distinctly, as Charles Lamb said:

> I confess myself utterly unable to appreciate that celebrated soliloquy in *Hamlet*, beginning, 'To be, or not to be,' or to tell whether it be good, bad, or indifferent; it has been so handled and pawed about by declamatory boys and men, and torn so inhumanly from its living place and principle of continuity in the play, till it has become to me a perfectly dead member.[1]

Perhaps we need not be too much dismayed; the

[1] Quoted in the Furness Variorum edition.

meaning may be simpler—even if in some ways subtler—than is commonly supposed. Since the speech is
crucial I must ask your indulgence whilst I read it,
indicating as best I may the stopping of the good
Quarto, which is considerably lighter than that in most
current editions.[1]

> To be, or not to be, that is the question,
> Whether 'tis nobler in the mind to suffer
> The slings and arrows of outrageous fortune,
> Or to take arms against a sea of troubles,
> And by opposing, end them, to die to sleep
> No more, and by a sleep, to say we end
> The heart-ache, and the thousand natural shocks
> That flesh is heir to; 'tis a consummation
> Devoutly to be wished to die to sleep,
> To sleep, perchance to dream, ay there's the rub,
> For in that sleep of death what dreams may come
> When we have shuffled off this mortal coil
> Must give us pause, there's the respect
> That makes calamity of so long life:
> For who would bear the whips and scorns of time,
> Th' oppressor's wrong, the proud man's contumely,
> The pangs of disprized love, the law's delay,
> The insolence of office, and the spurns
> That patient merit of th' unworthy takes,
> When he himself might his quietus make
> With a bare bodkin; who would fardels bear,
> To grunt and sweat under a weary life,
> But that the dread of something after death,

[1] It is hardly necessary for me to say that I am indebted to Professor Dover Wilson for calling attention to the punctuation of the
good Quarto. See *The Manuscript of Shakespeare's 'Hamlet'* pp. 192-215,
especially, in the present connexion, p. 210. In the New Cambridge
edition of the play Professor Wilson modifies the Quarto punctuation
slightly, whilst keeping the general fluid movement of the lines.

The undiscovered country, from whose bourn
No traveller returns, puzzles the will,
And makes us rather bear those ills we have,
Than fly to others that we know not of.
Thus conscience does make cowards of us all,
And thus the native hue of resolution
Is sicklied o'er with the pale cast of thought,
And enterprises of great pitch and moment,
With this regard their currents turn awry,
And lose the name of action. . . .

There is no need for me to do more than remind you
of the main puzzles. Does 'To be, or not to be' refer to
a contemplated action, to the continuation of Hamlet's
life, or to survival after death? When he speaks of 'The
undiscover'd country from whose bourn No traveller
returns', has he forgotten the Ghost, or has he given up
belief in its honesty? What is the meaning of that
'conscience' that makes cowards of us all, or indeed of
'thought'? And so on. It is of course clear that among
the thoughts in Hamlet's mind are thoughts of action
against the King, of suicide, and of the nature of life
after death, but the transitions are not clear, and as
soon as we attempt to give an exact paraphrase we
run into difficulties. At this point we may resort to
Dr Johnson, whose note on the passage begins:

Of this celebrated soliloquy, which bursting from
a man distracted with contrariety of desires, and
overwhelmed with the magnitude of his own purposes, is connected rather in the speaker's mind, than
on his tongue, I shall endeavour to discover the
train, and to shew how one sentiment produces
another.

This he proceeds to do, and I must say with considerable success, so far as success is possible; but the essential point is in his opening comment: it is the speech of a man 'distracted with contrariety of desires', and the connexions are 'rather in the speaker's mind, than on his tongue'. In other words it is not paraphrasable, and the reasons why it is not so are of some interest.

It is of course true that poetry that without loss of meaning could be put into other words would cease to be poetry. But we all know that there is a great deal of poetry of which we can usefully make for ourselves a tentative prose translation as a way of getting to grips with the full poetic meaning. Now there are passages in Shakespeare (as indeed in other poets) where even this tentative and exploratory procedure is of a very limited usefulness indeed, for what we are given is not the poetic apprehension of thought, but thought in the process of formation. Such a passage is the speech of Macbeth in the moment of temptation ('This supernatural soliciting Cannot be ill; cannot be good . . .') where we are directly aware both of the emotional and the bodily accompaniments of a state of being issuing in a conception that will not easily yield itself to conceptual forms ('my thought, whose murder yet is but fantastical . . .'). Such again is that other great soliloquy, 'If it were done, when 'tis done . . .' where the meaning is composed of an emotional current running full tilt against an attempted logical control. In the *Hamlet* passage the pace is more meditative, but such ideas as it contains are held loosely in relation to a current of feeling which is the main determinant of meaning. And this is important, because the thought that is struggling for expression is one that can only be clarified on certain conditions: the necessary condition, as we saw at the end of the last lecture, is an emotional integrity and a wholeness of the personality that Hamlet has not, so far, achieved, from which indeed, as soon as the soliloquy is ended, he decisively withdraws.

The thought struggling for expression to which I just now referred is contained in the arresting opening line, 'To be, or not to be, that is the question . . .' Dr Johnson expressed his sense of the opening in these words:

> *Hamlet*, knowing himself injured in the most enormous and atrocious degree, and seeing no means of redress, but such as must expose him to the extremity of hazard, meditates on his situation in this manner: *Before I can form any rational scheme of action under this pressure of distress*, it is necessary to decide, whether, *after our present state, we are* to be or not to be. That is the question, which, as it shall be answered, will determine, *whether 'tis nobler*, and more suitable to the dignity of reason, *to suffer the outrages of fortune* patiently, or to take arms against *them*, and by opposing end them, *though perhaps* with the loss of life.

Now I feel sure that Johnson is right in implicitly rejecting the idea of suicide at this point, and I think that the idea of immortality is indeed very close to the forefront of Hamlet's consciousness. But there is that in Johnson's phrasing which partially obscures the full implications of the crucial phrase. The primary thought is not whether 'after our present state' we are to be or not to be; it is the questions of present being.[1]

In the Fourth Book of Boethius's *Consolation of Philosophy*[2] there is a notable passage that throws some light on this. Wicked men, says Boethius, are fundamentally 'destitute of all forces'.

> For why do they follow vices, forsaking virtues? By ignorance of that which is good? But what is more devoid of strength than blind ignorance? Or do they know what they should embrace, but passion driveth them headlong the contrary way? So also intemperance makes them frail, since they cannot strive against vice. Or do they wittingly and willingly forsake goodness, and decline to vices? But in this sort they leave not only to be powerful, but even to be at all (*sed omnino esse desinunt*). For they which leave the common end of all things which are, leave also being. Which may perhaps seem strange to some, that we should say that evil men are not at all, who are the greatest part of men: but yet it is so. For I deny not that evil men are evil, but withal I say that purely and simply they are not.
>
> For as thou mayest call a carcase a dead man, but not simply a man, so I confess that the vicious are evil, but I cannot grant that they are absolutely. For that is which retaineth order, and keepeth nature, but that which faileth from this leaveth also to be that which is in his own nature.

I feel the more justified in invoking this passage for the light it may throw in so far as it is clear from *Macbeth*

[1] I am conscious of a debt here to Max Plowman. See 'Some Values in *Hamlet*', *The Right to Live*, pp. 156 ff.

[2] Book IV, Prose ii, which is said to be a paraphrase of Plato's *Gorgias*.

that Shakespeare was deeply familiar with the traditional doctrine of the nothingness of evil—*malum nihil
est*, evil is nothing, as Boethius says a few lines after the
ending of the passage I have just given. Not indeed that
evil deeds and evil passions do not exist; it is simply
that they lead away from what all men naturally desire,
and for which goodness and being are alternative
names.[1] Neither do I offer the passage as anything like
a direct source. I quote it simply as an indication of the
kind of ideas with which Shakespeare and his educated
contemporaries were likely to be familiar, and therefore of the implications of language that would be
present to them, but that we are likely to miss: in the
passage that I have quoted, in the translation of I.T.
of 1609, the words 'to be', 'are' and 'is' are used abso-
lutely to indicate essential being. The guiding theme of
the *Consolation* is that to be free of the shackles of passion
and ignorance is to rise superior to Fortune, so that
suffering itself becomes a positive act.[2] It is for this very
reasons we may notice, that Hamlet admires Horatio.

> Since my dear soul was mistress of her choice,
> And could of men distinguish, her election
> Hath seal'd thee for herself; for thou hast been
> As one, in suffering all, that suffers nothing;
> A man that Fortune's buffets and rewards
> Hath ta'en with equal thanks; and bless'd are those
> Whose blood and judgment are so well commingled

---

[1] On the relation of Shakespeare's thought to traditional doctrine
in this respect see W. C. Curry, *Shakespeare's Philosophical Patterns*
(Louisiana State University Press).

[2] For the relation of Boethius's fortitude and Christian attitudes to
suffering, see John F. Danby, *Poets on Fortune's Hill*, pp. 80-83. In
Chapter IV, '*King Lear* and Christian Patience', Professor Danby writes
well of the positive implications of Christian patience.

That they are not a pipe for Fortune's finger
To sound what stop she please. Give me that man
That is not passion's slave, and I will wear him
In my heart's core, ay, in my heart of hearts,
As I do thee.

Hamlet's deep underlying concern is with essential being.

What it seems to me that Hamlet is saying at the opening of the soliloquy is that what it means to be is the question of all questions; 'and this is so,' he goes on, 'whether we believe with Boethius that the blows of Fortune must be endured, or whether we think it better actively to combat evil—which, in my case, is likely to result in my own death'—

Or to take arms against a sea of troubles,
And by opposing, end them, to die to sleep
No more . . .

But by now there is no pretence of following a logical sequence of thought; one idea blends with another—killing Claudius, killing oneself, the well-nigh insupportable troubles of life, the fear of futurity—all carried by currents of half-expressed emotion, so that the thoughts that the Prince is trying to bring into some order are eroded and carried away on the stream of feeling. Now the strongest feeling, which takes charge with the equation of death and sleep, is, as we have seen, the regressive desire to evade, shuffle off, the complexities of consciousness. Of that I do not think there can be any doubt at all—

            'tis a consummation
Devoutly to be wished to die to sleep . . .

But if life is a load, death, or what may come after death, is even more to be feared. As Mr John Vyvyan has remarked in his recent book, *The Shakespearean Ethic*, 'Throughout the long soliloquy, every idea is negative. To live is to "bear the whips and scorns of time", to die is to fly to other ills "we know not of". Even the possibility of joy is excluded'; and 'when life loses joy, it also loses meaning'. For Hamlet, therefore, in his present state of conflicting feelings and restricted consciousness, no solution is possible, neither of his great problem, 'to be, or not to be', nor of the problems that entirely depend on an answer to that overriding question—the problems, I mean, of how to face life and death with something quite other than fear and aversion. What he reproaches himself with is excess of conscience—'Thus conscience does make cowards of us all'—whereas it is quite clear that, whether we take the word in the sense of reflection and consciousness or in the more usual sense of moral concern (and I agree with D. G. James that here both meanings are present), what Hamlet needs is not less of conscience but more.[1]

> Thus conscience does make cowards of us all,
> And thus the native hue of resolution
> Is sicklied o'er with the pale cast of thought,
> And enterprises of great pitch and moment,
> With this regard their currents turn awry,
> And lose the name of action. . . .

[1] Perhaps, in passing, we may recall that in *Richard III* it was one of the murderers of the Duke of Clarence who declared of conscience, 'it makes a man a coward . . . 'Tis a blushing shamefast spirit, that mutinies in a man's bosom; it fills a man full of obstacles: . . . it is turn'd out of towns and cities for a dangerous thing; and every man that means to live well endeavours to trust to himself and to live without it'.

It does not matter that in Hamlet's mind the thought of suicide merges with the thought of killing the king; what matters is the quite unambiguous sense of health giving way to disease, of a loss of purpose and a lapsing from positive direction. What the soliloquy does in short is to bring to a head our recognition of the dependence of thought on deeper levels of consciousness, and to make plain beyond all doubt that the set of Hamlet's consciousness is towards a region where no resolution is possible at all.

The soliloquy of course occupies a central point in the action. It is followed at once by the scene with Ophelia on which we have already had occasion to comment, and which makes fully explicit the direction of the emotional current of the soliloquy. To quote John Vyvyan again, the dialogue with Ophelia 'is really a continuation of the death theme; indeed, it is more, it is part of the long-drawn act of spiritual suicide'. What Ophelia says when Hamlet has left her is:

Oh, what a noble mind is here o'erthrown!
The courtier's, soldier's, scholar's, eye, tongue, sword;
The expectancy and rose of the fair state,
The glass of fashion and the mould of form,
The observed of all observers, quite, quite down!
And I, of ladies most deject and wretched,
That suck'd the honey of his music vows,
Now see that noble and most sovereign reason,
Like sweet bells jangled out of tune, and harsh;
That unmatch'd form and feature of blown youth
Blasted with ecstasy; Oh, woe is me,
To have seen what I have seen, see what I see!

That surely is quite explicit, and from now until the closing scene it seems to me that little detailed commentary is needed to enforce the view that I have been trying to define. Hamlet, with whatever excitements of his reason and his blood, is a man who has given himself over to a false direction of consciousness; and at each of the crucial points of the action Shakespeare leaves us in no doubt of the inadequacy—and worse— of Hamlet's basic attitudes. The play scene, which includes the obscene jesting with Ophelia, ends with the declaration,

'Tis now the very witching time of night,
When churchyards yawn, and hell itself breathes out
Contagion to this world; now could I drink hot
    blood,
And do such bitter business as the day
Would quake to look on . . .

—and indeed there is contagion from hell in the words addressed to the ostensibly praying Claudius. The scene with his mother includes the killing of Polonius and Hamlet's almost perfunctory repentance; whilst the attempt to break Gertrude's attachment to Claudius, to show her the truth of her false position, is subtly changed in character by Hamlet's obsessive preoccupation with what he denounces. Once more, before Hamlet disappears from the action for a time, he is allowed to reveal himself in a soliloquy which contains a firm though implicit placing judgment. It is, you remember, when Hamlet, about to embark for England, is informed of the expedition of Fortinbras— the same Fortinbras who, earlier in the play, had 'shark'd up a list of lawless resolutes' to regain the land lost by his father to the elder Hamlet. Dissuaded from that enterprise he is now leading his army against Poland,

> to gain a little patch of ground
> That hath in it no profit but the name.

It is by this expedition that Hamlet feels himself admonished—

> How all occasions do inform against me,
> And spur my dull revenge!

As before, our interest is evenly divided between what is said and what is implied. What Hamlet says is that these clear signs of making for a defined objective reproach his own inactivity:

> Sure he that made us with such large discourse,
> Looking before and after, gave us not
> That capability and god-like reason
> To fust in us unused . . .

—nor, we may add, to use for purposes such as those of the Fortinbrases of this world. And that surely is the dramatic point of the scene. As in the earlier soliloquy after the encounter with the Players, Hamlet is indulging himself with thoughts of a way out of his impasse that is no way out, and the terms in which he expresses his sense of inferiority indicate how far that ranging mind has allowed itself to be restricted.

> Examples, gross as earth, exhort me;
> Witness this army of such mass and charge,

> Led by a delicate and tender prince,
> Whose spirit with divine ambition puff'd
> Makes mouths at the invisible event;
> Exposing what is mortal and unsure
> To all that fortune, death and danger dare,
> Even for an egg-shell. Rightly to be great
> Is not to stir without great argument,
> But greatly to find quarrel in a straw
> When honour's at the stake.

Professor Dover Wilson paraphrases the last sentence: 'Fighting for trifles is mere pugnacity, not greatness; but it *is* greatness to fight instantly and for a trifle when honour is at stake'. Right enough; but this is arguing in a circle, for it leaves honour as no more than the prompting to fight instantly and for a trifle—

> a plot
> Whereon the numbers cannot try the cause,
> Which is not tomb enough and continent
> To hide the slain.

'Honour' here is not a defining word but a mere justifying blur. Since the author of *Henry IV*, Part I, was not likely to be uncritical of such 'honour', nor to believe that the ambition prompting Fortinbras was indeed divine, the purpose of the soliloquy can only be to define one further stage in the withdrawal of Hamlet's consciousness, a sacrifice of reason to a fantasy of quite unreflective destructive action; and indeed the soliloquy ends with explicit emphasis—

> O, from this time forth,
> My thoughts be bloody, or be nothing worth!

For three scenes Hamlet is absent from the action.[1] When he returns, he is shown first as brooding on death with an exclusive intensity, then as reacting to the poignant reminder of the love that he denied with a long outburst in which there is neither self-knowledge nor sincerity—

> Nay, an thou'lt mouth,
> I'll rant as well as thou.

Neither does the opening of the next scene, the final one of the play, do anything to restore our memory of the man whose own highest standards were made explicit in the noble eulogy of human potentiality—

> What a piece of work is a man, how noble in reason, how infinite in faculties, in form and moving, how like an angel in apprehension, how like a god!

Now, what we have instead is a demonstration of quickness of mind used in a triumph that is either barbaric or trivial. Rosencrantz and Guildenstern have been sent to their deaths 'not shriving time allowed', and 'they are not near my conscience'. As for the encounter with Osric, this serves both to demonstrate one more facet of King Claudius's world and at the same time to underline the only kind of relief that Hamlet now finds possible—a satirical display of the world's folly.

---

[1] Though he is kept in our minds not only by the frequent references to him and by his letters to Horatio and the King, but by Ophelia and Laertes: by Ophelia because her madness and death are the result of Hamlet's own actions, by Laertes because, as Mr John Vyvyan says, he represents the uninhibited vengeance to which Hamlet has now given himself up. On this, and the 'allegorical' overtones of these two figures see *The Shakespearean Ethic*, pp. 50 ff.

And now a strange thing happens, so strange that even those who by no means share the romantic idealization of Hamlet, feel justified in claiming that at the end his nobility is restored. This Hamlet, who has shown himself so torn and distracted, suddenly appears composed, with a fortitude that has in it nothing of the emotional heightening—of at times the near hysteria—that has accompanied his courage on former occasions. Osric has done his errand, the royal party is approaching, and there is a pause before the last desperate action.

> *Horatio.* You will lose this wager, my lord.
> *Hamlet.* I do not think so. Since he went into France, I have been in continual practice. I shall win at the odds; but thou wouldst not think how ill all's here about my heart—but it is no matter.
> *Horatio.* Nay, good my lord—
> *Hamlet.* It is but foolery, but it is such a kind of gain-giving as would perhaps trouble a woman.
> *Horatio.* If your mind dislike anything, obey it. I will forestall their repair hither, and say you are not fit.
> *Hamlet.* Not a whit, we defy augury. There is a special providence in the fall of a sparrow. If it be now, 'tis not to come—if it be not to come, it will be now—if it be not now, yet it will come—the readiness is all. Since no man, of aught he leaves, knows what is't to leave betimes, let be.

In my second lecture I made a truncated quotation from Professor C. S. Lewis which I must now give in its entirety. 'The world of *Hamlet* is a world where one has lost one's way. The Prince also has no doubt lost his, and we can tell the precise moment at which he finds it again'—it is the moment when he defies augury in those quiet, memorable but puzzling words that I have just quoted from the play. The Prince has lost his way, 'and we can tell the precise moment at which he finds it again'. Others have written to the same effect. But is it really so? If we take the view that this is a tragic hero who has indeed lost his way and who will shortly lose his life, but who has in some fundamental way come through, are we not in danger of losing sight of a fundamental principle of Shakespearean construction—of a fundamental principle indeed of all supreme works of art—that no passage has its full meaning in isolation from the whole of which it forms a part? Perhaps, for the last time, we may remind ourselves of other of Shakespeare's plays, so that comparison may help us to determine how we should take the matter before us.

In all the scenes in which Shakespeare's tragic characters confront their deaths there is a mystery that partially confounds our rational analysis and explanation. There is a profound remark of Blake's to the effect that we should distinguish between states and individuals in those states. Now whether we regard Shakespeare's characters as individuals or as dramatic embodiments of states of being, Shakespeare's generosity, his outgoing feeling for life in all its forms, even when life is perverted and self-defeated, plays about them at their end. All that can be said on their behalf *is* said, either directly or in the less explicit statement of the full dramatic action. There is, for example,

Brutus, whose funeral eulogy is so far from being merely formal:

> This was the noblest Roman of them all.
> All the conspirators save only he
> Did that they did in envy of great Caesar;
> He only, in a general honest thought
> And common good to all, made one of them.
> His life was gentle, and the elements
> So mix't in him, that Nature might stand up
> And say to all the world, 'This was a man!'

Or there is Coriolanus, whose foreknowledge of death gives dignity to his yielding to the instinct he had professed to despise:

> O mother, mother!
> What have you done? Behold, the heavens do ope,
> The gods look down, and this unnatural scene
> They laugh at. O my mother, mother! O!
> You have won a happy victory to Rome;
> But for your son, believe it, O, believe it,
> Most dangerously you have with him prevail'd,
> If not most mortal to him. But let it come.

Here indeed, in each instance, is nobility and genuine pathos. Yet neither of these passages stands in isolation: each of them comes at the culminating point of a dramatic structure of which the full force is now present to us—that is, unless we are prepared to sacrifice Shakespeare's complex meanings for the sake of some easy 'dramatic' effect. The word 'irony' tends to suggest some aloofness from life, a sort of pleasure in seeing through experiences that others find simply touching. Shakespeare's irony of course is not of this kind; it is simply part of his supreme intelligence; charity is not the less charity for being undeceived. In this sense, then, there is irony—a deeply tragic irony—in each of the scenes to which I just now referred. The abstract generality of Brutus's honest thoughts, the preoccupation with a political 'common good' at the expense of humanity—that is what the play taken as a whole has put in question. As for Coriolanus, neither the dignity of his mother's pleadings nor the fortitude and magnanimity of his decision can obscure what the play makes clear—that the patrician 'honour' in which Volumnia had reared him is an aggressive boy's pitiful and inadequate substitute for that integrity which is at once an individual and a civic virtue.

To all this—for examples could be multiplied—Hamlet's death is no exception. By what he says, by what others say about him ('noble Hamlet', 'noble heart', 'sweet Prince'), is recalled that other Hamlet whom Ophelia knew—'The expectancy and rose of the fair state'—but who has appeared so fitfully in the course of the present action, the 'sweet bells' of his reason being 'jangled out of tune, and harsh'. 'The readiness is all', he says, meaning, I take it, not simply preparedness for death but that quality for which Sir Thomas Elyot, declaring that English lacked a name for it, had taken from Latin the word 'maturity'.

'Maturum' in Latin may be interpreted ripe or ready, as fruit when it is ripe, it is at the very point to be gathered and eaten. And every other thing, when it is ready, it is at the instant after to be occupied. Therefore that word maturity, is trans-lated to the acts of man, that when they be done with such moderation, that nothing in the doing may be seen superfluous or indigent, we may say, that they be maturely done.[1]

Hamlet's 'readiness', then, is that maturity of the feeling, thinking being that enables a man to be 'as one, in suffering all, that suffers nothing'. The thought—as well as Elyot's phrasing—will be echoed in *King Lear*:

> men must endure
> Their going hence, even as their coming hither;
> Ripeness is all.

But whereas in *Lear* Edgar's sentence carries a large part of the burden of the play, indicating as it does that responsiveness to life in which 'the "I" in the individual' ceases to be in the centre of the picture and personal action takes on an almost impersonal quality, Hamlet's utterance can in no sense be regarded as indicating the goal towards which his consciousness, the central consciousness of the play, has been directed. What it represents rather is the paradoxical recognition of a truth glimpsed in defeat, and by this I mean defeat in terms of Hamlet's own highest standards. All that Hamlet is now ready for is to meet his death in playing the part of the avenger, the part imposed on him by that Ghost whose command had been for a sterile concentration on death and evil. Art, says Pasternak's Zhivago, 'has two constant, two unending preoccupa-

[1] Sir Thomas Elyot, *The Governour* (1531), Book I, Chapter xxii. Elyot is here beginning his exposition of the ways in which dancing may be an introduction to the cardinal virtue of Prudence, and the branch here indicated is the mean between celerity and slowness. The whole chapter has, I think, some bearing on Shakespeare's play.

tions: it is always meditating upon death and it is always thereby creating new life'. To recognize the truth in this it is necessary to supply an unspoken condition: that the meditation on death is no mere brooding but an energetic and transforming assimilation of the basic facts of the human condition. What Hamlet represents, on the other hand, is a fixation of consciousness—a condition in which neither death nor life can be truly known.

I said at the beginning that this account of *Hamlet* would be in some ways tentative, and I hope that no one will take my exposition as more than a challenge to re-read and re-think the play. What I have tried to do is to suggest that we are likely to see *Hamlet* more clearly if we see it as one of a series of studies of the mind's engagement with the world, of the intimate and intricate relations of self and world. In each of these plays—I have named *Othello*, *Timon*, and some others— there is an exploration of the ways in which 'being' and 'knowing' are related, so that failure in being, the corruption of consciousness, results either in a false affirmation, as with Othello, or in an inability to affirm at all, as with Hamlet. In *King Lear*, where so many lines of Shakespeare's thought converge, Lear only comes to 'see better' through a purgatorial progress of self-knowledge which enables him finally to respond to love. Perhaps we may say that Hamlet's consciousness is not unlike the consciousness of the unregenerate Lear, full of the knowledge of bitter wrong, of evil seemingly inherent in human nature. But Hamlet, unlike Lear—even if, initially, he is less greatly sinning —cannot break out of the closed circle of loathing and self-contempt, so that his nature is 'subdued to what it works in, like the dyer's hand'. The awareness that he embodies is at best an intermediate stage of the spirit, at worst a blind alley. Most certainly Hamlet's way of knowing the world is not Shakespeare's own.

2
Personality and Politics in
Julius Caesar

SHAKESPEARE wrote *Julius Caesar* in 1599, and the play was first performed in the new theatre, the Globe, which Shakespeare's company, the Lord Chamberlain's Men, had recently had built on the Bankside. Shakespeare, of course, got the material for his play from Plutarch's *Lives* of Caesar and Brutus. But, just as in gathering material for the English historical plays from Holinshed, he selected only what he needed as an artist dealing with the universal stuff of human nature, so here his purpose is not simply to reconstruct the historical situation in Rome in the year 44 B.C. The historical material is of interest only for what Shakespeare makes of it. That he made of it a pretty exciting drama is witnessed by the fact that the play is still being performed today, still capable of holding audiences not all of whom are compelled by the exigencies of university examinations. It is exciting; it is richly human; it holds the attention. It also happens to be an important work of art—which means that through the forms of a dramatic action it focuses a particular vision of life: the sequence of events, the dialogue, the interplay of different characters, are held together by an informing 'idea', so that all these elements contribute not solely to an evening's entertainment but to an imaginative statement about something of permanent importance in human life. What, at that level of understanding, is *Julius Caesar* 'about'? That is the question to which I want to attempt an answer.

Before tackling that question directly, there are two matters I want to touch on—one concerning the play's structure, the other its substance: they are, in fact, closely related. The action of *Julius Caesar* turns on a political murder, the assassination of

Caesar, which takes place in Act III, scene i—right in the middle of the play. Before the murder, attention is focused on the origin and development of the conspiracy—Caesar on one side, Cassius, Brutus, and half a dozen more, on the other. After the murder, attention is focused on the struggle between the conspirators (Brutus and Cassius) and the successors of Caesar (Octavius Caesar and Antony), on the failure and disintegration of the republican cause. It is possible to see a blemish here: the climax, it can be said, comes too early, and when Caesar has disappeared from the action, Shakespeare only contrives to hold our interest by such *tours de force* as Antony's oration and the quarrel between Brutus and Cassius. In fact, however, the play forms a coherent and tightly woven whole. The murder of Caesar is, if you like, the axis on which the world of the play turns. Up to that event, we are shown one half of that world, a hemisphere; as soon as the daggers are plunged into Caesar's body the world of the drama turns, and fresh scenes and landscapes come into view: but it is still one world. Dropping the metaphor, we may say that the interests aroused in the first part find their natural fulfilment in the second: that there is nothing in the presented action of the last two and a half acts (and action includes psychological as well as physical action) that is not a revelation of what was implicit, but partly concealed, in the conspiracy itself. There is no question here of a broken-backed play in which flagging interest must be maintained by adventitious means. The play is as much of a unity as *Macbeth*; and, like *Macbeth*, though less powerfully, it reveals the connexion between observable events in the public world and their causes in the deeper places of personal life—matters not so easily observed except by the eye of the poet.

My second preliminary observation concerns the nature of the interest enlisted by this play. In dealing with *Julius Caesar*, as indeed with other of Shakespeare's plays, there is a particular temptation to be guarded against—that is, the temptation to abstract from the play certain general issues and to debate them either in the abstract or in a context which Shakespeare has not provided for them. Criticism of *Julius Caesar* is sometimes confused by considerations that apply either to the historical situation at Rome at the time of Caesar's assassination, or else to specifically twentieth-century political situations, and the play is debated as though Shakespeare were putting before us the question of whether dictatorship or republicanism were the more desirable form of government. He is doing nothing of the kind; and perhaps the first thing to notice is how much of possible political interest the play leaves out. There is no hint of, say, Dante's conception of the majesty, the providential necessity, of the empire which Caesar founded. On the other hand, there is nothing that can be interpreted as a feeling for the virtues of aristocratic republicanism—in the way, for example, some of the first makers of the French Revolution felt when they invoked Roman example. We are not called on to concern ourselves with whether 'Caesarism' is, or was, desirable or otherwise. Instead, there is a sharp focus on a single, simple, but important question—on what happens when personal judgment tries to move exclusively on a political plane, where issues are simplified and distorted. I may say, in passing, that if we want a wider context for the play, we shall find it not in a realm of political speculation foreign to it, but in those other plays of Shakespeare—they include such different plays as *Troilus and Cressida* and *Othello*—where the dramatist is posing the question of how men come to deliver themselves to illusion, of how they construct for themselves a world in which, because it is not the world of reality but a projection of their own, they inevitably come to disaster. This means, of course, that the play offers no solution—it offers no material for a solution—of the question, Empire or Republic? dictatorship or 'liberty'? Shakespeare is studying a situation, bringing the force of his imagination to bear on it, not offering solutions, or not, at all events, political ones.

Yet—and this brings me to the substance of what I want to say—*Julius Caesar* does have important political implications. It takes up Shakespeare's developing preoccupation with the relation between political action and morality. 'Politics', I know, is an exciting word, and 'morality' is a dry word. But what I mean is this:—Politics are the realm where, whatever the particular interests involved, the issues are to some extent simplified and generalized, and therefore seen in abstract and schematic terms. Morality—and I mean essential living morality, not just copy-book maxims—has to do with the human, the specific and particular. Martin Buber, in his great book, *I and Thou*, has made us familiar with an important distinction —between the world of 'thou' (the world of relationship) and the world of 'it' (the world where things, and even people, are treated simply as objects, and manipulated accordingly). For the politician there is a constant temptation to lose sight of the 'thou' world, and Martin Buber's distinction may help us here.

Julius Caesar is a play about great public events, but again and again we are given glimpses of the characters in their private, personal, and domestic capacities. Caesar is concerned for his wife's barrenness, he faints when he is offered the crown, he 'had a sickness when he was in Spain', he listens to Calpurnia's dreams and fears. Brutus causes his wife concern about his health; we are told of his disturbed sleep; we see him forgetting his public cares and ensuring, with real tenderness, that his boy Lucius gets some needed sleep. And much more to a similar effect. Now Shakespeare at this time was nearing the height of his powers—*Hamlet* is only a year or two away—and it is unlikely that he put in these domestic scenes and glimpses because he didn't know what else to do. It is obvious that we are intended to be aware of some sort of a *contrast* between public life and private, and commentators have, in fact, noticed this. They point, for example, to the contrast between Caesar the public figure and Caesar the man:

> . . . for always I am Caesar.
> Come on my right hand, for this ear is deaf.

When Brutus, in his 'gown' (the symbol of domestic privacy) speaks gently to his boy, we are told that this 'relieves the strain' of the tragic action. And every account of the characters includes some reference to those aspects of Caesar, Brutus, and Cassius that are revealed in their more intimate moments and hidden or disguised in public. What seems not to have been recognized is the cumulative effect of these and many other reminders of a more personal life—the important part this pervasive but unobtrusive personalism plays, or should play, in our evaluation of the public action.

That we are intended to be aware of the characters as men, of the faces behind the masks, is clear enough. We may notice in passing that on occasion the contrast is emphasized in visual terms. At the beginning of II, ii, according to the stage-direction that makes every schoolboy laugh, Caesar enters 'in his night-gown' (a dressing-gown, or house-coat); then, as the conspirators prevail over his wife's entreaties, 'Give me my robe, for I will go.' Not only are all the main figures at some time divested of their public robes—those 'robes and furr'd gowns' that, according to King Lear, 'hide all'—and allowed to appear as husbands, masters of households and friends, but they all, in turn, emphasize each other's personal characteristics. 'He was quick mettle when he went to school,' says Brutus of Casca. A principal reason why Cassius thinks Caesar isn't fit for his exalted position is that he, Cassius, is the stronger swimmer, and that Caesar, like the rest of us, was hot and cold and thirsty when he had a fever. And although Antony, addressing the crowd, deliberately makes emotional capital out of Caesar's mantle, 'I remember,' he says,

> The first time Caesar ever put it on;
> 'Twas on a summer's evening, in his tent,
> That day he overcame the Nervii,

the touch of particularity, of revealed privacy, is intended for us, the audience, as well as for the Roman crowd. We notice, too, how often the word 'love' appears in this play. I haven't made a count, but it must be about two dozen times, which is perhaps rather surprising in a political play. Again and again the characters speak of their love—their 'dear love' or their 'kind love'—for each other, just as they seem to find a special satisfaction in referring to themselves as 'brothers'. Now the effect of all this is not only one of pathos or simple irony. The focus of our attention, I have said, is the public world: from the arena of *that* world, personal life—where truth between man and man resides—is glimpsed as across a gulf. The distance between these two worlds is the measure of the distortion and falsity that takes place in the attempt to make 'politics' self-enclosed.

The attempt—the attempt to make public action and public appearance something separate and remote from personal action—is common to both sides. Caesar constantly assumes the public mask. It seems to be a habit with him to refer to himself in the third person as 'Caesar'; and there is his speech, so charged with dramatic irony, when, immediately before the assassination, he rejects the petition of Metellus Cimber:

> I could be well mov'd if I were as you;
> If I could pray to move, prayers would move me;
> But I am constant as the northern star,
> Of whose true-fix'd and resting quality
> There is no fellow in the firmament . . .
> So in the world; 'tis furnish'd well with men,
> And men are flesh and blood, and apprehensive;
> Yet in the number I do know but one
> That unassailable holds on his rank,

> Unshak'd of motion: and that I am he,
> Let me a little show it. . . .

What this means, in the case of Caesar, is that in the utterance
and attitude of the public man we sense a dangerous tautness.
In the case of Brutus, a parallel divorce between the man and
the statesman results in something more subtle and more interesting. That a particular bond of affection unites Caesar and
Brutus, the play leaves us in no doubt. Almost the first words
that Brutus speaks of Caesar are, 'I love him well', and when,
after the murder, he insists again and again that Caesar was his
'best lover', there is no need to doubt his 'sincerity' in the
ordinary sense of the word. So, too, Cassius tells us, 'Caesar
doth bear me hard; but he loves Brutus'; and Mark Antony:

> For Brutus, as you know, was Caesar's angel:
> Judge, O you Gods! how dearly Caesar lov'd him.
> This was the most unkindest cut of all. . . .

It is this Brutus, the close friend of Caesar, who wrenches his
mind to divorce policy from friendship; and the way in which
he does it demands some attention.

It is, of course, true that on matters of public policy you may
have to take a firm stand against men whom on other grounds
you like and respect: you can see this in the government of a
university, for example, as well as in the government of a state.
Is Brutus doing more than follow this principle to a necessary
conclusion? Well, yes, I think he is. For the moment I want to
put on one side the scene in which Cassius (in Brutus's own
words later) 'whets' him against Caesar, and ask your attention
for the long soliloquy at the opening of Act II in which Brutus
reviews his own motives and intended course of action. This is
what he says:

> It must be by his death: and for my part,
> I know no personal cause to spurn at him,
> But for the general. He would be crown'd:

How that might change his nature, there's the question.
It is the bright day that brings forth the adder;
And that craves wary walking. Crown him! that!
And then, I grant, we put a sting in him,
That at his will he may do danger with.
The abuse of greatness is when it disjoins
Remorse from power; and, to speak truth of Caesar,
I have not known when his affections sway'd
More than his reason. But 'tis a common proof,
That lowliness is young ambition's ladder,
Whereto the climber-upward turns his face;
And when he once attains the upmost round,
He then unto the ladder turns his back,
Looks in the clouds, scorning the base degrees
By which he did ascend. So Caesar may:
Then, lest he may, prevent. And, since the quarrel
Will bear no colour for the thing he is,
Fashion it thus; that what he is, augmented,
Would run to these and these extremities;
And therefore think him as a serpent's egg
Which, hatch'd, would, as his kind, grow mischievous,
And kill him in the shell.

Now it is a principle of Shakespearean, indeed of Elizabethan, stage-craft, that when a character, in soliloquy or otherwise, develops a line of argument—as when Faustus, in Marlowe's play, produces a number of specious reasons for dismissing the traditional sciences—we are expected to follow the argument with some attention. Not, of course, that we follow such a speech merely as logicians. We are dealing with drama, which means that when a character expounds, say, his reasons for a course of action, what he says is intended to reveal some aspect of what he stands for and is committed to as a human being. And we are dealing with *poetic* drama, which means that even in an expository speech we are aware of much more than can be formulated in conceptual terms. But we do not, on this account, switch off our intelligence or such powers of logical thought as we may possess. As Virgil Whitaker says in his book, *Shakespeare's Use of Learning*, 'Like Marlowe, Shakespeare expected his audience to be able to detect a fallacy in reasoning.' With this in mind, let us turn back to Brutus's soliloquy. It is a curious argument, in which qualities known in direct contact between man and man ('I know no personal cause to spurn at him') are dismissed as irrelevant to public considerations; and it is precisely this that gives the air of tortuous unreality to Brutus's self-persuadings—full as these are of subjunctives and conditional verbs, which run full tilt against the reality that Brutus himself acknowledges:

> The abuse of greatness is when it disjoins
> Remorse from power; and, to speak truth of Caesar,
> I have not known when his affections sway'd
> More than his reason. . . .[1]

but:

> since the quarrel
> Will bear no colour for the thing he is,
> Fashion it thus. . . .

On this Coleridge shrewdly commented that what Brutus is really saying is that he 'would have no objection to a king, or to Caesar as a monarch in Rome, would Caesar but be as good a monarch as he now seems disposed to be'. In Brutus's mind, however, *what is* is now completely lost in a cloud of mere possibilities:

> And since the quarrel
> Will bear no colour for the thing he is,
> Fashion it thus; that what he is, augmented,
> Would run to these and these extremities;
> And therefore think him as a serpent's egg
> Which, hatch'd, would, as his kind, grow mischievous,
> And kill him in the shell.

[1] It may not be unnecessary to comment that 'remorse', here, means pity, and 'affections', passions.

Caesar is already, as Brutus describes him later, 'the foremost man of all the world'; he is not still 'in the shell', neither is he 'young ambition'. But it is by sophistries such as these that Brutus launches himself on what Clarendon was to call 'that fathomless abyss of Reason of State'.

Shakespeare, of course, was a very great psychologist, and what the play also shows—and I want to dwell on this for a moment before returning to the scene of Brutus's crucial choice and its consequences—is that personal feelings, which Brutus tries to exclude from his deliberations on 'the general good', are, in fact, active in public life. But they are active in the wrong way. Unacknowledged, they influence simply by distorting the issues. The famous quarrel scene between Brutus and Cassius certainly has this ironic significance. It is, of course, Cassius, in whom the 'taboo on tenderness' is strongest—who is scornful of 'our mothers' spirits' (I, iii, 83) and despises Caesar for behaving 'as a sick girl' (I, ii, 127)—who here displays the most pronounced 'feminine' traits—'that rash humour which my mother gave me' (IV, iii, 119). That the whole thing contrives to be touching should not obscure the fact that the causes of the quarrel—they had mainly to do with money—did demand a more impersonal consideration. Now the relevance of this is that it is above all in Cassius that the springs of political action are revealed as only too personal. What nags at him is simply envy of Caesar: 'for my single self', he says to Brutus:

> I had as lief not be as live to be
> In awe of such a thing as I myself. . . .
> . . . And this man
> Is now become a god, and Cassius is
> A wretched creature and must bend his body
> If Caesar carelessly but nod on him.

Caesar, he says to Casca, is:

> A man no mightier than thyself or me
> In personal action, yet prodigious grown.

And it is this man who acts as tempter to the 'idealizing' Brutus, skilfully enlisting what Brutus feels is due to his own 'honour'. I do not wish here to pursue the temptation scene in any detail; but that it *is* temptation the play leaves us in no doubt. At the end of the long, skilfully conducted second scene of the first act, Cassius is left alone and reveals his thoughts about the man whom we can only call, at this stage, his dupe:

> Well, Brutus, thou art noble; yet, I see,
> Thy honourable mettle may be wrought
> From that it is dispos'd; therefore 'tis meet
> That noble minds keep ever with their likes;
> For who so firm that cannot be seduc'd?

Editors disagree about the meaning of these lines. Some would have it that Cassius means that the noble disposition of Brutus may be, as it were, wrenched from truth by his friendship with Caesar, the dictator: the man of republican virtue should 'keep ever' with those like-minded to himself. It may be so; but I find it hard *not* to read the lines as a firm 'placing' comment on Cassius's own relations with Brutus: 'For who so firm that cannot be seduc'd—by specious reasoning? The most we can say for Cassius is that his appeals to Roman 'honour', to the 'nobility' of his associates, are not simply laid on for the benefit of Brutus, but are part of his own self-deception. The banished feelings have come in by the back door, thinly disguised by much talk of 'honour'.

It is of course true that the play does not present Caesar as an ideal ruler, and I myself think that Shakespeare would have agreed with Blake's gnomic verse:

> The strongest poison ever known
> Came from Caesar's laurel crown.

But when Brutus, the man of honour and high moral principles, accepts Cassius's arguments and enters the world of the conspirators, he enters a topsyturvy world—a world where 'impersonal' Reasons of State take the place of direct personal knowledge; and at the same time true reason, which is a function of the whole man, has given way to obscure personal emotion. Shakespeare leaves us in no doubt of the confusion of values and priorities in that world. We have noticed how often love and friendship are invoked in this play, indicating what men really want and need. What we also have to notice is how often the forms of friendship are exploited for political ends. When Caesar is reluctant to go to the Senate House, Decius inveigles him with protestations of 'dear dear love', and the conspirators drink wine with their victim before leading him to the Capitol; Brutus kisses Caesar immediately before the killing; Antony talks much of love and shakes hands all round as a way of deceiving the conspirators. It is this, therefore, that explains our sense of something monstrous in the action, symbolized by the storms and prodigies, and made fully explicit by Brutus in his garden soliloquy—for it is time to return to that—when, deserting the actual, he has given himself to a phantasmagoria of abstractions.

At this point, Brutus's self-communings are interrupted by his boy, Lucius, who brings him a letter—one of many such, purporting to come from the citizens of Rome asking for redress at his hands, but, as we know, manufactured by Cassius. 'O Rome!' says Brutus, not knowing that the letters do not represent 'Rome' at all,

> O Rome! I make thee promise;
> If the redress will follow, thou receiv'st
> Thy full petition at the hand of Brutus!

Then, as Lucius goes off once more to see who is knocking at the gate in the darkness:

> Since Cassius first did whet me against Caesar,
> I have not slept.
> Between the acting of a dreadful thing

> And the first motion, all the interim is
> Like a phantasma, or a hideous dream:
> The genius and the mortal instruments
> Are then in council; and the state of man,
> Like to a little kingdom, suffers then
> The nature of an insurrection.

The indications here—the insomnia, the fact that Brutus is, as he has said earlier, 'with himself at war'—are, if we remember *Macbeth*, clear enough. And the signs of a mind at war with itself, attempting to batten down its own best insights, which yet refuse to disappear, continue into Brutus's musings as the muffled conspirators are announced:

> O conspiracy!
> Sham'st thou to show thy dangerous brow by night,
> When evils are most free? O! then by day
> Where wilt thou find a cavern dark enough
> To mask thy monstrous visage? Seek none, conspiracy;
> Hide it in smiles and affability:
> For if thou path, thy native semblance on,
> Not Erebus itself were dim enough
> To hide thee from prevention.

Conspiracy is not only 'dangerous', it is 'monstrous', associated with night and darkness, with evils and Erebus. As J. I. M. Stewart has said, Brutus's words are those of a 'man over the threshold of whose awareness a terrible doubt perpetually threatens to lap'.

Brutus, of course, is not a deliberate villain as Macbeth is; but like Macbeth he is presented as losing his way in a nightmare world—'like a phantasma', something both horrible and unreal, 'or a hideous dream'. In other words, Brutus's wrong choice not only leads to wrong action, it delivers him to a world of unreality, for the 'phantasma', far from ending with the acting of the 'dreadful thing', extends beyond it. As the play proceeds, we are made aware not only of a complete lack of

correspondence between the professed intentions of the conspirators and the result of their act, but of a marked element
of unreality in the world which they inhabit. Let us take two
examples, for Shakespeare provides them, and he presumably
intended that we should take notice of what he provides.

Shakespeare often puts before the audience two different
aspects of the same thing, or suggests two different angles on it
—sometimes, but not always, in juxtaposed scenes. He makes
no obvious comment, but the different scenes or passages play
off against each other, with an effect of implicit comment,
for the audience itself is thus enlisted in the business of evaluation and judgment. I think of such things as Falstaff's description of his ragged regiment, following hard on the heels of
Hotspur's heroics about warfare, in the First Part of *Henry IV*;
or the way in which, in *Antony and Cleopatra* the summit
meeting on Pompey's galley is followed immediately by a
glimpse of the army in the field, with some irony from a
soldier about the High Command. In *Julius Caesar*, the murder
of Caesar is not only presented on the stage, it is described both
in prospect and in retrospect. You all remember the way in
which Brutus envisages the action to the conspirators in the
scene with which we have been dealing. Pleading that Antony
may be spared, he says:

> Let us be sacrificers, but not butchers, Caius.
> We all stand up against the spirit of Caesar;
> And in the spirit of men there is no blood:
> O! that we then could come by Caesar's spirit,
> And not dismember Caesar. But, alas!
> Caesar must bleed for it. And, gentle friends,
> Let's kill him boldly, but not wrathfully;
> Let's carve him as a dish fit for the gods,
> Not hew him as a carcass fit for hounds. . . .

Is that the way political assassinations are carried out? Before the battle of Philippi, Brutus taunts Antony, 'you very wisely threat before you sting', to which Antony retorts:

> Villains! you did not so when your vile daggers
> Hack'd one another in the sides of Caesar;
> You show'd your teeth like apes, and fawn'd like hounds,
> And bow'd like bondmen, kissing Caesar's feet;
> Whilst damned Casca, like a cur, behind,
> Struck Caesar on the neck.

Antony, of course, speaks as a partisan of Caesar, but the energy of the verse ('your vile daggers Hack'd one another in the sides of Caesar') leaves us in no doubt that Antony's account is nearer to actuality than Brutus's fantasy of a ritualistic sacrifice.

My second example is of even greater importance, for it concerns the whole sequence of events in the second half of the play—consequences, I want to insist once more, that are shown as flowing directly from what Brutus and the rest commit themselves to in the first part. As soon as Julius Caesar falls, Cinna cries out:

> Liberty! Freedom! Tyranny is dead!
> Run hence, proclaim, cry it about the streets.

And Cassius:

> Some to the common pulpits, and cry out
> 'Liberty, freedom, and enfranchisement!'

Then, as something of the mounting bewilderment outside the Capitol is conveyed to us ('Men, wives, and children stare, cry out and run As it were doomsday'), Brutus enforces the ritualistic action of smearing themselves with Caesar's blood:

> Stoop, Romans, stoop,
> And let us bathe our hands in Caesar's blood
> Up to the elbows, and besmear our swords:
> Then walk we forth, even to the market-place;
> And, waving our red weapons o'er our heads,
> Let's all cry, 'Peace, freedom, and liberty!'

The irony of that hardly needs comment, but the play does, in fact, comment on it with some pungency. I suspect that what I am going to say will be obvious, so I will be brief and do little more than remind you of three successive scenes. When, after the murder, Brutus goes to the Forum to render 'public reasons' for Caesar's death, it is his failure in the sense of reality, of what people really are, that gives us the sombre comedy of his oration: so far as addressing real people is concerned he might as well have kept quiet. 'Had you rather Caesar were living, and die all slaves, than that Caesar were dead, to live all free men?' he asks, and much more to the same effect. To which the reply is successively:

> —Live, Brutus! live! live!
> —Bring him with triumph home unto his house.
> —Give him a statue with his ancestors.
> —Let him be Caesar.

After this, the response of the crowd to Antony's more consummate demonstration of the arts of persuasion comes as no surprise: it is:

> Revenge!—About!—Seek!—Burn!—Fire!—Kill!
> —Slay!—Let not a traitor live!

Mischief, in the words of Antony's cynical comment when he has worked his will with the crowd, is indeed afoot; and the very next scene—the last of the third Act—gives us a representative example of what is only too likely to happen in times of violent political disturbance. It shows us the death of an unoffending poet at the hands of a brutal mob:

> —Your name, sir, truly.
> —Truly, my name is Cinna.
> —Tear him to pieces; he's a conspirator.
> —I am Cinna the poet, I am Cinna the poet.
> —Tear him for his bad verses, tear him for his bad verses.

The frenzied violence of this, with its repeated, 'Tear him, tear him!' is followed at once by a scene of violence in a different key. If the mob is beyond the reach of reason, the Triumvirs, Antony, Octavius, and Lepidus, are only too coldly calculating in their assessment of political exigencies:

> *Ant.* These many then shall die; their names are prick'd.
> *Oct.* Your brother too must die; consent you, Lepidus?
> *Lep.* I do consent—
> *Oct.*   Prick him down. Antony.
> *Lep.* Upon condition Publius shall not live,
>   Who is your sister's son, Mark Antony.
> *Ant.* He shall not live; look, with a spot I damn him.
>   But, Lepidus, go you to Caesar's house;
>   Fetch the will hither, and we shall determine
>   How to cut off some charge in legacies.

And, when Lepidus goes off on his errand, Antony and Octavius discuss the matter of getting rid of him, before they turn their attention to combating the armies now levied by Brutus and Cassius. These, then, are the more or less explicit comments on Brutus's excited proclamation:

> And, waving our red weapons o'er our heads,
> Let's all cry, 'Peace, freedom, and liberty!'

That peace and liberty could be bought with 'red weapons' was the illusion: the reality is mob violence, proscription, and civil war.

In following the story through to its end, Shakespeare was, of course, bound to follow his historical material; but, as an artist, he made this serve his own purposes. Many of you must have noticed how often Shakespeare, in his greater plays, makes the outward action into a mirror or symbol of events and qualities in the mind or soul: *Macbeth* is perhaps the most obvious instance of this. The last act of *Julius Caesar* certainly follows this pattern. Even before the battle of Philippi Brutus and Cassius appear like men under a doom; and, although defeat comes to each in different ways, it comes to both as though they were expecting it, and prompts reflections, in themselves or in their followers, that clearly apply not merely to the immediate events but to the action as a whole. Cassius asks Pindarus to report to him what is happening in another part of the field ('My sight was ever thick,' he says), and, on a mistaken report that his messenger is taken by the enemy, kills himself. On which the comment of Messala is:

> O hateful error, melancholy's child!
> Why dost thou show to the apt thoughts of men
> The things that are not? O error! soon conceiv'd,
> Thou never com'st unto a happy birth,
> But kill'st the mother that engender'd thee.

Harold Goddard, in his interesting chapter on *Julius Caesar*, says of this, 'The whole plot against Caesar had been such an error.'[1] We may add further that the play also enforces the close connexion between error and a supposed perception of 'things that are not'. As Titinius says to the dead Cassius a moment later, 'Alas! thou hast misconstrued everything.' As for Brutus, defeated and brought to bay with his 'poor remains of friends', he senses that this is no accident of defeat but the working out of the destiny to which he committed himself long before:

> Night hangs upon mine eyes; my bones would rest,
> That have but labour'd to attain this hour.

And then, as he runs on his own sword:

> Caesar, now be still:
> I kill'd not thee with half so good a will.

These last ten words—if I may quote Goddard once more—'are the Last Judgment of Brutus on a conspiracy the morality of which other men, strangely, have long debated'.[2] Earlier in the play, you may remember, Cicero had commented on certain portents and men's interpretation of them:

[1] Harold Goddard, *The Meaning of Shakespeare*, Vol. I, p. 329.
[2] Ibid.

> But men may construe things after their fashion,
> Clean from the purpose of the things themselves.

That seems to me an anticipatory summing-up of Brutus's whole political career, as the play presents it.

Let me repeat once more, Brutus was not, in any of the ordinary senses of the word, a villain; he was simply an upright man who made a tragic mistake. The nature of that mistake the play, I think, sufficiently demonstrates. Brutus was a man who thought that an abstract 'common good' could be achieved without due regard to the complexities of the actual; a man who tried to divorce his political thinking and his political action from what he knew, and what he was, as a full human person. Many of us remember the idealizing sympathy felt by liberal young men in the 1930s for the Communist cause. There had, it was felt, been excesses, but as against the slow cruelty of a ruthless competitive society, its degradation of human values, even violence might seem like surgery. 'Today,' said W. H. Auden, in his poem, 'Spain' (1937):

> Today the inevitable increase in the chances of death;
> The conscious acceptance of guilt in the necessary murder.

That, of course, was written before the Russian treason trials of 1938 and the subsequent purges, and Auden subsequently re-wrote the lines; but they serve to illustrate the matter in hand. 'General good,' said Blake, 'is the cry of the scoundrel and the hypocrite; he who would do good to another must do it in minute particulars.' There is some exaggeration in the first half of that aphorism, but it contains a profound truth, sufficiently demonstrated in many eminent figures in history. Shakespeare demonstrates it in the figure of a man who was neither a scoundrel nor a hypocrite:

> This was the noblest Roman of them all:
> All the conspirators save only he

> Did that they did in envy of great Caesar;
> He only, in a general honest thought
> And common good to all, made one of them.
> His life was gentle, and the elements
> So mix'd in him that Nature might stand up
> And say to all the world, 'This was a man!'

Shakespeare offers little comfort to those who like to consider historical conflicts in terms of a simple black and white, or who imagine that there are simple solutions for political dilemmas. In the contrast between the 'gentle' Brutus and the man who, for abstract reasons ('a general honest thought'), murdered his friend and let loose civil war, Shakespeare gives us food for thought that, firmly anchored in a particular action, has a special relevance for us today, as I suspect it will have at all times.

3
Timon of Athens

O NE OF THE most interesting problems in Shakespeare criticism —as indeed in the criticism of all great literature—is the problem of divergent interpretations. I do not refer to shifts of emphasis and approach inevitable as times change, or to the mysterious power of works of art to reveal *more* meaning in the course of centuries, but to radically incompatible accounts of 'the meaning' of a work among readers who respect each other's standards and general powers of judgment. A glance at the history of opinion about Shakespeare's *Timon of Athens*[1] suggests that the critic who chooses to write on this most puzzling of Shakespeare's plays must take especial care to expose the grounds of his judgment. An attempt to do this is my tribute to the author of *The Wheel of Fire* and *The Imperial Theme*, works which, more than any others available at the time, helped my generation in the arduous and endlessly rewarding task of reading Shakespeare for themselves.

There seems no doubt that *Timon of Athens* is an unfinished play: not in the sense that it lacks a formal conclusion, but in the sense that it has not been finally worked over for presentation on the stage.[2] It is, however, very much more than a mere draft; it is a play moving towards completion; and although the great variety of critical opinion warns us that it is not easy to get at the meaning, there is no reason why we should not trust our impression that Shakespeare is saying something important, and use our wits to determine what that something may be. Our best course, as usual, is to trust our immediate sense of dramatic power, to begin by concentrating on those parts where our minds and imaginations are most fully engaged, and to ask ourselves how these are related to each other and to the remainder of the play— to those parts of lesser intensity that serve to reinforce, to modify or to cast a fresh light on what is more prominent. I am not advocating simple concentration on dramatic highlights: all I am saying is that understanding has to start somewhere, and we run less risk of going astray if we start with whatever it may be that most engages us.

Timon is no exception to the rule that Shakespeare's plays are always superbly well planned. When we look back on *Timon*, after directly

experiencing it, we recall three episodes or phases of great dramatic
effectiveness. The first is the presentation of Timon in his prosperity,
surrounded by suitors, friends and parasites. This begins about a third
of the way through the first scene and continues throughout the second
(that is to say, to the end of the first Act). The second is the scene of
the mock banquet (III.vi), where Timon serves covered dishes of warm
water to the friends whose utter falseness has been exposed, denounces
them for the fawning parasites they are ('Uncover, dogs, and lap'),
beats them, and drives them out. The third is the exhibition of Timon's
misanthropy: this consists of the tirade of IV.i, and the tirades and
curses of IV.iii, when Timon is confronted, in turn, with Alcibiades,
Apemantus, the bandits, and other intruders on his solitude. There is in
addition a kind of prologue, when Poet, Painter, Jeweller and Merchant
congregate at Timon's house, and the Poet describes the common
changes and chances of Fortune's Hill; and a kind of epilogue, where
the cowed Senators of Athens submit to Alcibiades, Timon's death is
reported, and Alcibiades speaks a formal valediction.

All these major scenes, and all but one of the intervening scenes,
concentrate on Timon with an unremitting attention. The question
that any producer, like any reader, must ask himself is, how is Timon
presented? how are we to take him? Now it is obviously possible to
take him as a truly noble man, ruined by his own generosity—'Undone
by goodness', as the Steward says—someone, quite simply too good for
the society that surrounds him. Roy Walker, in an interesting review of
the Old Vic 1956 production, says, 'it was presumably the poet's intention to show how selfish society drives out true generosity.'[3] And
another critic writes as follows:

> In the first part of *Timon of Athens* Timon appears as a man full of
> warmth, geniality and overflowing humanity. He is the incarnation
> of charity and hospitality, and believes in the supreme virtue of
> friendship, which his generosity is intended to foster. Gold plays
> an immensely important part throughout the play, but for Timon,
> before his fall, it is completely the servant of 'honour' (another key
> word) and of brotherly love. In the great feast of I.ii, he comes very
> near to enumerating an ideal of benevolent communism in which
> money merely provides the opportunity for men to express charity
> towards one another: 'We are born to do benefits; and what better
> or properer can we call our own than the riches of our friends? O
> what a precious comfort 'tis, to have so many, like brothers, com-
> manding one another's fortunes' (I.ii. 105–9).[4]

Of remarks such as these I can only say that they seem to me completely to miss the point of the opening scenes. Timon is surrounded by
the corrupt and the self-seeking: this is made very plain, and he must

have been rather stupid or else possessed by a very strong emotional bias to have had no glimmer of it. Of course it is good to use one's money to redeem a friend from a debtor's prison or to enable a poor serving-gentleman to marry the girl of his choice. But it is not good to engage in a perpetual potlatch.

> No meed but he repays
> Seven-fold above itself: no gift to him
> But breeds the giver a return exceeding
> All use of quittance.   (I.i.288–91)

Gifts, to be meaningful and not part of a ritual of exchange or display, must be person to person. Timon, who does not pause to look at the Painter's picture or to glance at the Poet's book, hardly *attends* to anyone: in the words of one of the Lords, he simply 'pours it out' (I.i. 287). When, therefore, he voices the incontrovertible sentiments we have had quoted as an expression of his magnanimity—'We are born to do benefits. . . . O what a precious comfort 'tis, to have so many, like brothers, commanding one another's fortunes'—it is not moral truth that we recognize but self-indulgence in easy emotion. As for the significance of the great feast, Apemantus has already told us what to think of it:

> That there should be small love amongst these sweet knaves,
> And all this courtesy!   (I.i. 258–9)

And it is not long before the honest Steward sheds light retrospectively on the nature of Timon's hospitality:

> When all our offices have been oppress'd
> With riotous feeders, when our vaults have wept
> With drunken spilth of wine, when every room
> Hath blaz'd with lights and bray'd with minstrelsy. . . .
>   (II.ii. 167–70)

Compared with those who have idealized the early Timon for his generosity, the eighteenth-century critic, William Richardson, surely came nearer to the truth when he wrote:

> Shakespeare, in his Timon of Athens, illustrates the consequences
> of that inconsiderate profusion which has the appearance of liberal-
> ity, and is supposed even by the inconsiderate person himself to
> proceed from a generous principle; but which, in reality, has its
> chief origin in the love of distinction.*

* William Richardson, *Essays on Some of Shakespeare's Dramatic Characters*, Fifth edition (1797), p. 313. So too Dr. Johnson: 'The catastrophe affords a very powerful warning against that ostentatious liberality, which scatters

Tragedy of course takes us beyond bare moral judgment. But moral judgment necessarily enters into our experience of tragedy: and it is worth remarking how sharply, in this play, Shakespeare seems to insist on the moral issue, even to the extent of using techniques reminiscent of the morality plays. In the first part of the opening scene (in what I have called the Prologue) Timon's situation is presented with a formal simplification that suggests a moral *exemplum* rather than any kind of naturalistic portrayal. As the parasites gather—Poet, Painter, Jeweller, Merchant, and then certain Senators—the audience is invited (by one of them) to observe:

> See,
> Magic of bounty! all these spirits thy power
> Hath conjur'd to attend!   (I.i. 5–7)

In the Poet's fable of Fortune's Hill we are given due warning of what to expect

> When Fortune in her shift and change of mood
> Spurns down her late beloved . . .   (I.i. 84–5)

It is against this background that Timon appears and displays his undiscriminating, and ruinous, bounty; and it is here that the producer can help us a good deal, if he will let himself be guided by the hints that Shakespeare provides. The stage directions—both the explicit ones that seem to come direct from the author's working draft and those that are implicit in the text—are pretty clear indications of the intended theatrical effect. Timon's first entry is to the sound of trumpets. The 'great banquet' of the second scene is heralded by 'hautboys playing loud music'. And after the masque of Ladies as Amazons 'the Lords rise from table, with much adoring of Timon'. Throughout, there is much elaborate courtesy—'Serving of becks and jutting out of bums', as Apemantus puts it—and as the glittering pomp (which we now know can't be paid for) comes to an end, Timon calls for 'Lights, more lights' (I.ii. 234). All this obvious showiness serves the same purpose as similar elements in ballad or morality play: it tells us in straightforward visual terms that what we have before us is an example of vanity and pride of life decked out in tinsel. The last words of the scene are given to Apemantus:

> What needs these feasts, pomps, and vain-glories? . . .
> O that men's ears should be
> To counsel deaf, but not to flattery.
>   (I.ii. 248 ff.)

---

bounty, but confers no benefits, and buys flattery, but not friendship'. Johnson however thought that 'in the plan there is not much art'.

What we seem to be dealing with, then, is a play that, in some important ways, comes close to the Morality tradition. There is no attempt at characterization; many of the figures are simply representative types. When Timon, in need, appeals in turn to each of his false friends, all heavily indebted to him, what we watch is a *demonstration* of how right Apemantus had been when he said, at the feast,

> I should fear those that dance before me now
> Would one day stamp upon me. 'T'as been done.
> Men shut their doors against a setting sun.
> (I.ii. 148–50)

When Timon retires to the woods, naked and abandoned, he is Misanthropos, and his railings refer not to some sharply realized individual plight but to the human situation in general.

Now it is of course true that the tradition of didactic simplification was still active in Shakespeare's lifetime. A rather dull little Morality called *Liberality and Prodigality* was revived and acted before the Queen in 1601. As in our play Money is shown as in the gift of Fortune; Prodigality gets rid of Money with something of Timon's unthinking ease—

> Who lacks money, ho! who lacks money?
> But ask and have: money, money, money!

—and when Virtue hands over Money to 'my steward Liberality'—Prodigality having proved unworthy—her servant Equity preaches the golden mean ('Where reason rules, there is the golden mean') in the manner of Apemantus moralizing to Timon about 'the middle of humanity'. But we have only to put *Timon of Athens* beside *Liberality and Prodigality*, or beside a more sophisticated play in the same tradition such as Ben Jonson's *The Staple of News*, to see how inappropriate, here, any kind of Morality label would be. For myself I think we get closer to Shakespeare's play by recognizing the didactic elements than by a too ready responsiveness to Timon as the disillusioned idealist. But to see the play as straight didactic moralizing directed *at* Timon as Prodigality —as though he were merely an illustration of a moral thesis—that too feels inadequate. The verse is often too powerful to allow us that kind and degree of detachment as we judge.

We are still, then, left with the question on our hands: How is Timon conceived and presented? how are we to take him? Our answers so far have been mainly negative ones. If we want something more positive we must take a closer look at the play, paying special attention—as we always need to do—to those parts where we most find ourselves in difficulties of interpretation. There are various difficulties in *Timon*: and I mean more substantial ones than the identification of Timon's false friends, the name of the loyal Steward, or Shakespeare's confusion about the value of a talent.[5] One substantial difficulty concerns the dramatic function of III.v, where Alcibiades, failing to persuade the Senators to spare the life of his friend who has killed a man in hot blood, plans revenge against Athens. But this, together with the counterbalancing scene at the end, where Alcibiades is readmitted to the city, I want to put on one side for the moment in order to concentrate on Timon's invective, his display of satire and misanthropy in the fourth act.

The invective, of course, is largely about the power of money: and it has a superb force.

> O blessed breeding sun, draw from the earth
> Rotten humidity; below thy sister's orb
> Infect the air! Twinn'd brothers of one womb,
> Whose procreation, residence and birth
> Scarce is dividant—touch them with several fortunes,
> The greater scorns the lesser. Not nature,
> To whom all sores lay siege, can bear great fortune,
> But by contempt of nature.
> Raise me this beggar, and deny't that lord,
> The senator shall bear contempt hereditary,
> The beggar native honour.
> It is the pasture lards the brother's sides,
> The want that makes him lean. Who dares, who dares,
> In purity of manhood stand upright,
> And say this man's a flatterer? If one be,
> So are they all, for every grise of fortune
> Is smooth'd by that below: the learned pate
> Ducks to the golden fool . . .
>
> (IV.iii. 1–18)

Then, as Timon digs for roots and discovers gold:

> What is here?
> Gold? Yellow, glittering, precious gold?
> No, gods, I am no idle votarist.
> Roots, you clear heavens! Thus much of this will make
> Black, white; foul, fair; wrong, right;
> Base, noble; old, young; coward, valiant.
> Ha, you gods! Why this? this, you gods? Why, this
> Will lug your priests and servants from your sides,
> Pluck stout men's pillows from below their heads.
> This yellow slave
> Will knit and break religions, bless th'accurs'd,

Make the hoar leprosy ador'd, place thieves,
And give them title, knee and approbation
With senators on the bench. This is it
That makes the wappen'd widow wed again:
She whom the spital-house and ulcerous sores
Would cast the gorge at, this embalms and spices
To th' April day again . . .

(IV.iii. 24–41)

All this has an obvious relevance to the England of the late sixteenth
and early seventeenth centuries. Professor Lawrence Stone has docu-
mented very fully indeed the scramble for rewards at Court, the lavish
expenditure on all forms of conspicuous display, the heavy dependence
on credit and lucky breaks, the intense greedy competitiveness of those
for whom Fortune's Hill was a vivid symbol for a very present reality.[6]
There is no difficulty here. *Timon of Athens*, in so far as it is a direct
satire on the power of money, can be seen as Shakespeare's response to
certain prominent features in the economic and social life of his own
day. And the satire, as we have just seen, has the kind of bite that makes
it relevant to *any* acquisitive society, our own as much as Shakespeare's.
(It was almost inevitable that Karl Marx should quote Timon's denunciation of 'gold . . . this yellow slave' in an early chapter of *Capital*.)
But—and here comes the difficulty—when Timon first gives expression to his outraged feelings and curses Athens, in forty lines of invective the only reference to money is short, incidental and indirect (IV.i.
8–12). He does, on the other hand, have a lot to say about sexual corruption; just as in encouraging Alcibiades to destroy Athens his catalogue
of the city's vices, after a brief mention of usury, plunges into a lengthy
diatribe against an anarchic sexuality. Nothing in the play has prepared
us for this (apart from the dance of the Amazons in I.ii, Timon seems
to have lived in an exclusively masculine society). And although Timon
does of course denounce money, and although he subsequently gives
some of his new-found gold to Alcibiades to pay troops levied against
Athens, and some to the harlots to encourage them to spread diseases,
it is not money-satire, or satire on ingratitude, that forms the substance
of the long dialogue in the woods with Apemantus. In short, given the
obvious data of the play, and given the obvious grounds for Timon's
rejection of a society shown as corrupt and usurous, there is nevertheless something excessive in the *terms* of his rejection, just as there is
something strange (and, if you see the play solely in terms of a *saeva
indignatio* directed against society, even tedious) in the slanging match
with Apemantus in the woods. What, then, is Shakespeare up to?
I suggest that as in all the greater plays Shakespeare is using the outward action to project and define something deeply inward. I do not

mean simply that in *Lear* or *Macbeth* or *Othello* Shakespeare observes character with a rare psychological penetration, though he does of course do this. I mean that in a variety of ways he uses the forms of dramatic action, external conflict and event, to reveal inner conflicts and distortions, basic potentialities for good and evil, at a level where individual characteristics take second place to human nature itself. In short he demonstrates precisely what T. S. Eliot meant when he wrote:

> A verse play is not a play done into verse, but a different kind of play: in a way more realistic than 'naturalistic drama', because, instead of clothing nature in poetry, it should remove the surface of things, expose the underneath, or the inside, of the natural surface appearance.[7]

In *Timon*, as in *Lear* and *Othello*, Shakespeare is revealing what is 'underneath ... the natural surface appearance'—sometimes in a naïve Morality way (as when the mock feast of steam and stones instead of nourishment shows us what the earlier feast really was—not a feast at all), sometimes with the force and subtlety of the great tragedies.

In *Timon* the surface appearance is lightly sketched in the suggestions of a corrupt society, where the business of individuals is very much to feather their own nests: more firmly, though in a rather schematized way, in the presentation of Timon's friends and parasites. But the surface appearance on which, in the first Act, attention is most sharply concentrated is Man in Prosperity, the ego sustained in a fixed posture by an endless series of reflections which show it just as it thinks itself to be:

> All those which were his fellows but of late,
> Some better than his value, on the moment
> Follow his strides, his lobbies fill with tendance,
> Rain sacrificial whisperings in his ear,
> Make sacred even his stirrup, and through him
> Drink the free air.
>
> (I.i. 78–83)

That this picture—of what the Steward, allowing himself a touch of satire, calls 'Great Timon, noble, worthy, royal Timon'—has to be drawn again and again betrays a compulsive need. What supports Timon in his self-idolatry, what buys him reassurance ('You see, my lord, how amply y'are belov'd'), is of course his wealth. But the wealth is secondary in dramatic importance to what it serves: means to the same end could have been extorted professions of filial affection, as in *Lear*, or any of the familiar tricks that we use to cut a fine figure in our own eyes. Towards the end of Act II the Steward points the action:

Heavens, have I said, the bounty of this lord!
How many prodigal bits have slaves and peasants
This night englutted! Who is not Timon's?
What heart, head, sword, force, means, but is Lord Timon's,
Great Timon, noble, worthy, royal Timon?
Ah, when the means are gone that buy this praise,
The breath is gone whereof this praise is made,
Feast-won, fast-lost . . .

(II.ii. 173–80)

At virtually one stroke the props to Timon's self-esteem are removed,
and he is reduced to 'unaccommodated man'. He is stripped, so to
speak, of his protective covering, and, as in *Lear*, his physical appearance reflects an inner state. 'Nothing I'll bear from thee But nakedness,
thou detestable town!' (IV.i. 32–3).

There, I think, you have the central interest of the play. In a world
such as the men of great tragic vision have always known it to be, a
world where you clearly cannot remove all the threats—the inner and
the outer threats—to your security, how, quite simply, do you keep
going? Life only allows a limited number of choices. Either you live
by some kind of integrating principle through which even potentially
destructive energies can be harnessed, stability and movement combined; or, plumping for security—for 'a solid without fluctuation', like
Blake's Urizen—you seek artificial supports for a fixed posture. Unfortunately the concomitant of a fixed posture is unremitting anxiety to
maintain itself; and it is in the nature of artificial supports, sooner or
later, to break down. This is what happens to Timon. When his supports are removed, 'when the means are gone that buy this praise', he is
left, like Lear, with 'nothing'—nothing, that is, but a vision of a completely evil world that partly, of course, reflects a social reality, but is
also an expression of his own self-hatred and self-contempt:

. . . and his poor self,
A dedicated beggar to the air,
With his disease of all-shunn'd poverty,
Walks like contempt, alone.

(IV.ii. 12–15)

It is this, surely, that explains the nature of Timon's first great speech
of invective, where there is very little about money and nothing about
ingratitude, but much about sexual incontinence and general anarchy.

Let me look back upon thee. O thou wall
That girdles in those wolves, dive in the earth
And fence not Athens! Matrons, turn incontinent!
Obedience fail in children! Slaves and fools,

Pluck the grave wrinkled senate from the bench,
And minister in their steads! To general filths
Convert, o'th' instant, green virginity!
Do 't in your parents' eyes! Bankrupts, hold fast;
Rather than render back, out with your knives,
And cut your trusters' throats! Bound servants, steal!
Large-handed robbers your grave masters are,
And pill by law. Maid, to thy master's bed;
Thy mistress is o' th' brothel! Son of sixteen,
Pluck the lin'd crutch from thy old limping sire;
With it beat out his brains! Piety and fear,
Religion to the gods, peace, justice, truth,
Domestic awe, night-rest and neighbourhood,
Instruction, manners, mysteries and trades,
Degrees, observances, customs and laws,
Decline to your confounding contraries;
And yet confusion live! Plagues incident to men,
Your potent and infectious fevers heap
On Athens ripe for stroke! Thou cold sciatica,
Cripple our senators, that their limbs may halt
As lamely as their manners! Lust and liberty
Creep in the minds and marrows of our youth,
That 'gainst the stream of virtue they may strive
And drown themselves in riot!   (IV.i. 1–28)

It is a little like what Conrad's Marlow glimpsed on his voyage up the
river to the heart of darkness, though perhaps more specifically realized.
Timon's horror is of anarchic impulses that he knows within himself
when the picture of noble Timon is destroyed. It is true of course that
Timon presently denounces the inequalities bred by fortune, the corruption caused by money; and throughout the scenes in the woods,
when he is visited by Alcibiades and the harlots, the bandits, and various
former hangers-on who have heard of his newly discovered wealth, the
satire on money-lust continues. All this is clearly very near the dramatic
centre of the play. But to treat it as *the* controlling centre, *the* dominant
theme, is to see things entirely from Timon's point of view, from the
point of view of a man who feels unjustly treated by others,—as
of course he is. But the play only makes sense as a whole when we
see him as self-betrayed, his revulsion against the city as equally a
revulsion against himself.[*] Midway in the indictment of money that
I quoted from the opening of IV.iii Shakespeare drops the necessary
clue:

* John Wain speaks of the 'neurotic and self-feeding' nature of Timon's
tirades—*The Living World of Shakespeare*, p. 195.

> ... all's obliquy;
> There's nothing level in our cursed natures
> But direct villainy. Therefore be abhorr'd
> All feasts, societies, and throngs of men!
> His semblable, *yea himself, Timon disdains.*
> Destruction fang mankind! (IV.iii. 18–23)

If Shakespeare's intention was in fact, as I suppose, to portray self-revulsion, the shattering of an unreal picture and the flight from hitherto concealed aspects of the self that are found insupportable, this would also explain the drawn-out exchanges with Apemantus in the woods. In the opening of the play Apemantus, as professional cynic, is not an attractive figure. But he is no Thersites. It is from him, almost as much as from the Steward, that we get a true picture of Timon's 'bounty' and its effects:

> That there should be small love amongst these sweet knaves,
> And all this courtesy!
> (I.i. 258–9)
> What a sweep of vanity comes this way.
> They dance? They are madwomen.
> Like madness is the glory of this life,
> As this pomp shows to a little oil and root.
> We make ourselves fools, to disport ourselves ...
> (I.ii. 137–41)
> Thou giv'st so long, Timon, I fear me thou wilt give away thyself in paper shortly. What needs these feasts, pomps, and vain-glories?
> (I.ii. 246–8)

But if Apemantus is not Thersites, neither is he Lear's Fool, the dis-interested teller of unwelcome truths: the emotional bias, like the ostentatious poverty, is too marked. It is this that explains his dual and ambiguous role in the later scene. On the one hand he is the objective commentator, a mentor that Timon ignores at his peril; and since this is so clearly intended it is a mistake to play him simply as the abject and railing cynic. His pronouncements have authority:

> This is in thee a nature but infected,
> A poor unmanly melancholy sprung
> From change of fortune [F. future]
> (IV.iii. 202–4)
> If thou didst put this sour cold habit on
> To castigate thy pride 'twere well; but thou
> Dost it enforcedly. Thou'dst courtier be again
> Wert thou not beggar.
> (IV.iii. 239–42)

The middle of humanity thou never knewest, but the extremity of both ends.

(IV. iii. 300–1)

And th'hadst hated meddlers sooner, thou shouldst have loved thyself better now.

(IV. iiii. 309–10)

On the other hand, and simultaneously, he is a kind of mirror image of Timon. His first words on his reappearance are,

I was directed hither. Men report
Thou dost affect my manners, and dost use them, (IV.iii 198–9)

and not only is Timon's general manner identical in tone with that of Apemantus in the opening scenes, each echoes what, at another time, the other has said.[8] Geoffrey Bush remarks: 'Apemantus is what Timon becomes. . . . Even in the first three acts, though Apemantus and Timon are opposites, they are oddly drawn toward each other, as if they found a peculiar importance in each other's company. They go together . . . they are, as it were, two aspects of a single self, the extremes between which the personality of a human being can alternate'.[9] And it is not only cynicism about the world that they share. At the beginning of the play Apemantus was described as one 'that few things loves better than to abhor himself' (I.i. 59–60). Timon's echo of that we have already heard: 'His semblable, yea himself, Timon disdains' (IV.iii. 22). The final exchange of insults between the two, before Apemantus is driven off with stones—

—Would thou wert clean enough to spit upon!
—A plague on thee, thou art too bad to curse. . . . (IV.iii. 364 ff.)

reads like a monologue of self-hate.

Some of this, perhaps, is matter for dispute. What is abundantly clear is that Timon's misanthropy is in no essential way an approach to reality; it is primitive rage at the destruction of an ego-ideal, horror and hatred at what is revealed when support for that ideal picture is withdrawn. Denied the absolute and one-sided endorsement that he had claimed, the self-esteem that his wealth had enabled him to buy, he refuses to see his claims for what they were. Instead he projects on to the world at large his own desire to get what he wanted by means that were essentially dishonest. He has been, in effect, a thief. Confronted with the bandits, he declaims:

I'll example you with thievery:
The sun's a thief, and with his great attraction
Robs the vast sea; the moon's an arrant thief,
And her pale fire she snatches from the sun;
The sea's a thief, whose liquid surge resolves

The moon into salt tears; the earth's a thief,
That feeds and breeds by a composture stol'n
From gen'ral excrement; each thing's a thief . . .
                    (IV.iii. 438–45)

Shakespeare, who expected his audience to recognize a bad argument
when they heard one, knew that each of the elements mentioned here
in fact repays, or gives to another, what it takes. Timon, in becoming
nastier, has become sillier. But by now there is scarcely any pretence on
Timon's part that he is denouncing real corruption in a real world: he
is satisfying an emotional animus that can exhaust itself only in death.

Come not to me again; but say to Athens,
Timon hath made his everlasting mansion
Upon the beached verge of the salt flood,
Who once a day with his embossed froth
The turbulent surge shall cover . . .
Lips, let sour words go by and language end:
What is amiss, plague and infection mend!
Graves only be men's works and death their gain;
Sun, hide thy beams, Timon hath done his reign.
                    (V.i. 217–26)

I am of course aware that this unfavourable view of Timon has
against it not only the opinions of many critics but, more important,
certain pronouncements within the play itself—pronouncements that,
unlike the eulogies of the parasites, are disinterested, and must therefore be given due weight. There is the unwavering loyalty of the
Steward, for whom Timon is

Poor honest lord, brought low by his own heart,
Undone by goodness . . .

                    (IV.ii. 37–8)

and there is the eulogy by Alcibiades that virtually concludes the play:

Though thou abhorr'dst in us our human griefs,
Scorn'dst our brains' flow and those our droplets which
From niggard nature fall, yet rich conceit
Taught thee to make vast Neptune weep for aye
On thy low grave, on faults forgiven. Dead
Is noble Timon . . .

                    (V.iv. 75–80)

But I do not think that either substantially modifies the account that
I have given. The Steward, playing Kent to Timon's Lear, reminds us
in his devotion that love and loyalty see further than the eye of the mere
spectator; there is no need to doubt the potentiality of goodness that is

in Timon. But in the play it remains unrealized. The most that his old servant's undemanding devotion can wring from Timon is the recognition that his undiscriminating condemnation of mankind must allow of one exception:

> You perpetual-sober gods! I do proclaim
> One honest man. Mistake me not, but one,
> No more, I pray . . .
>
> (IV.iii. 503-5)

The current of his feeling remains entirely unchanged:

> Go, live rich and happy,
> But thus conditioned: thou shalt build from men;
> Hate all, curse all, show charity to none,
> But let the famish'd flesh slide from the bone
> Ere thou relieve the beggar . . .*
>
> (IV.iii. 532-6)

As for Alcibiades, the fact that his role is only roughly shaped forces us back on intelligent guessing. But the general intention seems clear. The point of the central scene in which he pleads unsuccessfully with the Senators for the life of the soldier who has killed a man in a brawl is partly to emphasize the greed and corruption of society (that much of Timon's indictment is true):

> . . . I have kept back their foes,
> While they have told their money, and let out
> Their coin upon large interest; I myself
> Rich only in large hurts. All those, for this?
> Is this the balsam that the usuring Senate
> Pours into captains' wounds?
>
> (III.v. 106-11)

---

* I find myself in complete agreement with Mr. H. J. Oliver when he writes in the Introduction to the New Arden edition (pp. l–li): 'The presence of the Steward among the characters, then, so far from being the puzzle or contradiction that Chambers found it, is essential to the meaning of the play and expressly forbids us from identifying *our* judgment (or Shakespeare's) with Timon's . . . Timon's misanthropy, like everything else in Shakespeare's plays, is part of a dramatized situation and is in no sense a lyrical statement of the poet's own belief; and Timon's invective for which the play has received most of such praise as has generally been given it, is all the more remarkable when one pauses to reflect that it states an attitude from which, through the presence of the Steward, Shakespeare has dissociated himself completely.' All I would add is that, as we have seen, it is not only the presence of the Steward that 'places' Timon's misanthropy.

But there is more to it than this. Both Alcibiades and the Senators are right in the general truths they enunciate:

> *Alcibiades* For pity is the virtue of the law,
>   And none but tyrants use it cruelly.
>
> *First Senator* He's truly valiant that can wisely suffer
>   The worst that man can breathe,
>   And make his wrongs his outsides,
>   To wear them like his raiment, carelessly . . .
>   (III.v. 8–9, 31–4)

What we are forced to question, by Alcibiades' special-pleading and the Senators' complacency, is the reliability of the speakers. Alcibiades' claim that his friend acted 'in defence' (l. 56), with 'sober and unnoted passion' (l. 21), is undercut by his own admission that the man 'in hot blood Hath stepp'd into the law' (ll. 11–12), and this not in self-defence but, 'Seeing his reputation touch'd to death' (l. 19). And although the Senators profess to stand for law and the virtues of restraint there is something very disagreeable in their legalistic morality.

> *First Senator* My lord, you have my voice to't; the fault's
>   Bloody; 'tis necessary he should die;
>   Nothing emboldens sin so much as mercy.
> *Second Senator* Most true; the law shall bruise 'em.
>   (III.v. 1–4)

Neither side is trustworthy. In this respect, then, the scene is a variation on the main theme. Much of what a man says may be true, as much of what Timon says is true; but what really matters is the integrity and self-knowledge, or the lack of these qualities, in the person speaking. If the Senators are clearly untrustworthy, Alcibiades does not represent an acceptable norm.

It is the recognition of this that prevents us from taking the last scene of all with the moral earnestness that both Alcibiades and the Athenians would like to impart. These eighty-five lines raise far more questions than they answer. Some of our perplexities may be due to the play's unfinished state. But if we take the scene in conjunction with III.v— the previous confrontation of Alcibiades with apparently representative Athenians—it suggests a world of hazy verbiage. (What right has Alcibiades to reproach Athens with being 'lascivious'? When last seen he was trailing about with a couple of mistresses. As for the Senators, anything goes, so long as they can save their skins and plaster the situation with appropriate platitude.) And this does not only contrast with Timon's blazing hatred, it offers a parallel. Men set themselves up for judges, when the underlying attitudes, from which their judgments spring, are distorted by evasions, self-exculpations, and lack of self-knowledge. All that is said in this final scene is, for Alcibiades and the Senators, an easy way out—the world's way when confronted with any kind of absolute, of negation or affirmation. In this context, 'Dead is noble Timon' suggests a bitter irony. Timon's self-composed epitaph was not noble; and his wholesale condemnation of the world, though not an easy way, was easier than the pain of self-recognition.

Presumably we shall never know when *Timon of Athens* was written, nor why it was not finally completed. The best of the verse puts it firmly in the period of Shakespeare's great tragedies. There are very many parallels—verbal and substantial parallels—with *King Lear*. Coleridge jotted down that it was 'an after vibration' of that play.[10] But why should a man try to repeat an unrepeatable masterpiece? My own guess, for what it is worth, is that *Timon* was drafted when *Lear* was already taking shape in Shakespeare's mind. Both plays are about a man 'who hath ever but slenderly known himself', who tries to buy love and respect, who has genuine reason to feel wronged, and whose sense of betrayal releases an indictment of the world that can't be shrugged off as 'madness' or 'misanthropy', but a man also whose sense of betrayal by others masks a deep inward flaw; in both the stripping away of all protective covering reveals with fierce clarity a world of evil. But there the major resemblances cease. *Timon of Athens* contains a loyal and decent Steward; it does not contain a Cordelia. Timon goes almost as far in hatred and revulsion as Lear; there is nothing in his mind that corresponds to Lear's gropings towards self-knowledge. And it is the active presence in *King Lear* of positive and affirmative elements that, paradoxically, makes its presentation of pain and evil so much more deeply disturbing. You can disengage from *Timon of Athens*, for all its power: you have to live with *King Lear*. And when the greater theme took possession of Shakespeare's mind, the more partial one could be abandoned: Timon had 'done his reign'.

NOTES

1 A full account is given in Francelia Butler's *The Strange Critical Fortunes of Shakespeare's 'Timon of Athens'* (Iowa State University Press, 1966).

2 The evidence of incompleteness is fully presented by H. J. Oliver in his Introduction to the New Arden edition of the play, which I have used for all quotations from the text.

3 Roy Walker, 'Unto Caesar: a Review of Recent Productions', *Shakespeare Survey*, 11; reproduced in part in Maurice Charney's edition of *Timon* (Signet Classics), p. 212.

4 R. P. Draper, '*Timon of Athens*', *Shakespeare Quarterly*, VIII, 2, Spring, 1957.

5 See Terence Spencer, 'Shakespeare learns the value of money', *Shakespeare Survey*, 6.

6 *The Crisis of the Aristocracy, 1558–1641.*

7 T. S. Eliot, Introduction to S. L. Bethell, *Shakespeare and the Popular Dramatic Tradition.*

8 See the New Arden notes at IV.iii. 279 and 394.

9 Geoffrey Bush, *Shakespeare and the Natural Condition*, p. 62.

10 Coleridge, *Shakespearean Criticism*, ed. T. M. Raysor (Everyman edition), Vol. I, p. 211.

4
"Integration" In *The Winter's Tale*

THERE is a good deal of rashness in a layman's speaking even to an "applied" section of the British Psychoanalytical Society. I have no more than a layman's and an ex-patient's knowledge of psychoanalysis and psychiatry, and I certainly shall not attempt a psychoanalytic account of the play that is my subject. Not only am I not equipped to do so, but I confess to a certain prejudice regarding attempts to apply psychoanalytical concepts to works of art. In such cases the literary critic who is not trained as an analyst can only rely on tools that have been shaped for him by others, which he may not know how to handle. The analyst who is not prepared to meet a work of art on its own terms before he applies what is essentially a clinical method may throw off some interesting observations, but he certainly runs the danger of forcing an abundant stream through the narrow channel that works his mill or—without metaphor—of imposing an interpretation that does not interpret. I think Ella Freeman Sharpe in her well-known essay "From *King Lear* to *The Tempest*" does this when she sees Lear's unruly knights as the baby's uncontrolled feces, or Lear's wandering on the heath as the emergence of an entirely supposititious event in Shakespeare's childhood. The essay does indeed remind us that the play *King Lear* reaches down to submerged layers of our consciousness—where, for example, we retain the first impact of rivalry with brothers or sisters, or a sense of early ambivalent relations between child and parent. But we might hope to attain these insights without such a drastic reduction of a masterwork of the philosophic imagination.

I do not of course mean that psychoanalytic and literary interests should be kept in separate compartments of our minds. The interpretation of literature demands a great variety of skills, and there is no reason why knowledge gained in clinical practice or in reading the work of psychiatrists should not enter into the reading of literature. The critical essays of D. W. Harding, for example, are the product of a fine *literary* sense; but clearly Harding could not have written as he has on, say, the guilt of Coleridge's Ancient Mariner, or on what he calls the hinterland of articulate thought, without a close acquaintance with psychology, including the psychoanalytic field. (See *Experience into Words*.) Conversely Freud's admiration—and I mean professional admiration—for Shakespeare and for Dostoevsky is well known. Recently I have noticed that D. W. Winnicott uses *Hamlet* to illustrate a theory about the balance of boy and girl elements in boy or girl—and does it in a way that (to me at all events) throws back light on the play itself. Perhaps a literary critic may take heart from Ernst Kris's remark that, at all events "in marginal areas," "there are problems of research which might be presented in better perspective were the testimony of the literary mind to be taken fully into account." Perhaps, however, the areas are not necessarily marginal.

No doubt others with a wider range than my own could produce very many examples of fruitful interplay between these two different fields of knowledge. My point is a very simple one: namely that useful insights are most likely to emerge when thought is allowed to *play* between them: there must be no forced marriages. Where literature is concerned it is necessary for every reader—whatever his professional or other preoccupations—to meet the play or poem on its own terms, as the curious complicated sort of thing it is, speaking with its own voice (which may be a blend of many voices), and governed by its own conventions of communication. As Harding says of one of Blake's more difficult poems, "repeated listening, with strict moderation in the use of intellectual ingenuities," is the likeliest way of getting at the pressures that shaped the words. There is indeed no substitute for attentive and repeated listening, without an overeagerness to "explain" in terms of some scheme not necessarily intrinsic to the poem. But when we have really listened in this way something may emerge that can be assimilated within a different field of interest by a psychiatrist, a teacher or administrator, or even a politician.

I want to suggest the kind of thing that is going on in *The Winter's Tale*. I shall use some ideas that I have got from reading outside the field of literary studies. But I don't want to pretend to knowledge that I do not possess; and I shall probably be most useful if I speak of the play simply and directly, leaving others to decide how, if at all, the play (and what I say about the play) engages with other interests, such as an interest in psychoanalysis.

Shakespeare's last plays (which he may not have known were his last) in some ways form a group different from the tragedies that preceded them not only because they have happy endings. They are sometimes misleadingly known as romances—misleadingly because the term doesn't do justice to their firm connection with the actual: a connection that we see both in the language—which is firm, pithy, and incisive as well as complex and subtle—and in the nature of the interests aroused: the magic island of *The Tempest*, for example, is a microcosm of the world, and the play is about colonization and politics as well as about the attempts of an aging man to reach some kind of peace with himself. Neither are these plays a homogeneous group: *Pericles* and *Cymbeline* are experiments, and *The Winter's Tale* and *The Tempest* are different from these two plays and from each other.

All the same the last plays do share certain common features. Serious issues are raised—the nature and consequences of human sin and frailty—but all end "happily." Relationships are shattered and renewed. Lost children are found again, and attention is directed not to the "generation gap" (as in *King Lear*) but to the positive effect of young people in bringing some renewal of life to the world of the middle-aged or old. Instead of following through the potentially disastrous consequences of wrong choice, perverted energy, or the clash of rival value-systems, reversal from disaster is brought about through developed insight, repentance, forgiveness, and reconciliation. "Pardon's the word for all": the words of the king in *Cymbeline* cannot be applied with any easy complacency, but they suggest the direction in which these plays are moving.

All these themes are presented in a special way. It is not merely that plot and action violate probability, that magic plays a part (oracles warn and exhort), and that there are improbably successful disguisings and impossible adventures. Most of these features could be paralleled in earlier plays, and if we want to grasp the distinguishing features of the technique of the last plays we need to glance at Shakespeare's whole career. We may put it like this. In the earliest plays you are asked to *observe* a world. It isn't a world of course: it is a play world. But the point is that you are asked to observe. You are interested, you feel sympathy and antipathy, you almost necessarily make judgments—and to that extent you are involved. But in the main you are an onlooker. You may feel, "There, but for the grace of God, go I"; but you don't feel that the play is directly evoking your own potentialities, your own conflicts, and all that life of the emotions which can be handled only through myth, symbol, or poetry. As the plays succeed one another we not only feel that more of our world—the world of shared human experience—is involved in the action, but we sense that the kind of thing the action does tends to become different. It is used to project an inner truth in which each one of us finds some aspect or potentiality of himself. To be sure, when Yeats said that in great tragic drama "it is always ourselves that we see upon the stage," he did not mean that we identify ourselves with the hero, or that we discard our interest in forms of experience other than our own and look for some idealized—or at all events beglamored—ego-image on the stage: any true work of art demands some going out of ourselves, some stretching of the selves that we are, or think we are. Nevertheless the increasing inwardness of Shakespearean drama means that the action as a whole is more designed to embody and make comprehensible universal forms of inner experience, or potential experience, than it is to reflect or correspond to experience in its outward forms. This is a simplification; and the plays themselves don't make a neat pattern of development. For example *Coriolanus* is concerned with the public and observable world, even though it traces public attitudes and actions to their sources in the personal life: it is not in any sense a myth or parable of the inner life. But *King Lear*, in a sense, is; and it is *King Lear*, more than any other of the great tragedies, that looks forward to the final plays. In these, it seems to me, there is a sense in which it is true to say that certain characters and events are part of the experience of a central character, and therefore stand for—or evoke—aspects of the spectator's own personality as he is absorbed in the play. In *Cymbeline* certain sides of the hero, Posthumus, are reflected in the black Iachimo and in "that irregulous devil" Cloten; and all three reflect something in ourselves. Not that this is entirely new in Shakespearean drama. In one sense Iago is an unrecognized part of Othello; and in *King Lear* it is not only the daughters who represent different aspects, or possible aspects, of Lear's own character. It is simply that in the later plays this feature of Shakespeare's drama becomes more insistent. One way of putting it might be to say that the plays move closer to the dream, in which the dreamer is *all* the characters; but I don't want to suggest that the plays are in any way "dreamy" or mere wishful fantasy. In *English Dramatic Form* M. C. Bradbrook speaks of the way in which a play can affect the "internal society" of each individual spectator:

Participation may correspond to the therapeutic function of a dream, and the final result will not by any means

123

be just a fantasy gratification. The play dynamically frees and flexes relatively fixed and rigid images of the inner society. Therefore, if several roles attract identification, the plot becomes an exercise in the dynamics of adjustment, uniquely assisted by the fact that participation in drama is itself a social act. Conflicts can be projected more directly and more intensively.[1]

Miss Bradbrook is speaking of drama generally, but I think her words are especially apt in relation to Shakespeare's last plays. In these Shakespeare is exploring possible alternatives to disruption and tragedy; he is trying to define the life-enhancing energy that paradoxically was released by the great tragedies, but defining it now not as something glimpsed in and through defeat, but as something that *could* be actualized in daily living. He is especially concerned with what, borrowing the term from psychiatry, we may perhaps call integration, considered both as something taking place within the individual and as a function of relationship between persons.

If you knew *The Winter's Tale* only from an outline of the plot you would conclude that it is a very silly play. The same of course could be said of other great plays in which unlikely stories frame significant human actions. But Shakespeare did more than infuse human interest into a plot adopted from Greene's *Pandosto*. We should see *The Winter's Tale* not primarily as a dramatic action, following the fortunes of certain people, but instead as a poetic and dramatic representation of two contrasting "states" of the human soul and an exploration of the possibility of "metamorphosis" of one state into the other. It seems significant that one of Shakespeare's favorite books, the *Metamorphoses* of Ovid, was much in his mind at this time.[2]

[1] I am not sure that *identification* is the right word.

[2] J.M.P. Pafford refers to the *Metamorphoses* in his discussion of sources in the New Arden edition of *The Winter's Tale*, but there are even more reminiscences of Ovid than Pafford lists.

We can best get the sense of what the play is doing if—instead of bothering about probability or even much about characterization—we put side by side two passages in which the poetry is most powerful. They form a contrast on which the whole play turns—and I don't mean contrasts of character; I mean contrasting mental states.

> Thou want'st a rough pash, and the shoots that I have
> To be full, like me: yet they say we are
> Almost as like as eggs; women say so,
> (That will say anything.) But were they false
> As o'er-dyed blacks, as wind, as waters; false
> As dice are to be wish'd, by one that fixes
> No bourn 'twixt his and mine; yet were it true,
> To say this boy were like me. Come (Sir Page)
> Look on me with your welkin eye: sweet villain,
> Most dear'st, my collop: Can thy dam, may't be
> Affection? thy intention stabs the centre.
> Thou dost make possible things not so held,
> Communicat'st with Dreams (how can this be?)
> With what's unreal: thou coactive art,
> And fellow'st nothing. Then 'tis very credent,
> Thou may'st co-join with something, and thou dost,
> (And that beyond commission) and I find it,
> (And that to the infection of my brains,
> And hard'ning of my brows.)

The Folio punctuation which I have used for this passage is not unalterable, but I assume that it comes close to Shakespeare's intentions. It is, in any event, impossible to "straighten out" the speech and make it conform to ordinary syntactical forms: the point is its disjointedness. The marked caesuras and the frequent parentheses produce a panting, heaving movement which tells you what to think of the appearance of argument with which Leontes tries to establish his belief.

The "thinking" is entirely guided by passion. This speech has been described (by Mark Van Doren in his *Shakespeare*) as "the obscurest passage in Shakespeare," but the general drift is clear. Whatever the precise meaning is of "affection" or "intention," Leontes is trying to establish the validity of an emotional bias by claiming how very reasonable it is to accept it. After all, he says, a strong feeling that a thing is so can sometimes be more valid than common sense ("dost make possible things not so held"), and our intuitions can find truth in dreams. Dreams are "unreal," are "nothings," so if affection can work on such unsubstantial material, how much more likely that it can join with what is actually there. In his concluding lines his mind fairly pounces on his "proof": "Then 'tis very credent, /Thou may'st co-join with something, *and thou dost.*"

It is completely illogical, of course; for it is the existence of the "something" that needs to be proved. But it has a kind of spurious or neurotic logic; and this drive of Leontes' mind is strengthened by the images of great physical intensity, here and elsewhere, through which it is expressed. I do not think we need bother ourselves with the question of the causes of Leontes' disease. I can find no support in the play for J.I.M. Stewart's suggestion that Leontes is projecting on to Hermione his own repressed homosexual feelings for Polixenes. It seems more likely that his jealousy is rooted in a revulsion against his own sexuality and therefore against sexuality in general. But Leontes here is a type of irrational self-justifying suspiciousness that in real life could have many causes. What Shakespeare defines with great clarity in Leontes is, so to speak, a type case of disordered passions. In "The Grammar of Jealousy" J. P. Thorne has shown by a detailed linguistic analysis of Leontes' "insane" speeches how ambiguity, broken syntax, and a kind of fissure in the deep structure of the sentences are used to express a distortion and *parti pris* in the preverbal levels of his thinking.

126

I shall return to this speech; but now consider the passage I have selected for contrast, again retaining the folio punctuation.

> What you do,
> Still betters what is done. When you speak (Sweet)
> I'ld have you do it ever: when you sing,
> I'ld have you buy, and sell so: so give alms,
> Pray so: and for the ord'ring your affairs,
> To sing them too. When you do dance, I wish you
> A wave o' the sea, that you might ever do
> Nothing but that: move still, still so:
> And own no other function. Each your doing,
> (So singular in each particular)
> Crowns what you are doing, in the present deeds,
> That all your acts, are queens.

The rhythm is obviously very different from that of Leontes' disordered speech. Leontes had said, "My heart dances, But not for joy—not joy." Here the movement and the patterning suggest a dance, even before the word is mentioned. There is a basic order given by the repetitions of the structure ("When you speak, Sweet," "when you sing," "When you do dance") and by the repetition of words ("do" and "doing"—the barest and simplest indication of activity—and "so" and "still"). But there is no monotony: as in a dance there are repetition and variety, order and vitality. The actions that are the objects of this loving attention are all of the simplest and commonest kinds—speaking, singing, buying and selling, giving alms, saying prayers, ordering household affairs; but the "common" is invested with grace and power and appears in all its irreplaceable uniqueness in the present moment.

When you do dance, I wish you
A wave o' the sea, that you might ever do
Nothing but that: move still, still so:
And own no other function.

Here not only does the line-movement suggest the movement
of the wave ("move still, still so"), but the image brings with
it further suggestions: just as the breaking of the wave on
the shore has behind it the force of the deeper movements
of the ocean, so the grace of the dancer is associated with
deep "impersonal" forces. In short what the poetry gives you
is an image of natural energy, patterned and ordered into
expressive forms. And Perdita, we notice, is described—or
evoked—in poetry that implies a widening circle of relationship. Leontes' speech is disjointed, broken, passion-
ridden; and it comes to a climax on "I" ("and I find it"). It
spins on itself with an insane frenzy. Florizel is entirely absorbed in contemplation of the loved person.

These two speeches, then, are polar opposites, representing
radically contrasting possibilities of experience, and, put in
conjunction, they indicate the inner movement that determines the play's dramatic structure. It is always dangerous
to talk about "what Shakespeare intended"; but you can say
that the play seems to ask, and to attempt an answer to, the
question: How, if at all, is it possible for the man who utters
the first speech to recognize the health of, and so reach out
toward, what is represented in the second? What is the possibility of radical metamorphosis?

Acts 1 to 3—the long first movement—are mainly given to
creating a sense of Leontes' unbalanced self-enclosure. Poetry
and action go together. Throughout the greater part of this
movement nothing is in relation. Things are broken off
abruptly and without ceremony, like Polixenes' visit and the
tale Mamillius begins to tell his mother, which gets no further than "there was a man dwelt by the churchyard." They
are seen in sharp contrast, as the domestic quiet of the open-

ing of act 2 is destroyed by the eruption of Leontes' mad fury. There are denial and rejection, as Hermione is repudiated by Leontes, the baby Perdita cast out, and the message of the oracle at first denounced as false. There is a special significance in the contrast, so often insisted on, between infancy and youth on the one hand and adult life on the other. A striking example is when the newly born babe is laid at the feet of the madly jealous Leontes (2. 3). Paulina describes it in some detail, so that for a few moments it is vividly there to our imaginations—a physical presence, genuine new life and, Paulina insists, in a clear relationship to the father. But Leontes denies it; he will have the child cast away—in a sense, therefore, denying his own age of innocence.

There is much more in these first three acts that deserves attention—especially the bewildered expostulations of the courtiers as they try to make contact with Leontes' mind; the strangely serene and moving poetry in which Apollo's island of Delos is described (the oracle, says John Vyvyan in *The Shakespearean Ethic*, is "a message to the passions from the spirit"); and Hermione's dignified speech at her trial, where she shows a legitimate concern for her honor, but is less concerned for herself than for her husband. All of this not only acts as a contrast to, and therefore defines, Leontes' paranoiac suspiciousness but will play a part in the total pattern of the play. Above all there is the last scene of act 3, in which, in a setting of storm and disaster, the castaway baby is found by the old shepherd: "Thou met'st with things dying," he says to his son, "I with things new-born." But I must go on to speak, briefly and inadequately, of the great pastoral scene that, after a gap of sixteen years, forms the greater part of act 4.

It isn't easy to say what one wants to about the sheepshearing scene, because there are no critical terms immediately available. Clearly you can't use psychological terms appropriate to the analysis of character; and at the same time you have to avoid any suggestion of mere allegory. It is a unique achievement, and I don't know anything quite like it, even in Shakespeare. Act 4, scene 4, is devoted to presenting nothing less than a whole, complex but unified, attitude to life. It does this by building up a pattern of relationships, not in any abstract way, but through the movement of our minds and feelings and imagination as we respond to what is concretely given in the dramatic action and the poetry. It is by attending to that pattern, responding to it as fully as we can, that we become aware of new possibilities of living that form the direct antithesis of what has been presented in Leontes. The characteristics of his state of mind, we saw, were self-enclosure, chaos, and the projection of his fantasies. What is given in the evocation of Perdita is a grace of human living, felt intensely in an individual presence, but *related* both to a wider human context and to impersonal forces of generation and growth. The whole of the scene is devoted to giving body to that relationship—not only in the idiom and reference, which range from the homely to the highly imaginative, from the rural and local to the classical and mythological. And all is pervaded by a full and intimate sense of "great creating Nature." Our sense of Perdita comes in the first place from the poetry that she speaks or that is spoken to her. There is no doubt about the grace that lives in her, but she is not in any way cut off from the life that surrounds her. Her speech can be as homely and direct as that of Autolycus and the rustics. Again and again she refers to the everyday things and processes of rural life—the gardener's "dibble," grafting, planting slips, starved sheep in winter, "Whitsun pastorale." It is this that links her to the rustic earthiness of the shepherds, though she goes beyond it. There is nothing of the prude or the flirt in the expression of her love for Florizel.

Perdita and Florizel only exist in the living context that Shakespeare has provided for them. From the opening exchange of the lovers there is a sense of the relation of man, nature, and the "gods." We are constantly but unobtrusively reminded of the daily and seasonal cycle. In late summer Perdita evokes the flowers of the spring.

> O Proserpina,
> For the flowers now that, frighted, thou let'st fall
> From Dis's waggon! daffodils,
> That come before the swallow dares, and take
> The winds of March with beauty; violets, dim,
> But sweeter than the lids of Juno's eyes
> Or Cytherea's breath.

Classical myth—and it is especially appropriate that Proserpine should be invoked—is re-created in terms of the English countryside; and with only a little exaggeration we may say that the whole of an English spring is caught in the two lines about the daffodils—which are tough and resilient ("take/ The winds of March") as well as beautiful. It is immediately after this that we have Florizel's lines, "What you do,/Still betters what is done," of which I have already spoken. But a moment later we are back to jokes about garlic ("to mend your kissing with"), "homely foolery," with ballads, rounds, and a dance of twelve satyrs.

It would be easy to see the central contrast embedded in the play as one between neurosis bred by or within civilization and a purely natural spontaneity and directness of living. But the matter is more complicated than that. If we don't take the full force of all that is suggested by Autolycus's song, "The red blood reigns in the Winter's pale"—which, so to speak, carries over into the love-making that follows—we certainly don't possess the play. But equally we don't possess it if we see *only* that. I don't know the current status of the will in psychoanalytical thinking. Certainly a patient can't dissolve a neurosis by will alone: the spurred horse always shies at the same fence. But equally you can't talk about health in any meaningful way without invoking the conception of intent. Lionel Trilling in "Freud and Literature" says:

What may be called the essentially Freudian view assumes that the mind, for good as well as bad, helps create its reality by selection and evaluation. . . . The reality to which Freud wishes to reconcile the neurotic patient is, after all, a "taken" and not a "given" reality. It is the reality of social life and of value, conceived and maintained by the human mind and will. Love, morality, honour, esteem—these are the components of a created reality.

Such considerations seem relevant here. When, toward the end of this scene, Polixenes, in terms that suggest something like elderly jealousy of the young, forbids the marriage, the poetry moves to the celebration of faithfulness—a quality that is not merely natural but human:

> Not for Bohemia, nor the pomp that may
> Be thereat gleaned; for all the sun sees, or
> The close earth wombs, or the profound seas hide
> In unknown fathoms, will I break my oath
> To this my fair beloved.

It is only with this, the assertion of a love that, very credibly, is not Time's fool, that we can pass to the final image of integration in the last act.

What is meant by integration here is something that can be defined only in terms of a close study of the action and the poetry. We are not dealing with the working out of a plot in terms of a sequence of cause and effect. We are dealing with two contrasting states of the human soul; and when we ask how the one can be changed into the other we find our answer not in the descriptive and analytic terms of psychology, but in terms of a poetry and symbolism that evoke, without fully rationalizing, the deeper movements of mind and feeling. The play's second movement has given us a state of being that offered the strongest possible contrast to the state displayed by Leontes in the opening acts—a spring and summer opposed to Leontes' winter. When the lost daughter returns, she brings with her all the richness of positive living that has been so strongly associated with her. She represents an order of experience that is now, I was tempted to say, available to Leontes. That would be a wrong way of putting it. Instead it is an order of experience within which Leontes can be included. For the image of integration of which I spoke, although it can find a reflection in the mind of each individual beholder, is something that goes beyond the separate characters of the drama. It is composed, enacted, by the whole dramatic pattern, and—contrary to Leontes' jealousy—it is established in a widening circle of relationships.

At the opening of act 5 Leontes' penitence belongs to the same order of experience as Florizel's and Perdita's affirmation of faithfulness and Hermione's legitimate concern for her honor: it is a recognition of absolute human values. It is only with the full and continued recognition of what he has done—resolutely assisted by Paulina—that we hear at his court the note of new life with the entry of the young lovers, who are "welcome hither,/As is the spring to the earth." Florizel, asking for help, links the past and present:

> Beseech you, sir,
> Remember since you owed no more to time
> Than I do now,

—which recalls both "grace and remembrance be to you both" and the nostalgic memories of boyhood that, early in the play, contrasted so markedly with Leontes' adult folly. But the youthful past is no longer felt as simple contrast, and there is no need either to regret or to disown it. I think it is true to say that in these later scenes you have a poetic enactment of Erik Erikson's account in *Insight and Responsibility* of the mutual support and creative interplay that exist between the generations. Jung says in *On the Nature of the Psyche* that the maturing personality "must assimilate the parental complex," a statement that needs to be complemented by one that, as it were, goes in the other direction. The maturing personality must somehow, in Coleridge's words (in *The Friend*), "carry on the feelings of childhood into the powers of manhood." "To find no contradiction in the union of old and new, to contemplate the Ancient of Days with feelings as fresh, as if they then sprang forth at his own fiat, this characterises the minds that feel the riddle of the world, and may help to unravel it." (Blake's poem "The Echoing Green" is a beautiful image of the kind of experience I have been pointing to.) It is not for nothing that, a little later, the old shepherd is described as standing by "like a weather-beaten conduit of many kings' reigns"; the simile suggests a succession of generations that, in the forms of culture, stretches far beyond the span of father and mother and child.

The second scene of the last act consists of the relation of the discovery of Perdita's birth, in which Shakespeare forestalls the objections of literalist critics:

> such a deal of wonder is broken out within this hour, that ballad-makers cannot be able to express it.

> they looked as they had heard of a world ransomed, or one destroyed.

> Every wink of an eye some new grace will be born.

Some of the phrases have religious associations, but the scene as a whole has a down-to-earth quality that relates the profound and the commonplace. On the sea-voyage Perdita had been "much sea-sick," and Florizel "little better." And at the end of the scene we have the naïve pride of the shepherd and his son, a pride that is tempered by the shepherd's natural good breeding, "for we must be gentle, now we are gentle-men." When the shepherd's son expounds the relationships between himself, his father, and their new royal "kindred," the effect is comic but not merely comic: for when, in the clown's words, "the prince my brother and the princess my sister called my father father," we have an echo of Perdita's

> I was not much afeard; for once or twice
> I was about to speak and tell him plainly,
> The selfsame sun that shines upon his court
> Hides not his visage from our cottage, but
> Looks on alike.

As for the final scene, obviously it is possible to see it as a conventional happy ending with a few striking lines of poetry interspersed. But, again, we need to see it in relation to the whole dramatic pattern. Instead of the racy prose of the preceding scene we have poetry with a solemn, cere-monious quality: a rite is being performed. The tempo of the previous scene was one of mounting excitement: here there is a hushed stillness as all eyes center on the supposed statue and the final transformation of the play is enacted. The statue, the wife who for a time had ceased in Leontes' eyes to be the person she was (significantly she is far more wrinkled than when he saw her last), steps down. Within the conventions of the play this is a symbol of that renewal of life which is the main theme of *The Winter's Tale*. The characters, restored to each other in a new naturalness of affection, are restored to life lived in the present, free from the usual mechanisms of distortion. Paulina's words, to the accompaniment of music, are:

> Come!
> I'll fill your grave up: stir, nay, come away:
> Bequeath to death your numbness; for from him
> Dear life redeems you.

There is an echo here of Autolycus's song about the daffodils and the red blood. He is not present at the final revelation; but he is, very properly, in Sicily, and not far off.

After the winter of sin and separation, however, it is not merely "red blood" or natural impulse that reigns: it is natural impulse purified by something for which Shakespeare uses the religious word *grace*. Northrop Frye says (in *Fables of Identity*) that "such grace is not Christian or theological grace, which is superior to the order of nature, but a secular analogy of Christian grace which is identical with nature." I am sure Frye is right to make the distinction between grace as used in *The Winter's Tale* and theological grace. But grace in the play's sense isn't really "identical with nature." There is no divorce and absolute discontinuity between them. Grace, here, is a consummation of that naturalness and spontaneity that were so beautifully evoked in the pastoral scene. It can only enter when nature has been, not disowned, but enlisted in the cause of "honesty" and "honour," love and trust—human values and commitments of which nature by itself knows nothing.

With the paradoxical combination of intimacy and distancing characteristic of great dramatic art, *The Winter's Tale* works in two different ways to one end. Insofar as the different characters represent different possibilities of experience for the individual self, it explores some of the ways of growing into wholeness, which involves not only the—sometimes painful—withdrawal of projections, but also a continuing openness to different kinds of life. Although the play as a whole is received by different individual minds (just as it was created by one mind), it is received *as if* it enacted relations between persons inhabiting a common world; and to grasp it in the second of these aspects is, curiously, the best way of understanding it as a *psychomachia* or internal "conflict of the soul." And in this way, as in others, art "imitates" life. In *Organic Unity in Coleridge* Gordon McKenzie comments on Coleridge's idea of individuation in his essay "Theory of Life":

To the common-sense view, individuality frequently means that which is unique or peculiar to one person; its essence lies in something strong in itself and sharply detached from life around it. Individualism or individuality is often directly opposed to universality or catholicity. This is not true of Coleridge, who looks upon individuality as something strong in itself, to be sure, but more particularly as a force which reaches out and makes new connections and relations. The greatest individuality is that which has the greatest degree of organization, the largest quantity of relations.*

That, however, is merely statement, admirably as it is made. Shakespeare's play, by calling out the energies of the mind, makes us—in ways that are not fully open to introspection— *live through* movements of mind, feeling, sympathy, that have to be experienced as parts of ourselves. No more than *The Tempest* does *The Winter's Tale* offer a "solution" that can be applied. It is simply that in responding, trying to understand, the mind *grows toward* the experience of which the play is a living image: it moves toward an idea of wholeness that can nourish our living, even when we are—as is usually the case—not whole.

*In Coleridge's own words "this tendency to individuate cannot be conceived without the opposite tendency to connect" (*Miscellanies*). In our own time the relation between integrity in the individual and mutual affirmation between persons is of course central to the thought of Erik Erikson.

5
The Tempest

OF ALL THE greatest works of art it seems true to say that they contain an element of paradox, that what imposes itself on our imaginations as a unified and self-consistent whole contains contradictory elements tugging our sympathies—and therefore our judgments— in different ways: part of the continuing life of the great masterpieces springs from the fact that they will not allow the mind of the reader to settle down comfortably with the sense that he has finally reached *the* meaning which can now be put in a pocket of the mind with other acquired certainties producible at need. More than is the case with any other of Shakespeare's plays, with the exception of *King Lear*, paradox is of the essence of *The Tempest*, a fact that is reflected in the history of Shakespeare criticism. I am not referring to the truism that every work of art, without exception, 'means' something different for every age and every reader, but to the completely contradictory accounts that have been given of this play. It is not so long since critics, identifying Prospero with Shakespeare, saw the play either as embodying the serene wisdom of age or as a deliberate turning aside from the harsh realities of life to the more easily manageable world of romantic fantasy. More recently the views to which I have alluded have been sharply challenged, most notably by Jan Kott—in *Shakespeare our Contemporary* —for whom *The Tempest* is 'a great Renaissance tragedy of lost illusions', its ending 'more disturbing than that of any other Shakespearean drama'. Others have written to much the same effect. And even for those who are not unduly swayed by critical opinion there is difficulty in saying simply and clearly where one feels the play's greatness to reside. Because of its obvious impressiveness and mystery, and because it is probably Shakespeare's last play without a collaborator, there is a temptation to read in large significances too easily, as I think we may tend to do with *Cymbeline*. On the other hand, to say that *The Tempest*, like *Cymbeline*, points to more than it contrives to grasp and hold in a unified dramatic structure—that also feels wrong. Perhaps we should start by pondering what everyone would agree to be there, in the play: I mean prominent aspects of the play's dramatic mode, its technique. Not everyone will agree as to the significance to be attached to these, but to consider them may clear the ground for criticism. I. A. Richards has remarked of the interpretation of poetry that 'whatever accounts are offered to the reader must leave him—in a very deep sense—free to choose, though they may supply wherewithal for exercise of choice'. This, he added, 'is not . . . any general licence to readers to differ as they please. . . . For this deep freedom in reading is made possible only by the widest surface conformities'; for 'it is through surfaces . . . that we have to attempt to go deeper'.[1]

There are four aspects of 'surface' technique that deserve attention. The play observes the unities of time and place; it is related to the contemporary masque; it makes great use of music and song; it employs a very great variety of modes of speech.

Alone among Shakespeare's plays the action of *The Tempest* keeps well within the limits of a natural day: indeed Prospero is rather insistent on getting the whole business completed in three or four hours. Clearly this means compression, and it is compression of a particular kind. There are plays that keep the unities that obviously have great depth and spaciousness, for example *Oedipus*, or *Phèdre*. Here the effect is different—as though important experiences were rendered by a rather spare, and at times almost conventional, notation, that only gets its effect when the reader or spectator is prepared to collaborate fully, to give apparently slight clues full weight. We notice in particular two things. (i) There is a form of symbolism developed out of the earlier plays (notably *King Lear*), as when Stephano and Trinculo fall for the 'trumpery' hung up on the line (or linden tree); and the potentially healing and cleansing power of the tempest is indicated by the information about the shipwrecked party—'On their sustaining garments not a blemish, But fresher than before'; and 'Though the seas threaten, they are merciful' (which it may not be fanciful to associate with Jung's dictum, 'Danger itself fosters the rescuing power'). Or again, love's labours are simply represented by Ferdinand carrying logs. (ii) Psychological states are briefly, even if pungently, represented. We know that Antonio was ambitious ('So dry he was for sway') and that Sebastian is a would-be murderer; but neither state of mind is developed as it might have been in the tragedies. Alonso undergoes a storm in which he learns to listen to his own guilt; but this is reduced to,

O, it is monstrous, monstrous!
Methought the billows spoke, and told me of it;
The winds did sing it to me; and the thunder,
That deep and dreadful organ-pipe, pronounc'd
The name of Prosper: it did bass my trespass. . . .

So too with the young lovers: compared with Florizel and Perdita they have very little to say to or about each other, but what they do say is often telling and beautiful; and the harmony in diversity of the sexes is given in a simple tableau—'Here Prospero discovers Ferdinand and Miranda playing chess'. It remains to be seen whether we are justified in giving to these brief 'notations' the kind of weight that I have implied we should give.

The Tempest is also distinguished from Shakespeare's other late plays in its relation to the contemporary masque. Apart from the formally presented masque of Ceres at the betrothal in Act IV, there are various masque-like tableaux, as when 'several strange shapes' bring in a banquet for the shipwrecked party, and then, as they approach it: 'Thunder and lightning. Enter Ariel like a Harpy; claps his wings upon the table; and, with a quaint device, the banquet vanishes'. This has been often noticed;[2] and indeed Shakespeare had often used what is seen on the stage to emphasize what is said, as in the formal and cere-monious grouping of his characters, their pairing off or drawing apart; but *The Tempest* puts a special emphasis on modes of formal, masque-like, presentation, and we need to be fully aware of the language of visual suggestion that is developed in the play.

'Suggestion': the critic does well to be careful when he uses the word, but he can hardly avoid it when speaking of a play in which music and song have so important a part. Ariel sings to Ferdinand, to the sleeping Gonzalo, to Prospero as he robes him and anticipates his own freedom; Stephano sings 'a scurvy song'; Caliban sings. At key points in the action Ariel plays music to the actors. The banquet is presented to the King's party with 'solemn and strange music' and vanishes to the sound of thunder. The masque of Ceres is accompanied by 'soft music' and vanishes 'to a strange, hollow and confused noise'. In short 'the isle is full of noises . . .'. Now not only is music—harmony—the polar oppo-site of tempest, as Professor Wilson Knight has rightly and so often reminded us,[3] it is the art furthest removed from the discursive mode. In all Shakespeare's plays music and song had been functional to the action, and so they are here; but they make their contribution to the changing moods of the play by unexpected and almost undefinable means, as W. H. Auden has pointed out in his essay, 'Music in Shake-speare'.[4] Perhaps we may have to allow to the play as a whole a power of controlled suggestion greater than any formulable meaning we can attach to it.

Finally, in this brief glance at 'technique'—the surface characteristics which everyone would agree to be there, whatever the interpretation attached to them—we should notice the great range in the aural manner: from the delicate allusiveness of Ariel's songs to the decidedly *not* delicate speech of the 'low' characters; from the slightly stylized verse of the masque to the passionate intensity of some of Prospero's speeches. Nor is it only the low characters who command a pithy

idiom directly related to everyday speech. It is Antonio who gives
us,

> For all the rest,
> They'll take suggestion as a cat laps milk;
> They'll tell the clock to any business that
> We say befits the hour;

and it is Ariel himself who describes the effect of his music on the
drunken butler and his followers—'they prick'd their ears . . . lifted up
their noses As they smelt music'. In the poetry of the play there is at
least as much of the earthy as there is of the ethereal.

With this, of course, we find our attention focusing on far more than
'technique'. To the range of style there corresponds an equal range of
interest and awareness. It is well known that the play makes direct
reference to contemporary matters. It is, among many other things, a
contribution to the debate on 'nature' and 'nurture'; and F. R. Leavis,
making the point that *The Tempest* is 'much closer [than *The Winter's
Tale*] to the "reality" we commonly expect of the novelist', is clearly
right in saying that 'Caliban . . . leads the modern commentator, quite
appropriately, to discuss Shakespeare's interest in the world of new
discovery and in the impact of civilization on the native'.[5] Important as
this is, it is even more important to see how much of 'the real world'
comes into the play by way of reference, imagery and allusion. The
opening storm proves to be merciful, but, as Gonzalo says,

> Our hint of woe
> Is common; every day, some sailor's wife,
> The masters of some merchant, and the merchant,
> Have just our theme of woe. . . .

Ariel's songs are balanced by the coarse life of Stephano's song.
Gonzalo's Utopia, remembered from Montaigne, inevitably calls to
mind its opposite—the more familiar world of 'sweat, endeavour,
treason, felony, Sword, pike, knife, gun . . .'. The masque of Ceres
conjures up images of the English countryside at its most peaceful:

> You sunburn'd sicklemen, of August weary,
> Come hither from the furrow, and be merry:
> Make holiday; your rye-straw hats put on, . . .

but we are also reminded of the wilder, undomesticated, aspects of
nature—not only the storm-tossed waves, the 'roarers' that 'care
nothing for the name of King', but 'long heath, broom, furze . . .', 'the
green sour ringlets . . . whereof the ewe not bites', the lightning-cloven
oak. The island, for all its magical qualities is very much a part of the
everyday world: even one of the most delicate of Ariels songs has for

burden, 'Bow wow' and 'Cock a diddle dow . . . the strain of strutting chanticleer', as though it were dawn in an English village. And at the centre of these specific references is a vision of 'the great globe itself', which, with all its towers, palaces and temples, as Prospero reminds us, is as transient as 'this insubstantial pageant faded'. In other words, the island mirrors, or contains, the world; what we have to do with is not exclusion and simplification but compression and density, vibrant with its own unique imaginative life. The point has been well put by Dr. Anne Barton:

> Spare, intense, concentrated to the point of being riddling, *The Tempest* provokes imaginative activity on the part of its audience or readers. Its very compression, the fact that it seems to hide as much as it reveals, compels a peculiarly creative response. A need to invent links between words, to expand events and characters in order to understand them, to formulate phrases that can somehow fix the significance of purely visual or musical elements is part of the ordinary experience of reading or watching this play.[6]

With so much, perhaps, all readers would agree. Any attempt to say more, to define the centre of interest to which these different aspects of Shakespeare's technique direct our attention, is unavoidably personal and partial. As so often when a play has made a strong impact on the mind and we know we are still far from understanding, it is useful to face directly the more obvious difficulties. Consider, for example, the abrupt ending of the masque that Prospero had arranged for Ferdinand and Miranda.

> *Enter certain Reapers, properly habited: they join with the Nymphs in a graceful dance; towards the end whereof Prospero starts suddenly, and speaks; after which, to a strange, hollow, and confused noise, they heavily vanish.*
>
> Pros. [*Aside*] I had forgot that foul conspiracy
> Of the beast Caliban and his confederates
> Against my life: the minute of their plot
> Is almost come [*To the Spirits*] Well done! Avoid; no more!
> Fer. This is strange: your father's in some passion
> That works him strongly.
> Mir.   Never till this day
> Saw I him touch'd with anger, so distemper'd.

It is indeed strange, and Professor Kermode finds the motivation inadequate, wondering 'that Prospero should so excite himself over an easily controlled insurrection'.[7] But it is only strange if we forget that

Caliban, like Ariel, stands in some kind of special relationship with Prospero. ('We cannot miss [i.e. do without] him', and, near the end of the play, 'This thing of darkness I Acknowledge mine'.) Caliban, although his mother was a witch, is also a 'native' of new-found lands who raises the whole question of man before civilization and of the relation of 'natives' to European settlers. It is also Caliban, who knows the island better than anyone else, who speaks' some of the most beautiful poetry in the play:

> Be not afeard; the isle is full of noises,
> Sounds and sweet airs, that give delight, and hurt not.
> Sometimes a thousand twangling instruments
> Will hum about mine ears; and sometimes voices,
> That, if I then had wak'd after long sleep,
> Will make me sleep again: and then, in dreaming,
> The clouds methought would open, and show riches
> Ready to drop upon me; that, when I wak'd,
> I cried to dream again.

But he is also a brute 'on whose nature nurture can never stick'; and the play gives us no warrant for supposing that each man has not a Caliban inside himself—even Prospero. In the passage I have referred to we have had an elaborate, slightly artificial masque of Ceres—a vision of nature fertile and controlled. But life isn't as simple as that: Caliban, pure instinct, is still plotting; and it is the sudden memory of this that puts Prospero into a 'passion That works him strongly'. No one is put into that kind of temper by external danger (especially when the danger, such as it is, is largely represented by a couple of drunks), only by self-insurrection. Perhaps we have here an explanation of Prospero's tensed-up attitude towards Caliban at the beginning of the play and his spiteful and childish punishings of him—'I'll rack thee with old cramps, Fill all thy bones with aches. . . .' What I am suggesting is that the play is mainly the drama of Prospero, a man who, even by Elizabethan standards, is not old, but one who is looking towards the end of his days, trying to sort out and to come to terms with his experiences. Prospero is not simply above the action, controlling it, he is intimately involved. The play is about what Prospero sees, and, above all, what he is and has it in him to become. 'Prospero,' says Harold Goddard, 'when expelled from his dukedom, is a narrow and partial man. Thanks to his child, the island, and Ariel, he gives promise of coming back to it something like a whole one. But an integrated man is only another name for an imaginative man.'[8]

I have said that no single, clearly defined interpretation can be extracted from—much less put upon—this play. But when it is seen in some such way as this the action at least falls into an intelligible shape, which still allows the working of other promptings. Consider briefly a few major phases in the action. The play opens with a storm, conjured up by magic, but real enough not to make its nautical technicalities out of place. In some sixty lines Shakespeare—as in all his masterful openings—is doing several things simultaneously. The human characteristics of various people who will play a part in the subsequent action are revealed—from the detachment of Gonzalo to the panicky blustering of Antonio and Sebastian. The storm is also a reminder of fundamental equalities—'What care these roarers for the name of King?'. But like all Shakespearian storms it carries overtones: indeed it is explicitly related (I, ii, 207 ff.) to inner storms. The second scene is sometimes regarded as a contrast to the first, and so—in some ways—it is; but it is also a continuation. The storm has prepared us for something in the mind of Prospero, a mental turmoil that is sharply contrasted with the music of Miranda's compassion—'O, I have suffered with those that I saw suffer.' The tortured syntax of many of his speeches, with their abrupt dislocations, his interjections to Miranda (more, surely, than a clumsy attempt by the dramatist to hold the attention of the audience throughout a long exposition)—these mark the tumultuous strength of his anger against his brother: 'I pray thee, mark me, that a brother should Be so perfidious', 'Thy false uncle—Dost thou attend me?'. And underneath the anger (which to be sure is natural enough) is an admission of at least partial responsibility.

> I pray thee, mark me.
> I, thus neglecting worldly ends, all dedicated
> To closeness and the bettering of my mind
> With that which, but by being so retir'd,
> O'er-prized all popular rate, in my false brother
> Awak'd an evil nature. . . .

The New Arden note on this passage, rightly admitting that 'no paraphrase can reproduce its involved urgency', offers as the main sense: 'The fact of my retirement, in which I neglected worldly affairs and dedicated myself to secret studies of a kind beyond the understanding and esteem of the people, brought out a bad side of my brother's nature. . . .' Apart from the fact that a ruler's business is to rule—not at all events to be 'all dedicated' to study—the paraphrase misses the point. In the phrase, 'in my false brother Awak'd an evil nature', the verb has a subject, and it is not 'the fact of my retirement' but the pronoun 'I'. Auden is surely right when in *The Sea and the Mirror* he makes Prospero say, 'All by myself I tempted Antonio into treason.' From at least as early as *Richard II* Shakespeare had used incoherence *dramatically*; and Prospero's involutions contain at least some admission of hidden guilt.

The main movement of the play, it has been suggested, is Prospero's movement towards restoration, renewal of the self. He is certainly human enough—not simply the wise controller of other people's fate— to make us interested in his fluctuations of mood. True, as white magician he is in some ways analogous to the artist, and within the conventions of the play his magic can control much of the action. But even within the play magic cannot do what is most essential. It is not magic that determines Gonzalo's decency or the falling in love of Ferdinand and Miranda. Magic can help to demonstrate how evil mistakes the goal or desires what proves to be trash, just as art can set out telling *exempla*. But magic cannot help Prospero in his most extreme need. When, in the passage already referred to, he breaks off the masque because he has recalled the 'foul conspiracy of the beast Caliban and his confederates', his 'old brain' is genuinely 'troubled', and he needs to walk 'a turn or two . . . To still my beating mind'. The conspiracy, as it turns out, is easily dealt with: the conspirators are very stupid, and Prospero certainly puts too much effort and too much venom into punishing them. To 'a noise of hunters heard', Caliban and his associates are hunted by dogs, one of whom is called 'Fury' and another 'Tyrant'. Prospero clearly relishes the hunting:

> Go charge my goblins that they grind their joints
> With dry convulsions; shorten up their sinews
> With aged cramps; and more pinch-spotted make them
> Than pard or cat o' mountain.

It is not the first time that he has appeared like a bad-tempered martinet, so that you want to ask, What is he afraid of? It is immediately after his grim enjoyment at handing out punishment that he announces,

> At this hour
> Lies at my mercy all mine enemies.

Any actor playing the part of Prospero would have to ask himself, What is the *tone* of this? It certainly isn't a calm announcement of a further stage in the magician's demonstration: to my mind it is very close to the lines immediately preceding. The question of what Prospero intends to do with his enemies (which means also, What is he going to do with himself?) is a genuine one, and at this stage we have no right to assume that the answer will be comfortably acceptable.

If we agree that in this play comparatively slight clues do in fact bear a great weight of implication, then the opening of Act V, which immediately follows the hounding of Prospero's minor enemies, is a genuine crisis, and we miss what Shakespeare is doing if we see it as leading smoothly into a pre-ordained 'happy ending'. Everything now depends on how Prospero handles the situation. When the Act opens he is tugged two ways. Miranda—'a third of mine own life'—loves his enemy's son, and he furthers and approves, though putting mock obstacles in the way. But he has been in a thundering bad temper (which he has tried to overcome); he wants to get his own back—to hunt his enemies with the dog, Fury. The question is whether he can stop dwelling on his own wrongs, real as these are, stop nagging about Caliban, and trust his best self. That, surely, is the significance of the opening exchange with Ariel—his intuitive self. Ariel describes the plight of the King of Naples and his party.

> Your charm so strongly works 'em,
> That if you now beheld them, your affections
> Would become tender.
> *Pros.*   Dost thou think so, spirit?
> *Ari.* Mine would, sir, were I human.
> *Pros.*   And mine shall.
> Hast thou, which art but air, a touch, a feeling
> Of their afflictions, and shall not myself,
> One of their kind, that relish all as sharply,
> Passion as they, be kindlier mov'd than thou art?
> Though with their high wrongs I am struck to th' quick,
> Yet with my nobler reason 'gainst my fury
> Do I take part: the rarer action is
> In virtue than in vengeance: they being penitent,
> The sole drift of my purpose doth extend
> Not a frown further. Go release them, Ariel:
> My charms I'll break, their senses I'll restore,
> And they shall be themselves.*

It is *after* this—and in the acting there should be a marked pause before 'And mine shall'—that Prospero can 'abjure' 'this rough magic', and we hear the 'heavenly music' that he has called for. As Goddard points out, not only does Prospero obey Ariel, instead of commanding him— 'Music replaces magic'.[9]

What follows is of great importance. Once more, music and formal movement add an undefinable suggestion to the spoken word. But the words are clear enough. The royal party, shepherded by Ariel, enter to

---

* It is interesting—though not, I think, essential for our understanding of the play—to note that some of Prospero's lines are a direct translation from the opening paragraph of Montaigne's essay 'Of Cruelty'. I owe this reference to Miss Eleanor Prosser; see her *Hamlet and Revenge*, (Stanford University Press) pp. 83–4, and 'Shakespeare, Montaigne and the "Rarer Action"', *Shakespeare Studies* I (1966) pp. 261–6.

'a solemn music', Alonso 'with a frantic gesture', and 'all enter the circle which Prospero has made'. As they come to themselves the feeling is of a more-than-individual return to consciousness.

> The charm dissolves apace;
> And as the morning steals upon the night,
> Melting the darkness, so their rising senses
> Begin to chase the ignorant fumes that mantle
> Their clearer reason.

(It is the same image as in George Herbert: 'As the sun scatters with his light All the rebellions of the night'.)

> Their understanding
> Begins to swell; and the approaching tide
> Will shortly fill the reasonable shore,
> That now lies foul and muddy.

Prospero is not simply *arranging* this: as 'one of their kind, that relish all as sharply, Passion as they', he is himself involved. As the King's party come to themselves, so he resumes his full human nature, not as magician but as man:

> I will discase me, and myself present
> As I was sometime Milan.

The often quoted 'the rarer action is In virtue than in vengeance' is of course the key. Prospero has come to terms with his experience, and —so far as their individual natures permit—with his enemies. There is a special emphasis on the rejoicings of the good Gonzalo.

> O, rejoice
> Beyond a common joy! and set it down
> With gold on lasting pillars: in one voyage
> Did Claribel her husband find at Tunis,
> And Ferdinand, her brother, found a wife
> Where he himself was lost, Prospero his dukedom
> In a poor isle, and all of us ourselves
> When no man was his own.

Prospero 'found his dukedom' in a more than literal sense 'in a poor isle', and you certainly have to include him among those who 'found' themselves 'when no man was his own'. But Gonzalo is not Shakespeare's chorus to the play. Antonio makes no reply to the 'hearty welcome' that Prospero offers all (V.i. 110–111), and it is his silence that comes between Prospero's first address to him—'Flesh and blood, You, brother mine. . . . I do forgive thee'—and the second, where 'forgive' is used in the barest legal sense:

For you, most wicked sir, whom to call brother
Would even infect my mouth, I do forgive
Thy rankest fault,—all of them; and require
My dukedom of thee, which perforce, I know,
Thou must restore.

It is with some reason that Auden, quoting these lines, finds that the play ends 'more sourly' than *Pericles, Cymbeline*, or *The Winter's Tale*. I myself don't feel that 'sourly' is the word. The harmony that is achieved is valuable,—but there is no final all-embracing reconciliation. Prospero may draw his circle of relationship, but some people will choose to stay outside, and Prospero will somewhat tartly respond. The music remains something that Caliban dreams of, and that humans hear from time to time—and can sometimes actualize in their own lives. The play claims no more than that. The end is an acceptance of the common conditions and common duties of life: 'Every third thought shall be my grave'. Those characters who have proved themselves capable of it have undergone a transforming experience. Now they go back to the workaday world, to confront once more the imperfect, paradoxical and contradictory nature of life.

Paradox runs through the play. Again and again the double and contradictory nature of things is insisted on. To Miranda's question, 'What foul play had we, that we came from thence? Or blessed was't that we did?' Prospero answers, 'Both, both, my girl'. Miranda's 'O brave new world, That has such people in't' is counterpointed by Prospero's ''Tis new to thee', which is not merely cynical and disillusioned. And the great speech in which Prospero dwells on the transience of all things human, which it would be both perverse and simple-minded to see as 'pessimistic',* begins,

You do look, my son, in a mov'd sort,
As if you were dismay'd: be cheerful, sir . . .

It is in these tensions that man has to live. Gonzalo, we remember, had tried to cheer up his king by painting a picture of the ideal commonwealth:

All things in common Nature should produce
Without sweat or endeavour: treason, felony,
Sword, pike, knife, gun, or need of any engine,
Would I not have; but nature should bring forth,
Of its own kind, all foison, all abundance,
To feed my innocent people.

---

* 'Prospero's great speech is an utterance neither of pessimism nor of ennui but of awe'—Enid Welsford, *The Court Masque*, p. 346.

Life, however, is more stubborn and intractable than that, and part of the greatness of *The Tempest* is that it forces us to recognize it. It helps us to face with something that is neither wishfulness nor despair—with something that is both resigned and positively affirming—the intractabilities and the limitations of our lives.

NOTES

1 I. A. Richards, *Internal Colloquies: Poems and Plays* (Harcourt Brace Jovanovich, N.Y., 1971: Proem to 'Goodbye Earth and Other Poems', 1958), pp. 76–77.

2 For example, by Enid Welsford in *The Court Masque*, chapter 12, 'The Masque Transmuted', and by Frank Kermode in the Introduction to his New Arden edition of the play.

3 Especially in *The Shakespearean Tempest*.

4 The essay was first published in *Encounter*, December, 1957; it is in Auden's collection of critical essays, *The Dyer's Hand* and in the World's Classics volume, *Shakespeare Criticism, 1935–60*, ed. Anne Ridler.

5 F. R. Leavis, 'Shakespeare's Late Plays', *The Common Pursuit*, p. 79. See also Professor Kermode's Introduction to the New Arden edition; D. G. James, *The Dream of Prospero*; Philip Brockbank, '*The Tempest*: Conventions of Art and Empire', *Shakespeare Survey* 8; and the commentary of Henri Fluchère, *Poèmes de Shakespeare, Suivis d'Essais Critiques sur l'Oeuvre Dramatique* (Bibliothèque de la Pléiade), pp. 581ff.

6 Anne Barton, Introduction to the Penguin edition of *The Tempest*, p. 19.

7 Frank Kermode (ed.), *The Tempest*, p. 103.

8 Harold Goddard, *The Meaning of Shakespeare* (Chicago University Paperbacks), Vol. II, p. 290.

9 *Op. cit.*, p. 284.

6
Shakespeare's Politics: with Some Reflections on the Nature of Tradition

AS my rather cumbersome title indicates, this lecture is an attempt to bring together two interests—an interest in the nature of Shakespeare's political wisdom, and an interest in the nature of tradition. Shakespeare, as is proper, will get most of the attention, but I should like to begin by indicating the wider concern. There is no need to emphasize the importance for us in these days of an understanding of the nature of a living tradition. It is something which literary studies and studies in the background of literature should foster. But there are two dangers that—it seems to me—are insufficiently guarded against. There is the danger of allowing the 'background' metaphor to dominate our thinking. We need to think in terms of promptings and incitements to decent living and clear thought, rather than in terms of assumptions that are merely accepted and taken for granted, which is what 'background' tends to suggest. The second danger is inherent in the increased availability of information about a past age. One result of the accumulation of 'background' studies—even of necessary and valuable studies—is to suggest that what was peculiar to an age, what can only now be recovered by thinking our way into past systems of thought, is what we most need to know if we are to enter fully into the imaginative achievements of that age. Certainly we need, at times and according to our capacities, to make ourselves into Elizabethans, and to think in terms like those that Dr Tillyard, for example, has made generally available in *The Elizabethan World Picture*. But I sometimes suspect that in concentrating on what was peculiar to the age, on categories of thought that can only be reconstructed by an effort of the historical imagination, we are in danger of losing sight of something even more important. May it not be that what was most nourishing of creative achievement in the past was what, in the tradition of the time, is—or should be—most available for us now? It is towards some understanding of one aspect of tradition in the sixteenth century—the promptings, namely, that lie behind Shakespeare's individual approach to political issues—that this inquiry is directed. I use the word 'directed' deliberately: neither the time at my disposal nor my own severely limited equipment will allow me to do much more than to lead up to the questions that I should like to see answered.

When we speak of Shakespeare's politics there are possibilities of misunderstanding to guard against. 'Policy', 'politic', and 'politician' are words that occur in Shakespeare, sometimes with a pejorative implication—'a scurvy politician', 'base and rotten policy'—that might tempt us to suppose a context like that of the modern political platform. The supposition would of course be wrong. 'Politics' (which Shakespeare does not use) only acquired its most frequent modern meanings—'political affairs', 'political principles or opinions'—much later, with the rise of the parties. If you had said to Shakespeare, 'Do you take any part in politics?' or 'What are your politics?' he would probably have been puzzled. 'Politics' still implied systematic thought on the constitution of states and the art of government —a matter for philosophers: our 'politics', the conduct of internal affairs of state, together with the observation of 'who's in, who's out', and plans to reverse that order—these were matters for the men who did the work, of constant interest only to them, to those with special interests to press, and to a fringe of Politic Would-be's. Shakespeare, like the great majority of his fellow-countrymen, 'had no politics': he had too many other things to think about. The fact remains, however, that although he made no arbitrary separation between what is politics and what is not (and this, to anticipate, is a notable aspect of his political wisdom), he showed throughout his career a lively concern with men not only in their private and personal, but in their public and formal, relations. And this concern included questions of power and subordination, of mutual relations within a constituted society, of the ends and methods of public action, so that we may properly speak of Shakespeare's political philosophy—so long, that is, as we remember that this philosophy is not something ready formed once for all, and applied or exhibited in varying circumstances, but a part of that constant search for meanings that informs his work as a whole.

A recent writer on the history of political thought has called Shakespeare 'a superb interpreter of group psychology and an almost unrivalled observer of political behaviour'.[1] I doubt whether these phrases quite do justice to Shakespeare's political wisdom. They do, however, call attention to one element in it, namely its realism. Shakespeare's political realism is not of course Machiavellian or modern realism ('How realistic is the realist?' is a question that the plays force us to ask), but it is certainly based on a clear perception of the actualities of political situations. Consider for example the implicit comment made by the play *Richard II* on the wishful thinking of a king for whom words and dramatic postures take the place of action; the explicit comments of the Bastard on 'commodity' in *King John*, and the place his comments have within the larger political action; or the sombre demonstration in *King Henry IV* of

[1] Christopher Morris, *Political Thought in England: Tyndale to Hooker* (H.U.L.), p. 103.

what is involved in getting and keeping power: the recognition
of inevitable consequences by the dying Bolingbroke

—For all my reign hath been but as a scene
Acting that argument—

enforces the same political moral as Marvell's Horatian Ode

—The same Arts that did gain
A Power must it maintain—

and enforces it with a similar effect of irony. But Shakespeare's
realism goes further than this; fundamentally it is a refusal to
allow the abstract and general to obscure the personal and
specific. After the earliest plays on English history Shakespeare's
political plays are not shaped by a predetermined pattern of
ideas: like the rest of his work they are the result of a full exposure to experience. If they unavoidably raise moral issues it is
because of the felt pressure of life itself.[1] If they clarify for us
Clarendon's phrase about 'that fathomless abyss of Reason of
State', it is because they insist on setting every 'political' action
in the widest possible human context and so—implicitly, if not
always explicitly—assessing it in relation to that context. It is of
especial significance that the political action of *Henry IV* has for
setting scenes in which the actions of great ones take on a quite
different appearance, in which the assumptions of the dominant
groups are by no means taken for granted, and which therefore
act as a challenge to those assumptions.

In the two political plays that follow *Henry IV*, in *Henry V*
and *Julius Caesar*, Shakespeare continues the questioning of what
statesmen are likely to accept without question. It is one of the
curiosities of literature that *Henry V* should have been seen so
often as a simple glorification of the hero-king. I am not suggest-

[1] I have in mind the passage in Henry James's Preface to *The Portrait of a
Lady*, where he speaks of 'the perfect dependence of the "moral" sense of a
work of art on the amount of felt life concerned in producing it'.

ing that we should merely reverse the conventional estimate. It is simply that, on the evidence of the play itself, Shakespeare's attitude towards the King is complex and critical. As M. Fluchère has said, 'While making the necessary concessions to patriotic feeling ... Shakespeare lets us see ... that the political problem, linked with the moral problem, is far from being solved by a victorious campaign and a marriage with happy consequences for the country.'[1] In other words, the political problem, purely at the level of politics and the political man, is insoluble. In *Julius Caesar*, freed from the embarrassments of a patriotic theme, and with the problem projected into a 'Roman' setting, Shakespeare examines more closely the contradictions and illusions involved in political action. The matter cannot be properly argued here, but it seems to me undeniable that the play offers a deliberate contrast between the person and the public persona, the face and the mask; that tragic illusion and error are shown to spring from the wrenching apart of the two worlds—the personal and the public; and that Brutus, in particular, is a study in what Coleridge was to describe as the politics of pure—or abstract—reason, with the resulting sophistries and inevitable disappointments.[2]

I hope that even from so cursory a survey of some of the plays preceding the great tragedies one point has become clear: that even in plays where the political interest is most evident, it is never exclusive or, as it were, self-contained. The implied question, What does this political action or attitude mean? is invariably reduced to personal terms: How does this affect relations between men? What kind of man acts in this way? How does he further make himself by so acting? Swift says of

[1] Henri Fluchère, *Shakespeare*, p. 204. I also agree with Mr D. A. Traversi that the effect of the play is 'to bring out certain contradictions, moral and human, inherent in the notion of a successful king'. *Shakespeare: from 'Richard II' to 'Henry V'*, p. 177.
[2] See *The Friend*, First Section, 'On the Principles of Political Knowledge'.

the party man, 'when he is got near the walls of his assembly he assumes and affects an entire set of very different airs; he conceives himself a being of a superior nature to those without, and acting in a sphere, where the vulgar methods for the conduct of human life can be of no use.'[1] It is Shakespeare's distinction that, when dealing with rulers and matters of state, he constantly brings us back to 'the vulgar methods for the conduct of human life', that he refuses to accept a closed realm of the political. Indeed, it is only by a deliberate focusing of our interest for a particular purpose that we can separate 'political' from 'non-political' plays, the two kinds being in fact linked by common themes and preoccupations. Thus in the Second Part of *Henry IV* Shakespeare's interests are plainly setting away from his ostensible subject towards a more fundamental exploration of the human condition that points towards the great tragedies; and *Julius Caesar* shares with later, non-political plays, a preoccupation with the ways in which men give themselves to illusion. So too, from *Julius Caesar* onwards, it is possible to trace Shakespeare's political themes only in plays that, with the exception of *Coriolanus*, are not primarily political plays.

Troilus and Cressida, King Lear, Macbeth—each of these, in one of its aspects, takes the political theme a stage further. *Troilus and Cressida* makes a simple but far-reaching discovery: it is that the sixteenth-century commonplace of the necessity for order and degree might mean much or little according as the reason that formulated it was, or was not, grounded in the responsiveness to life of the whole person. I refer especially to what might be called the dramatic status of Ulysses' well-known speech on 'degree'. In the context of the whole play—the clash of varied attitudes to life which forces us to a judgment—this speech appears as something other than the expression of an

[1] Swift is speaking of 'those, who in a late reign began the distinction between the personal and politick capacity'. *A Discourse of the Contests . . . between the Nobles and the Commons in Athens and Rome* (1701), chap. V.

unquestioned standard: for the significant thing is that it is spoken by Ulysses, and Ulysses is the chief exponent of a reason and policy that do not, any more than Troilus' emotionalism, commend themselves to us. To put it simply, just as emotion, divorced from reason, is reduced to appetite ('And the will dotes that is inclinable To what infectiously itself affects . . .'), so reason, divorced from intuition, is reduced to cleverness: statecraft, for Ulysses, is the manipulation of men. Political order and authority—so the play as a whole forces us to conclude—are not concepts to be accepted without question, independent of some prior ground from which they draw their justification.

That ground is explored in *King Lear*; it is taken for granted in *Macbeth* and *Coriolanus*. What I mean is this. *King Lear* is not a political play; it is a play about the conditions of being human, and it seeks to answer the great question put by Lear as Everyman, 'Who is it that can tell me who I am?' But at the same time it has marked political implications. A play in which 'the king *is* but as the beggar' was bound to raise the social question, and to do rather more than hint that 'distribution should undo excess'. It was almost bound to raise the question of justice: why should the half-witted vagrant be whipped from tithing to tithing, or the farmer's dog be an image of authority? But the political implications go further than that. In a lecture on 'The Politics of *King Lear*' Edwin Muir has suggested that Goneril, Regan, and Edmund have in common a way of seeing people which lacks a dimension. For Edmund, as A. C. Bradley had remarked, men and women are 'divested of all quality except their relation to [his] end; as indifferent as mathematical quantities or mere physical agents'. So too, says Mr Muir, Goneril and Regan 'exist in this shallow present'; without memory, they are without responsibility, and their speech 'consists of a sequence of pitiless truisms. . . . Their shallowness is ultimately that of the Machiavellian view of life as it was understood in [Shakespeare's] age, of "policy". . . . We need not shrink from regarding Edmund and his confederates as political types'.[1] This, if we do not push it too far, suggests one of the ways in which the group opposed to Lear may properly be regarded. And the converse also holds. *King Lear* establishes the grounds of any politics that claim to be more than a grammar of power. Behind hierarchy and authority, behind formal justice and public order, is a community of persons bound by 'holy cords. . . . Which are too intrinse t'unloose'. The basic political facts of this play are that men can feel for each other, and that this directness of relationship—expressing itself in the humblest of ways as well as in the most exalted forms of loyalty and sacrifice—is the only alternative to a predatory power-seeking whose necessary end is anarchy. Ulysses, it will be remembered, had foretold how chaos would follow the 'choking' of degree:

> Then everything includes itself in power,
> Power into will, will into appetite;
> And appetite, an universal wolf,
> So doubly seconded with will and power,
> Must make perforce an universal prey,
> And last eat up himself.

In *King Lear*, Albany, envisaging the same state of chaos, significantly shifts the argument:

> That nature, which contemns it origin,
> Cannot be border'd certain in itself;
> She that herself will sliver and disbranch
> From her material sap, perforce must wither
> And come to deadly use . . .

---

[1] 'The Politics of *King Lear*', *Essays in Literature and Society*, pp. 39–42. See also J. F. Danby's *Shakespeare's Doctrine of Nature: a Study of 'King Lear'*, especially, in this connexion, p. 38.

If that the heavens do not their visible spirits
Send quickly down to tame these vile offences,
It will come,
Humanity must perforce prey on itself,
Like monsters of the deep.

We hardly need to put each passage back in its context to see
that the later one draws on a far deeper sense of what it is that
sanctions the human order.[1] Lear's discovery of his kinship with
the naked poor is both a moral and a political discovery: it is a
king who says, 'O! I have ta'en too little care of this.'

That is what I meant by saying that *Macbeth* takes for granted
the ground established in *King Lear*. Evil in *Macbeth* is more than
tyranny; but tyranny is part of the evil, and it is defined in
terms of a violation of those bonds—the 'holy cords'—that are
essential to the being of man as man. We cannot fail to be
affected by the varied images of concord, of mutual service and
relationship, through which we are made aware that behind the
disintegration and dissolution of Macbeth's state—of his 'single
state of man' and of the state at large—are contrasting possibilities of order. And it seems to me that the conception of
order—as we are given it, in the play—draws on a different
dimension of experience from that envisaged in the 'degree'
speech of Ulysses. In *Macbeth* institutional life—all that is indicated and symbolized by churches, castles, 'humane statute'—
guards and guarantees a living system of relationships ('honour,
love, obedience . . .'), which in turn are related to more than
human sanctions. Thus the evocation of the temple-haunting

---

[1] In *The Allegory of Love* (p. 110) C. S. Lewis translates some lines from
the Latin *Architrenius* of Johannes de Altavilla which curiously sum up the
central movement of *King Lear*, including its political meaning:

This must I do—go exil'd through the world
And seek for Nature till far hence I find
Her secret dwelling-place; there drag to light
The hidden cause of quarrel, and reknit,
Haply reknit, the long-divided Love.

martlets, of the birds that securely build and breed, is an image
of life delighting in life, and it subtly and powerfully contri-
butes to our sense of the ideal presence of a life-bearing order
in the human commonwealth—in what the play calls 'the
gentle weal'.[1]

In *Coriolanus*, which is the last of the great tragedies and also
the last overtly political play, Shakespeare takes up again from
the earlier 'histories' the theme of the Governor. Those earlier
plays were largely, though not exclusively, studies of rulers
who failed because they were isolated within an arbitrary conception of power or privilege: and I think one could deduce
from them that Shakespeare saw the good ruler as not merely
set over the people whom he ruled (though rule is necessary),
but linked with, and in some sense expressive of, the society
for whose sake he performs his office.[2] In *Coriolanus* the main
subject is the relation between a member of the ruling class, a
Governor, and the political society to which he belongs; and
the handling of it results in a breaking-down of any over-simple
distinction we might be tempted to make between what is
'individual', on the one hand, and what is 'social' and 'political'
on the other. It is clear that if individual qualities are partly the
result of social pressures (behind Coriolanus is Volumnia, and
behind Volumnia is the patrician class), the political crisis is,
to say the least, exacerbated by the personal disorders that play
into it. The isolation and over-development of one quality in

[1] These values are of course positively present to our minds and imaginations even in the explicit denial of them by the protagonists—in Macbeth's
great invocation of chaos in IV, i, for example.
[2] In the simple moralizing of the gardeners' scene in *Richard II* (III, iv)
the King's function is explicitly to 'trim and dress' his land, 'as we this
garden': that is, not to impose his mere will, but to foster what is given in
accordance with the laws of its nature. We may compare Burgundy's
speech in *Henry V*, V, ii. In *Measure for Measure* Escalus, unlike Angelo—
and this helps to define the Deputy—has a side of himself open to the rather
foolish Elbow: Angelo talks about abstract justice; Escalus patiently sifts the
evidence in an apparently unimportant case.

the hero is not only analogous to the failure of connexion and integration in the social group ('Rome and her rats'), the one is shown as having a direct bearing on the other. The play thus draws on the same established affirmations as *Macbeth*: the state is not simply an embodiment of power, it is society in its political or public aspect; and society is a mutual relation of persons who, by and large, need each other if they are to come to anything like maturity. What the play emphasizes is the challenge of difference and diversity. There is no suggestion that the social distinctions between patricians and plebeians ought not to exist: it *is* suggested that the diversified social group, the body politic, is in danger of corruption to the extent that *what lies behind diversity* is lost sight of. 'What lies behind' is of course simple humanity. It is Coriolanus's defective humanity that makes him a defective governor.

If I have spoken as though these plays offered us a simple political moral or message, my excuse must be that the necessary qualifications are sufficiently obvious. Indeed it might be claimed that my simplifications have all been in the interest of a recognition of complexity. Shakespeare's political thought, I have insisted, is not a body of abstract principles to be applied and illustrated. It is part of a continuous exploration and assessment of experience: it grows and develops. And in any one play it is part of a complex organization whose very nature it is, as work of art, to challenge each individual reader to become imaginatively alive: the political meanings are only *there* to the extent that we do so respond. So long as we keep this clearly in mind, simplification may have its uses. What I most want to suggest, then, is that Shakespeare's political meanings—the things he tells us about politics—are inherent in and inseparable from his method, his way of presenting his political material. Aware as he is of the need for mutual relationships within society, he does not merely preach this: rather he explores— with a maximum of concreteness and immediacy—the nature of mutuality and its opposite. Thus the distrust that he shows, from first to last, for individualism—for the attitude expressed in Richard of Gloucester's 'I am myself alone'—is based on a sure grasp of the self-mutilation inherent in egotism and isolation, of the inevitable denaturing effect of an attitude that wilfully blinds itself to the fact that personal life only has its being in relationship: Macbeth as tyrant inevitably 'keeps alone'. The converse of this is the pervasive sense that we find in the plays that the foundations of political organization are in the realm 'beyond politics', in those varied relationships that are the necessary condition of individual growth: it is only a Caliban (and Caliban drunk at that) who can wish for an untrammelled 'freedom'. What we may call the idea of the state in Shakespeare is thus fundamentally opposed to the Renaissance conception of the state as a work of art.[1] Nor can it be adequately expressed by the conventional analogy of the bees,

> Creatures that by a rule in nature teach
> The act of order to a peopled kingdom.

Shakespeare probed further and more subtly than the political Archbishop of *Henry V*. What he went on to ask—what, I think, he was already asking when he wrote *Henry V*—was, what are the foundations of a living order? Both *Macbeth* and *Coriolanus* confirm the maxims,

> If a man have not order within him
> He can not spread order about him . . .
> And if the prince have not order within him
> He can not put order in his dominions:

the disordered man makes for disorder, not only in his more

---

[1] See Burckhardt, *The Civilization of the Renaissance*, Part I, 'The State as a Work of Art'.

immediate circle but in his wider social relations.¹ And the contrasting positive values? Shakespeare does not sum things up for us, but I think that a few sentences from Boethius' *De Consolatione Philosophiae* (in the English of Chaucer) come close to the spirit of his political philosophy: '. . . al this accordaunce of thynges is bounde with love, that governeth erthe and see, and hath also commandement to the hevene. . . . This love halt togidres peples joyned with an holy boond, . . . and love enditeth lawes to trewe felawes.'² The love that is in question is not of course simply a matter of feeling; it includes a neighbourly tolerance of differences and a sense of mutual need; and in its openness to life, its willingness to *listen*, it is allied to that justice which gives each man his due, looking towards what he is, or can become; and there is delight superadded.³ Shakespeare's abundance, his feeling for uniqueness and variety, his imaginative grasp of what makes for life—these qualities ensure that when political issues are handled in the plays we sense behind them a concern for the 'trewe felawes' (Boethius' *sodales*), for the living body politic in all its variety. We are inevitably prompted to a clearer recognition of the fact that a wholesome political order is not something arbitrary and imposed, but an expression of relationships between particular persons within an organic society. The 'concord' that Shakespeare invokes as

¹ Ezra Pound (Canto XIII) puts these words into the mouth of a Chinese sage. The idea, I suppose, is common in Western philosophy; my point is that Shakespeare does not merely invoke the idea, valuable as it is, he makes vividly present the kind of actuality from which the idea springs. Professor D. W. Harding, writing on the psychological aspects of war in *The Impulse to Dominate*, has reminded us that a mass phenomenon like war is not something that simply *happens* to a community, that in the last analysis it is rooted in individual habits that make part of the texture of normal 'peaceful' existence.

² Book II, Metrum 8.

³ Paul Tillich's *Love, Power and Justice*, describing the intrinsic and necessary relation between these three concepts, will be found to clarify the meaning of love in social—as well as in directly personal—relations. On listening as a function of creative justice see especially pp. 84–5.

the alternative to both tyranny and anarchy in *Macbeth*[1] has this depth of meaning behind it.

In this last part of my lecture I want to look beyond Shakespeare and to ask some questions. None of Shakespeare's greater plays can be adequately 'explained' by anything outside itself; each is its unique self, with its own virtually inexhaustible depth of meaning—'so ramm'd with life It can but gather strength of life with being'. But no work of art, above all no major work, is entirely original: promptings and insights from the past have helped to make it, so that to apprehend it is in some measure to apprehend them. Shakespeare, undoubtedly, was receptive to what his age had to offer, and we have had valuable studies showing his awareness of the current modes of political thinking.[2] But Shakesepeare's politics cannot be defined simply in terms of the Tudor view of history and the commonplaces of order and degree. When he inquired most deeply into the nature of political life what incitements were offered him to the affirmation, or reaffirmation, of positives transcending the political?

I am not a medievalist, but even a slight acquaintance with earlier literature suggests that the characteristics of Shakespeare's political wisdom, which I have tried to define, had some correspondence with older forms of thinking about politics and social life.[3] There was, for example, the medieval habit of dis-

[1] *Macbeth*, IV, iii, 97–100.

[2] For example, Alfred Hart's pioneering *Shakespeare and the Homilies* (1934) and E. M. W. Tillyard's *Shakespeare's History Plays*.

[3] Professor F. P. Wilson says of Shakespeare, 'The evidence suggests that when a theme took possession of his mind, especially a theme with a long tradition behind it, he read widely—not laboriously, but with a darting intelligence, which quickened his invention. . . . Somehow, like all thinking

cussing politics in terms not of masses but of men, and of men
not only in one specialized aspect but in relation to all their
needs, spiritual as well as material, as human beings. Thus R. W
and A. J. Carlyle, writing of political theory in the thirteenth
century, speak of the general conviction that 'the end and purpose
of the state is a moral one—that is, the maintenance of justice,
or, in the terms derived from Aristotle, the setting forward of
the life according to virtue, and that the authority of the state
is limited by its end—that is, by justice'.[1] Similar considerations
of course lie behind the medieval formulations of economic
ethics, as Professor Tawney and others have shown. This I
suppose is sufficiently well known. What I should like to add
is that if medieval political thought is ethical through and
through, what is in question is not the legalistic application of a
formula but the bringing to bear of spiritual penetration and
moral insight. If Dante in the *De Monarchia* is medieval in his
use—and abuse—of formal logic, he is also, I suppose, representative when he insists on the necessary connexion between
love and justice:

> Just as greed, though it be never so little, clouds to some extent
> the disposition of justice, so does charity or right love sharpen and
> brighten it. . . . Greed, scorning the intrinsic significance of man,
> seeks other things; but charity, scorning all other things, seeks God
> and man, and consequently the good of man. And since, amongst
> the other blessings of man, living in peace is the chief . . . and
> justice is the chiefest and mightiest accomplisher of this, therefore

[1] R.W. Carlyle and A. J. Carlyle, *A History of Medieval Political Thought in
the West*, Vol. V, *The Political Theory of the Thirteenth Century*, p. 35.

men in his day, he acquainted himself with that vast body of reflection upon
the nature of man and man's place in society and in the universe which
his age inherited in great part from the ancient and medieval worlds.'
—'Shakespeare's Reading', in *Shakespeare Survey III* (pp. 18, 20). Professor
Wilson well suggests the innumerable ways in which any one aspect of 'the
tradition' might reach Shakespeare. Cf. also M. D. H. Parker, *The Slave
of Life: a Study of Shakespeare and the Idea of Justice*, p. 196.

charity will chiefly give vigour to justice; and the stronger she is, the more.[1]

Similarly St Thomas Aquinas, discussing the advantages of just rule and the basic weakness of tyranny, remarks, 'there is nothing on this earth to be preferred before true friendship'; but 'fear makes a weak foundation'.[2] The significance of such comments is that although they are in the highest degree relevant and acute, they spring from an insight that is spiritual, moral, and psychological rather than political in any limited sense.

It is the same with the medieval conception of the nature and purpose of the state. For Aquinas man is by nature a social and political animal, destined therefore to live in a society which supplies his needs in far more than a merely material sense. Life in a community, he says, 'enables man to achieve a pleni-tude of life; not merely to exist, but to live fully, with all that is necessary to well-being'.[3] This way of thinking not only re-minds us of the social character of politics, it helps to bring out the implications of the great traditional metaphor (which has behind it both Plato and the New Testament) of the body politic: the implication, above all, of co-operation and mutual-ity not as a vague ideal of universal benevolence but as the necessary condition, intimately felt, of individual development in its diversity. I think that John of Salisbury, in whose *Poli-*

[1] *De Monarchia*, Book I, Chap. 11, Temple Classics edn., p. 153. A similar passage is the opening of Book I, Chap. 13, where Dante shows 'that he who would dispose others best must himself be best disposed'—which is Duke Vincentio's

> He who the sword of heaven will bear
> Should be as holy as severe;
> Pattern in himself to know . . . (*Measure for Measure*, III, ii.)

[2] Aquinas, *Selected Political Writings*, translated by J. G. Dawson, edited by A. P. d'Entrèves, pp. 55, 59. The whole passage is relevant to *Macbeth* in its political aspect.
[3] *Selected Political Writings*, p. 191. On Aquinas' conception of the State as 'the highest expression of human fellowship' see Professor d'Entrèves' Introduction, p. xv.

craticus (1159) the organic conception of the state is prominent,[1]
gives life to the metaphor, reveals its sharp immediacy, when
he tells how Philip of Macedon, advised to beware of a certain
man, replied, 'What, if a part of my body were sick, would I
cut it off rather than seek to heal it?'—or when, speaking of the
prince's reluctance to administer even necessary punishment, he
asks, 'Who was ever strong enough to amputate the members
of his own body without grief and pain?'[2] The temptation for
the modern reader is to regard the metaphor simply as a
rhetorical or conventional flourish. Taken in its context it does
not seem to be so, but rather to spring from a perception of the
foundations of political and social life in 'the real spirit of
helpfulness'.[3]

> Then and then only will the health of the commonwealth be
> sound and flourishing when the higher members shield the lower,
> and the lower respond faithfully and fully in like measure to the
> just demands of their superiors, so that each and all are as it were
> members one of another by a sort of reciprocity, and each regards
> his own interest as best served by that which he knows to be most
> advantageous for the others.[4]

[1] *The Statesman's Book of John of Salisbury* (selections from the *Policraticus*),
translated with an Introduction by John Dickinson (Political Science
Classics Series). The editor speaks of 'the absence of any clear distinction
in John's thought between the social and the political; abuse of public
power is conceived simply in terms of a breach of personal morality'
(p. lxvii).

[2] Op. cit., pp. 37-8. 'It was [Trajan's] habit to say that a man is insane
who, having inflamed eyes, prefers to dig them out rather than cure them'
(p. 39).

[3] Op. cit., p. 95.

[4] Op. cit., p. 244. In *English Literature in the Sixteenth Century* (p. 36) C. S.
Lewis gives an interesting summary of an aspect of Calvin's social thought
which has a similar revealing power: 'a Christian must not give "as though
he would bind his brother unto him by the benefit". When I use my hands
to heal some other part of my body I lay the body under no obligation to
the hands: and since we are all members of one another, we similarly lay
no obligation on the poor when we relieve them.'

The social and moral bias of medieval political thought also appears in the conception of the nature and duties of the ruler, who is ideally concerned not only with his own power, nor simply with the power of the state, but with the common good: 'for albeit the consul or king be masters of the rest as regards the way, yet as regards the end they are their servants'.[1]

These are random examples, I know, but it does seem that Shakespeare, in his thinking about politics, is closer to John of Salisbury than he is, say, to Hobbes: closer not only when he speaks explicitly of 'the king-becoming graces' in the great traditional terms,

> As Justice, Verity, Temp'rance, Stableness,
> Bounty, Perseverance, Mercy, Lowliness,
> Devotion, Patience, Courage, Fortitude,[2]

but also in his whole conception of a political society as a network of personal relationships, and of the health or disease of that society as ultimately dependent on the quality and nature of those relationships. If this is so, one question is how the great commonplaces of medieval political and social thinking were kept alive into the sixteenth century. By the great commonplaces I do not refer only to explicit political formulations. From the principles deriving from Greek, Roman, and Christian sources diverse political theories could be drawn; and although some of the explicit theories such as that of the ruler's responsibility to God and to his people were still alive in the sixteenth century,[3] there were also, with the changing circumstances of the age, major shifts of emphasis and direction, I refer also, and perhaps above all, to a manner of approach, and to a cast of

[1] Dante, *De Monarchia* (Temple Classics), I, 12, p. 159.

[2] *Macbeth*, IV, iii, 91 ff.

[3] On the general question of the continuity of political thought see A. P. d'Entrèves, *The Medieval Contribution to Political Thought*; J. W. Allen, *A History of Political Thought in the Sixteenth Century*, Part II, Chap. III ('A Very and True Commonweal'); and Christopher Morris, *Political Thought in England: Tyndale to Hooker*.

mind. Mr Christopher Morris says of Tudor Englishmen that they did not find it easy to think of politics except in terms of persons: they 'were still medieval enough to persist in discussing political matters in what to us are not political terms'.[1] So that our inquiry would not only take the form of an investigation into the number of times that medieval formulations reappear in political tracts and the like. It would be less concerned, for example, with the elaboration of correspondences between the individual and the state than with habits of mind implying a direct perception of mutual need, of what Hooker called 'a natural delight which man hath to transfuse from himself into others, and to receive from others into himself especially those things wherein the excellency of his kind doth most consist';[2] it would be concerned with those habits of mind without which the commonplaces remain lifeless. The great metaphors ('the body politic'), the great moral sentences ('Without justice, what are states but great bands of robbers?') not only provoke thought; for their fullest efficacy at any time they demand a habit of active apprehension. An important part of our inquiry, then, would be into the tradition of vividness and particularity in the handling of social and political questions: a tradition of which the tendency was to transform the political into the social, and the social into the religious—the tradition (shall we say?) of *Piers Plowman*.[3]

Of the habits helping to constitute the tradition something,

[1] Op. cit., pp. 1–2.
[2] *Of the Laws of Ecclesiastical Polity* (Everyman edition), I, x, 12.
[3] Of that poem it can be said, as Coleridge said of religion in *The Statesman's Manual*, that it acts 'by contraction of universal truths into individual duties, as the only form in which those truths can attain life and reality'. It would be interesting to know who bought and read *Piers Plowman* in the various editions put out by Robert Crowley in 1550—'the sense', it was thought, 'somewhat dark, but not so hard, but that it may be understood of such as will not stick to break the shell of the nut for the kernel's sake'. There were three impressions in 1550; a further edition appeared in 1561. See Skeat's edition of the poem, Vol. II, pp. lxxii–lxxvi.

clearly, was due to the characteristic features of communities not yet large enough to obscure direct dealing between men with impersonal forms. But social life alone did not make the tradition: it was made by proverbs and preachings, by ballads and plays, by words read and listened to; in Elizabethan England it was largely made by the Bible.

Shakespeare's contemporary, Richard Hooker—who is also, like Shakespeare, a great representative figure—may help to direct our thoughts. In Hooker, so far as I am acquainted with him, there is not only the familiar 'medieval' insistence on the subordination of politics to ethics and religion; not only the sense that civilization, 'a life fit for the dignity of man',[1] is based on 'the good of mutual participation'[2] (and co-operation is with the dead as well as among the living): there is a disposition of mind that springs from and fosters a lively responsiveness to the actual. Hooker's sense of history, for which he is so rightly admired, is a sense of being in a concrete situation: it is allied with and encourages an unruffled acceptance of complexity,[3] and his work is a permanent antidote to the doctrinaire, simplifying mind—puritan or other. Yet the insistence on change, on the element of convention in human undertakings, is balanced by a firmness of principle that springs from an assurance of the continuity of the great affirmations. Hooker's attitude to the Bible is of interest not only to theologians and

[1] *Of the Laws of Ecclesiastical Polity* (Everyman edition), I, x, 1.
[2] 'Civil society doth more content the nature of man than any private kind of solitary living, because in society this good of mutual participation is so much larger than otherwise. Herewith notwithstanding we are not satisfied, but we covet (if it might be) to have a kind of society and fellowship even with all mankind' (I, x, 12).
[3] 'The bounds of wisdom are large, and within them much is contained.... We may not so in any one special kind admire her, that we disgrace her in any other; but let all her ways be according unto their place and degree adored' (II, i, 4). As Hooker says elsewhere, 'Carry peaceable minds and ye may have comfort by this variety', 'A Learned Discourse of Justification', op. cit., Vol. I, p. 75.

students of church history. Completely free from what Professor d'Entrèves calls 'the narrow and intolerant scripturalism of the puritans',[1] Hooker's appeal to the Bible is that of a free and reasonable mind for which the Bible has a special authority. And the relevance of this fact to our inquiry into the more-than-political tradition becomes clear when we recall *The Statesman's Manual* of Coleridge. The Bible, he said, was 'the best guide to political skill and foresight' because its events and prescriptions demand a response of the whole man, because they embody universal principles in the sharply particular. 'In nothing', he said, 'is Scriptural history more strongly contrasted with the histories of highest note in the present age, than in its freedom from the hollowness of abstractions': its symbolic actuality ('incorporating the reason in images of the sense') offers the strongest possible contrast to histories and political theories produced by the 'unenlivened generalizing understanding'.[2] Remembering this, we may perhaps understand why 'the strange immediacy of scriptural history'[3] in the age of Shakespeare had a very decided bearing on the way in which the best minds sought to understand political situations.

What bearing this, and the other matters I have touched on, had on the practice of the age would be a separate study. When we think in turn of the adult political wisdom of Shakespeare and the tradition informing that wisdom, then of certain aspects of Elizabethan-Jacobean political life, its greed, faction and unscrupulousness,[4] inevitably a question confronts us. A

[1] *The Medieval Contribution to Political Thought*, p. 104.

[2] See *The Statesman's Manual*, in *Political Tracts of Wordsworth, Coleridge and Shelley*, ed. R. J. White, pp. 18, 24, 28 and *passim*. Mr White's Introduction gives a valuable account of this aspect of Coleridge's thought.

[3] David Mathew, *The Jacobean Age*, p. 14. 'The biblical characters were very close and they overshadowed the chronicles and the heraldry' (p. 15).

[4] See, for example, the closing pages of Professor J. E. Neale's Raleigh Lecture for 1948, 'The Elizabethan Political Scene', *Proc. Brit. Acad.*, vol. xxxiv.

cynical answer would be out of place. The passion of Dante does not prove that he came from a just city: rather, as we know, the reverse. Yet how much it meant that Italy in the thirteenth century, even in the conditions we know, should produce a Dante! Mr T. S. Eliot, borrowing the term from Canon Demant, speaks of 'the *pre-political* area', where the imaginative writer exercises his true political function. 'And my defence of the importance of the *pre-political*', he says, 'is simply this, that it is the stratum down to which any sound political thinking must push its roots, and from which it must derive its nourishment.'[1] That in the imperfect conditions of Elizabethan-Jacobean England something was kept alive in the pre-political area that was of the greatest importance for the health of a political society, Shakespeare's plays (and not these alone) are the living witness. When we try to define what it was that was kept alive we find ourselves with a renewed sense of the meaning and nature of a tradition whose significance for us today should need no arguing. Towards the end of the Third Satire Donne says,

> That thou mayest rightly obey power, her bounds know;
> Those past, her nature, and name is chang'd; to be
> Then humble to her is idolatry.

Shakespeare's political plays are creative explorations of conceptions such as power, authority, honour, order, and freedom, which only too easily become objects of 'idolatry'. Their real meaning is only revealed when political life is seen, as Shakespeare makes us see it, in terms of the realities of human life and human relationships. As Aristotle said long ago, 'Clearly the student of politics must know somehow the facts about soul.'[2]

---

[1] 'The Literature of Politics', in *To Criticize The Critic*.
[2] *Ethics* (translated by W. D. Ross), I, xiii.

7
The Thought of Shakespeare

EVEN to a superficial view, it is clear that in Shakespeare's plays a mind of unusual power is at work: the structure and patterning of even the earliest plays is evidence enough that they were not done without thinking; and when we recall many of the best-known passages—Hamlet's 'To be or not to be', for example, or Polixenes' speech in *The Winter's Tale* on the relation of art and nature—we cannot deny that thought in the usual sense of the word has gone into them. But none of this justifies us in using my title phrase as though we were talking about something self-evident and requiring no explanations. 'The thought of Shakespeare' suggests a consecutive development of discursive reasoning—as we speak of the thought of Francis Bacon or Descartes or, at a less abstract level, the thought of George Bernard Shaw: something that can be followed from point to point, argued with, or even—without too much distortion—summarized. Obviously this is something we do not find in Shakespeare. Shakespeare read widely—far more widely than used to be supposed; he may even have read Hooker; but his handling of the laws of nature in *King Lear* is very different from anything we find in *The Laws of Ecclesiastical Polity*. And even when the plays—or characters within the plays—seem to be offering 'thought', we take it, not at its face value, and not as we should take the thought of a moralist or philosopher, but as one ingredient in something wider, and other.

Consider for a moment Ulysses' famous speech on degree in *Troilus and Cressida*.

> The heavens themselves, the planets, and this centre
> Observe degree, priority, and place,
> Insisture, course, proportion, season, form,
> Office, and custom, in all line of order . . .
> Take but degree away, untune that string,
> And, hark! what discord follows. . . .

Here surely is a piece of Shakespearian 'thought'. Not only does it reflect a good deal of Elizabethan teaching about the necessity of order and due subordination, it is an eloquently persuasive passage of ratiocination; and it ends with a strong imaginative vision of the chaos that comes 'when degree is suffocate'.

> Then every thing includes itself in power,
> Power into will, will into appetite;
> And appetite, an universal wolf,
> So doubly seconded with will and power,
> Must make perforce an universal prey,
> And last eat up himself. . . .

If we are looking for evidence of Shakespeare's thought on a matter of great and permanent concern it would be difficult to find anything more striking. And yet there are various considerations that forbid us to take the speech as straightforward rational exposition, a direct expression of its author's mind, as we might take a comparable passage in Hooker. To start with, it is always hazardous to jump to conclusions about what Shakespeare was thinking just because we find parallels to various passages in the writings of his contemporaries. Shakespeare's plays have been regarded as a treasury of Elizabethan commonplace on such matters as the heinousness of rebellion and the need for order in the state. But this—since we are dealing with a man of remarkable intelligence—is to see the matter too simply.[1] Ulysses' speech occurs in a particular dramatic context. It is almost immediately followed by the rather underhand plot against Achilles, in which Ulysses takes the lead, and Shakespeare takes particular pains to ensure that we shall not see the Greek generals quite as the dignified elder statesmen that they envisage themselves as being. As Aeneas says, enquiring for Agamemnon so that he may deliver his message,

> How may
> A stranger to those most imperial looks
> Know them from eyes of other mortals?

And even if we attend simply to the speech itself there is something in the tone—the prepared, oratorical, public manner—that prompts some questions about its validity. True, it offers a positive conception of public rule, but we do find ourselves wondering whether Greek reason, thus expressed, is an entirely satisfactory alternative to Trojan impulsiveness, which is also given careful exposition. Perhaps I can make my point by remarking that another tradition of thought—other, I mean, than that contained in the Elizabethan commonplaces of degree—was also available to Shakespeare. I quote from *The Consolation of Philosophy* of Boethius, using Chaucer's translation:

> . . . all this accordaunce of thynges is bounde with love, that governeth erthe and see, and hath also commandement to the

hevene. . . . This love halt togidres peples joyned with an holy
boond, and knytteth sacrement of mariages of chaste loves; and
love enditeth lawes to true felawes.

(Book II, verse 8)

When, with some familiarity with Shakespeare's other plays, we listen
to Ulysses' speech, it is at least open to us to reflect that 'order' is not
a simple concept, that creative order cannot be divorced from love,
and that love needs for its expression something other than a rhetoric
that clearly has no roots in a personal life.

Similar considerations apply to every passage in Shakespeare where
an argument is pursued or a line of thought put forward. The kind and
degree of endorsement that we give the 'thought' is determined not
only by subtleties of tone, manner and implication—by expression in a
poetic form that is precisely so and not otherwise—but by the particular
context into which it enters. I think of such things as Richard II on the
divine right of kings, Brutus on the necessity of tyrannicide, and
Macbeth on the futility of life. What this means is that you cannot
equate Shakespeare's thought with the explicit thought of any of his
characters. Much less can you get at his thought by assuming that the
plays simply reflect contemporary ideas. And when you cast more widely
for what might be called the thought of a play, you find that you are
taking into account far more than 'thought'—far more, that is, than
discursive thought: you bring into focus the attitudes embodied in the
different speakers in their complex relationships, the implicit comment
of action on profession, emotional overtones, perhaps things even
more elusive.

Do we have to say, then, that there is no such thing as 'the thought
of Shakespeare'? Did he simply let his mind be a thoroughfare for all
thoughts? Do his plays simply reflect the richness and variety of life,
without—in Matthew Arnold's sense—offering a 'criticism' of it? An
affirmative answer to these questions also feels wrong. 'The poetical
Character,' said Keats in a famous passage, 'has no self—it is everything
and nothing—it has no character—it enjoys light and shade; it lives in
gusto, be it foul or fair, high or low, rich or poor, mean or elevated—it
has as much delight in conceiving an Iago as an Imogen. What shocks
the virtuous philosopher, delights the chameleon Poet.' There is, I
think, much truth in this. But to think of Shakespeare *simply* as a
'chameleon Poet', changing colour, as it were, according to the circumstances that he himself creates, to do this is to ignore the feeling of
coherence that we have when we contemplate not only a single play but
all the plays considered as a single work: it is to ignore the imaginative
drive that runs through Shakespeare's plays from first to last. Perhaps
what we have to do is to attempt to re-define 'thought'.

First of all, then, if by 'thought' we mean 'the formation and arrangement of ideas in the mind', then it is plain that there are other modes of thought besides the familiar discursive mode. In discursive thought the mind abstracts from the rich variety of experience, and the thinking consists of an orderly progression of ideas thus abstracted. It is this progression that, in spoken or written argument, is offered for inspection, so that each step of the mind may be tested before a conclusion is reached. But thought is not limited to what can be offered— abstractly, explicitly and discursively: it can also be stimulated. The way a great artist stimulates ideas is by the presentation of particulars. And these particulars are not simply presented in a temporal or linear succession like steps in an argument: they fall into a pattern which—ideally speaking—the mind perceives in a single complex act of attention.

One way in which Shakespeare promotes ideas is by the patterning of his plot. Professor Hereward T. Price, in an excellent study of *Construction in Shakespeare*,[2] says:

> The point that I want to make is that Shakespeare had an eminently constructive mind. . . . Shakespeare's work is a strict intellectual construction developed from point to point until he brings us to the necessary and inevitable conclusion. *He interrelates part to part, as well as every part to the whole. His main idea is manifested in an action, with which it is intimately fused, so that the crises in the action which move us most deeply reveal at the same time the inner core of Shakespeare's thought.* [My italics.]

One of Professor Price's examples is the way in which, in the First Part of *King Henry VI*, formal ceremony is three times interrupted, at the beginning of the first, third, and fourth acts, by dissension and disorder. What this means is, as Mr. Cairncross puts it in the Introduction to his edition of the play: 'Ceremony and degree have lost their hold. Not only is an extended ceremony not wanted dramatically in a play like this; there is just no place for it in the nature of things.'[3] Further—and stronger—examples are the pattern of retribution in *Richard III*, and the careful alternation of main plot and subplot in the central scenes of *King Lear*, so that Yeats could say:

> We think of *King Lear* less as the history of one man and his sorrows than as the history of a whole evil time. Lear's shadow is in Gloucester . . . , and the mind goes on imagining other shadows, shadow beyond shadow, till it has pictured the world.

But thought in Shakespeare is generated not only by a pattern of incidents, but by what may be called—rather pedantically—a pattern of attitudes embodied in different characters: different attitudes towards

Honour in *Henry I V*, Part I, towards liberty and restraint in *Measure for Measure*, towards Nature in *King Lear*. And when we attempt to elicit the thought of these plays we rarely find that it can be summed up in the explicit utterance of any of the characters: it lies behind the clash of opposites and needs the whole play for its expression; so that in *The Tempest*, for example, the question of 'nature' and 'nurture' isn't simply settled on the side of nurture: Caliban, we are made to feel, has his rights.

When we speak of Shakespeare's thought, then, we mean something that emerges from a dramatic pattern, that inheres in that pattern and is inseparable from it. What I now want to add is that Shakespeare's thought—his poetic thought—is far more than thought as commonly conceived. The point is a difficult one, but for my present purpose it can be put quite simply. *As You Like It* rings changes on the contrasting meanings of 'natural' (*either* 'adequately human' *or* 'close down to the life of instinct') and 'civilized' (*either* 'well nurtured' *or* 'artificial'), especially in relation to the passion of love. In a play by Shaw the ideas would be put forward in the form of argument and counter-argument. Shakespeare is subtler. His characters do not only advance ideas, they embody attitudes to life that lie deeper than 'ideas', and our judgment is directed not only to *what* they say but to *how* they say it: it is the *how* that reveals the feelings, tone, and—as it were—life-style that comes to expression in their explicit formulations about experience. Thus Jacques' melancholy world-view is not simply an intellectual ingredient. Our response to his famous speech on the seven ages of man, for example—'All the world's a stage . . .'—is not determined exclusively by the substance, as though Shakespeare himself were offering us a little homily on life: it is determined by our awareness of the weary cynicism, the languor and preening self-regard that is finally 'placed' so neatly and effectively by Rosalind.[4] In play after play—in relation to Richard II, Brutus, Hamlet, Troilus, Othello—Shakespeare plumbs the recesses of the mind beyond 'thought', so that a character's conscious and deliberate formulation of any matter of urgent interest and concern—

> —For every man that Bolingbroke hath press'd
> To lift shrewd steel against our golden crown,
> God for his Richard hath in heavenly pay
> A glorious angel. . . .

> —It must be by his death, and for my part,
> I know no personal cause to spurn at him,
> But for the general. . . .

> —It is the cause, it is the cause, my soul. . . .

> —Life is a tale told by an idiot. . . .

—all such formulations are seen as having their full meaning only in the complex tissue of thoughts, feelings, desires, motives, valuations, and actions from which they emerge.

It is this hinterland of articulate thought—thought, often, in the very process of formation—that Shakespeare's developed verse can present so superbly. And this applies not only to the imputed thought of the major characters, so that every utterance of Othello or Macbeth carries something of a subliminal meaning, something from the fringes—or from beyond the fringes—of consciousness.[5] It applies also to all that is conveyed by the pervasive poetic medium within which the characters have their being, so that they can echo and re-echo each other without any sense of incongruity, as though they were—what indeed they are—symbols and projections of one mind actively constructing, or growing into, a single unified vision of life. Lady Macbeth's 'Come thick night' and Macbeth's 'Light thickens', Duncan's 'the air Nimbly and sweetly recommends itself Unto our gentle senses' and Malcolm's 'Your leavy screens throw down. And show like those you are', are not simply the utterances of individual characters: they are related aspects of a single vision of good as freedom and clarity, and evil as that which hinders and impedes. It is this 'pattern behind the pattern' that above all expresses itself in modes that may be impervious to the rational understanding—in imagery, rhythm, overtone, and suggestion —though they speak directly to the imagination.

When we speak, therefore, of the 'thought' of a Shakespeare play— the controlling 'idea' that determines not only the over-all design but the minutest details—we refer to a movement of mind, of imagination, that emerges *from* the structure of the plot, *from* the interplay of the characters and of the varied attitudes to experience that they represent; and we refer to a depth and energy of apprehension that, uniting all the characters in a single vision of life, enlists not only our cognitive and conceptual faculties but as much of our own wholeness as we can bring to bear. Shakespeare's thought is not something that can be paraphrased or summarized: it is something we imaginatively apprehend and assimilate to our own most personal life in a lifetime of discovery.

When this is recognized, and only when it is recognized, we are free to speak of Shakespeare's thought and to point to some of its main lines of growth. In the remainder of this paper I shall try, very briefly, to say something about the ways in which Shakespeare's mind and imagination grappled with the subject of power.

It was not an accident that Shakespeare's earliest plays, the three parts of *Henry VI* and *Richard III*, were concerned with power—power in the simple and obvious sense of who, in the state at large, gives orders to whom. It is important to realize this simple fact and to realize what the focus of attention really is. These plays take as their immediate subject events in England's still recent past—the faction and dynastic rivalry that began immediately after the death of Henry v, that broke out in the Wars of the Roses, and that culminated in the bloody triumph of the Yorkist Richard III, who in turn was overthrown by Henry Tudor at Bosworth Field. But they are not straight chronicle plays. Chronicle material is selected from, compressed, altered and added to, to form dramatic structures that are not designed solely to endorse the Tudor view of history. Even the first Part of *Henry VI*, as Professor Price observes, is not, as commonly supposed, 'artless, chaotic or merely discursive'; on the contrary, 'Shakespeare is imposing upon a body of historical data a controlling idea, an idea that constructs the play.' The idea is simple: it is that private faction undermines public order and the common cause—a process symbolized not only in the repeated scenes of interrupted ceremony to which I have already referred, but in the death of Talbot, who is betrayed by the rivalry of Somerset and York. 'This jarring discord of nobility . . . doth presage some ill event. . . . There comes the ruin, there begins confusion' (iv.i). In the two remaining Parts the pattern is equally schematic but the moral is less simple. It is as though the question, What is it that undoes the state?— answer: faction—were replaced by a further question, What is the nature of faction? The answer is given in the repetition and parallelism of the plot, in the apparently endless succession of revenges for wrong done. York kills Old Clifford; Young Clifford kills York's son, Rutland—'Thy father slew my father; therefore, die'—and joins the other Lancastrians in exulting over the defeated York, whose head is placed on the city gates; Young Clifford is killed in his turn, and his head replaces York's, for 'Measure for Measure must be answered.' And the whole senseless process is summed up in the two famous stage directions (*3 Henry VI*, II.v), 'Enter a son that has killed his father, dragging in the dead body', and 'Enter a father that has killed his son, bringing in the body'. *Richard III* is the most powerful and vivid member of this sequence of plays, but it grows directly from its predecessors. The victorious Yorkists are themselves divided and their dynastic triumph serves only to establish the dominating figure of Richard of Gloucester, in whom all the self-seeking of the earlier plays finds it fullest embodiment. Richard, however, does not stand alone; he is at the centre of what A. P. Rossiter calls "a basic pattern of retributive justice".[6] Mutual revenge is now seen as mutual punishment. Nemesis presides over the play, not as a convenient fiction, but because this is the way things happen: 'Wrong hath but wrong, and blame the due of blame.'

All this is obvious enough. What is, I think, equally obvious, though it gets less attention, is the total imaginative effect of these plays, which sometimes depends on hints and glimpses that cannot be subsumed in the rather rigidly controlled patterns of which I have spoken. In other words, to become aware of a play's main structural lines is only the beginning of understanding; even in dealing with these early plays whose pattern, as Professor Price says, can appear 'as schematic as the black and white squares on a chess board,' you have not really done very much when you have established the more obvious correspondences of plot structure. Even the Henry VI plays are something much more than pageant accompanied by illustrative dialogue. Structure includes, but is more than, a structure of events: it is a structure of value judgments, and value judgments are conveyed by words. For example, the contrast between the simple bloody-mindedness of most of the nobles—York's

> I will stir up in England some black storm
> Shall blow ten thousand souls to heaven, or hell—

and the religiously toned positives of the old Protector, Gloucester, or Henry himself,

> Thrice is he arm'd that hath his quarrel just,
> And he but naked, though lock'd up in steel,
> Whose conscience with injustice is corrupted

even though the play puts the King's ineffective virtue in an ironic light—such a contrast is at least as integral to the pattern as the simpler effects of action. Nor indeed can we expect even the early Shakespeare to hand over his meanings with the explicitness of a morality play. As soon as we have recognized that living structure comes into being only when we ourselves are actively engaged, we see that the necessary process of putting two and two together—of holding in one focus different attitudes towards the main action—involves what is implied as well as what is explicit. Shakespeare from the start expects from his audience some alertness towards tone and implication. Take a small example from the third Part. At Act II, scene iii, the Yorkists have suffered defeat at Towton. In addition to the familiar cry for revenge ('Warwick, revenge! brother, revenge my death!') there is Warwick's blasphemous vow 'to God above' to fight

> Till either death hath closed these eyes of mine
> Or fortune given me measure of revenge.

Edward of York then joins him on his knees, and applies to God—'Thou setter up and plucker down of kings'—terms that, as C. H. Herford pointed out, were popularly assigned to Warwick himself, and that are in fact used by Margaret when addressing Warwick in a later scene—'Proud setter up and puller down of kings.' Shakespeare couldn't say more plainly that for these men God can only be envisaged —when He is envisaged at all—as a kind of super-Warwick. Of course, you hear what he is saying only when you make the connexion for yourself. But to make connexions is a main part of the understanding of Shakespearian drama.

There is a further point to make here. The Henry vi plays are structured so as to embody a controlling idea, and you can learn from them something of how to approach later and more complicated plays. But just as you have to be alert to what is implied, rather than explicitly stated or presented, so—even from the start—you have to notice not only the more or less obvious pattern, but also what breaks into or goes beyond it, or in some way doesn't fit in. Cast back for a moment to the simplest play of the series, the first Part of *Henry VI*. The play's latest editor quotes Alfred Harbage to the effect that this 'is a play about the courage, prowess and assumed righteousness of the English as represented by such loyal and able leaders as Salisbury, Bedford, Warwick, and, above all, Lord Talbot; and about the opportunism, treachery, and fox-like success of the French as represented by the fraud and moral depravity of La Pucelle' (New Arden edition, Introduction, p. xl). No doubt this fairly represents the general background of assumptions against which the theme of internal faction is developed. But it is not the whole story. Talbot is indeed presented for our admiration as the embodiment of English patriotism; but there are also suggestions that Talbot's single-minded patriotism, although it serves to measure the depravity and self-seeking of the factious nobles, is not an absolute standard: it is not, by itself, sufficient to measure the causes of chaos in a world given to violence. Nor is it simply assumed that values are embodied in the English cause if only the English would give up quarrelling among themselves. In Act III, scene iii, when Joan persuades the Duke of Burgundy to desert the English and return to his French allegiance, her speech has a genuine authority.

> Look on thy country, look on fertile France,
> And see the cities and the towns defac'd
> By wasting ruin of the cruel foe;
> As looks the mother on her lowly babe
> When death doth close his tender dying eyes,
> See, see the pining malady of France. . . .

I am not pretending that this is great poetry; but it is not the speech of a character intended only for contempt. Joan is indeed later presented as contemptible; but I hope it is not only hindsight if I say that just at this point something breaks through the prevailing tenor of English patriotism and points forward to the great speech of the Duke of Burgundy, in *Henry V*, when he pleads for peace.[7] And we recall how much else there is in the later play—though less than ten years later—to qualify the simple patriotic interpretation that is often put on it. You can see too how in *Richard II* conflicting values are held in tension with each other, forming a pattern of meanings of great complexity.[8] In *1 Henry VI* we can hardly speak of complexity; there is rather, when we keep the last scenes presenting La Pucelle in mind, simple contradiction. But the point I am making is a simple one: you can't extract the structure from a Shakespeare play like the backbone from a kipper. Shakespearian structure is a living thing; it emerges only as we relate this to that; it cannot be summed up in an easy formula. That is why we need to be alert not only to the main lines of development of a play but of what cuts across them, and makes us reassess the pattern of meaning we thought we had found.

And now there is one last thing I should like to say about these early plays before leaving them. It is in fact rather obvious, but not the less important for that, especially if we keep the later plays in mind. The meaning of the three parts of *Henry VI* may begin to become clear as we attend to dramatic structure—a pattern of events and of attitudes towards those events (at the same time not ignoring what cuts across and complicates the more obvious orderly arrangement). But even here —at all events in the second and third Parts—the total imaginative effect depends also on hints and glimpses that cannot be subsumed in any formal pattern. We are here of course in the realm of individual and intuitive, but not lawless, judgment. It seems to me, then, that what we are most aware of is the unending clash of tight, self-contained egos, without any reaching out towards 'the other', or towards anything that transcends the self. And the feeling we get as we read or watch is that life is delivered over to automatism because of a radical misdirection of energy. Public life is private life writ large (that truth came to Shakespeare early), and Richard of Gloucester is explicit:

> And am I then a man to be beloved?
> O monstrous fault, to harbour such a thought!
> Then, since this earth affords no joy to me,
> But to command, to check, to o'erbear such
> As are of better person than myself,
> I'll make my heaven to dream upon the crown.

The pursuit of power is a substitute gratification, and it is in Richard that Shakespeare reveals something of what happens in the person when power is envisaged as the sole desirable end. The soliloquy I have just quoted from *3 Henry VI*, III, ii continues:

And I,—like one lost in a thorny wood,
That rends the thorns and is rent with the thorns,
Seeking a way and straying from the way;
Not knowing how to find the open air,
But toiling desperately to find it out,—
Torment myself to catch the English crown.

In that central image Shakespeare puts into words the sense of nightmare and frustration that pervades these plays—a process in which there is literally *no end*, only a sterile and meaningless repetition: 'a perpetual and restless desire of power after power, that ceaseth only in Death.' Early in the last act of this same play Warwick—'Proud setter up and puller down of kings'—meets defeat and death at the hands of the Yorkists at Barnet. His last words are a formal, rhetorical lament on the vanity of power:

Thus yields the cedar to the axe's edge,
Whose arms gave shelter to the princely eagle,
Under whose shade the ramping lion slept. . . .

But before the end the speech shifts into another mode:

For who lived king, but I could dig his grave?
And who durst smile when Warwick bent his brow?
Lo, now my glory smear'd in dust and blood!
My parks, my walks, my manors that I had,
Even now forsake me, and of all my lands
Is nothing left me but my body's length.

Instead of rhetorical figures there is now the simplest and most natural expression of human feeling — 'my parks, my walks, my manors that I had . . .' The result is both a deepening of perspective (something that comes to be a major characteristic of the later historical plays[9]), and an intensification of the ironic light in which we see the play's conclusion. Warwick's words are still echoing in our minds when we hear the victorious Edward announce his security with that bland short-sightedness that we shall meet again (with different tones) in other of Shakespeare's 'successful' men of action.

And now what rests but that we spend the time
With stately triumphs, mirthful comic shows,
Such as befits the pleasure of the court?
Sound drums and trumpets! farewell sour annoy!
For here, I hope, begins our lasting joy.

Since Richard of Gloucester has just announced his intention of 'blasting' that 'harvest', the irony here is inescapable. But even without Gloucester's melodramatic asides, Edward's crude assumptions about the fruits of kingship are sufficiently placed, within the context of the play, as vanity. And the obviousness of the irony shouldn't prevent us from seeing the significance of it. Other princes in the Shakespearian drama—Henry Bolingbroke at the end of *Richard II* and again at the end of *I Henry IV*, Henry V at the end of his play—will be compelled to stand in the same steady light, of which they themselves are unaware. And this may serve as a reminder that Shakespearian irony is not simply a dramatic device. What it manifests is an intelligence that is at the same time a commitment to life and life's realities; and against *these* all kinds of sham, self-deception, substitute values—however loudly endorsed by society—must show themselves for what they are.

It seems plain, then, that in these early plays we have the beginning of much of Shakespeare's thought on the subject of power, even though it is not explicitly formulated *as* thought. The process in which, in play after play, he traces the intricacies of political power is far too large a subject for a single paper, much more for a concluding section. We will merely note that in the sequence of Shakespeare's plays there are four characteristics that bear directly on our question of what Shakespeare's 'thought' is on the question of power. First, there is the tendency (most marked in *Henry IV*) to put the political action in a wider setting that in various ways reflects back on it: there is an increase in depth and perspective. Second, for an explanation of conflict and failure at the political level we are more and more directed towards conflict and failure at the personal level: here the line runs from Richard II, to Brutus, to Coriolanus. Third, there is a growing sense of the inadequacy of action that is merely political, merely concerned with power, as in *Henry V*. Finally—and this is in some ways inseparable from the other three—the deepening insight into the inadequacies of power goes hand in hand with what may be called the celebratory aspects of Shakespeare's art, in which all is finally subsumed: the celebration, I mean, of life-values against which the distortions and subterfuges of partial life may be measured. This, too, was a long process, and it started early. Harold Goddard, remarking that in the reign of Henry VI Shakespeare came face to face with chaos, 'a subject that continued to enthral him to the end of his days,' says: 'It would be folly to try to subsume Shakespeare's works under one head, but, if we were forced to do so, one of the least unsatisfactory ways would be to say that they are an attempt to answer the question: 'What is the cure for chaos?'[10] That answer is to be found, not in the overtly political dramas but in the tragedies and final plays. Here, Shakespeare's handling of power, when it occurs, is always part of something far wider; it is always in implicit or explicit relation to positive values; and it can be defined only in terms of a total dramatic and poetic structure. His 'thought' about power, in short, is—inescapably—a function of the imagination: 'a man in his wholeness, wholly attending.'

At the end of a paper that has been necessarily discursive I must not attempt to dwell in any detail on one of the great tragedies, but we may briefly call to mind *Macbeth*. *Macbeth*, in one of its aspects, is a study in tyranny: dominative power, seeking to establish and support itself by violence, is traced as never before or since as a progress towards meaninglessness and chaos. It is not merely that Macbeth creates confusion around him; from the moment he yields to 'that suggestion Whose horrid image doth unfix my hair,' he *is* confusion. And what the poetry tells us in its imagery of unnatural strain and hysterical effort is, unmistakably, that violence towards another is violence towards the self—towards that innermost self that exists only in relationship—in the world where one gives and takes 'honour, love, obedience'. It tells us more too: not only that, as Martin Foss says, 'he who wants to possess will himself be possessed,'[11] but that apparent firmness and single-minded concentration on a purely egocentric purpose covers an underlying disintegration. But the telling is entirely in terms of the awakened imagination, that holds in one complex act of attention explicit thought, dramatic action, and symbolism, and all that is presented or suggested by rhythm and imagery.

> This castle hath a pleasant seat; the air
> Nimbly and sweetly recommends itself
> Unto our gentle senses.
>
>   This guest of summer,
> The temple-haunting martlet, does approve,
> By his lov'd mansionry, that the heaven's breath
> Smells wooingly here; no jutty, frieze,
> Buttress, nor coign of vantage, but this bird
> Hath made his pendent bed, and procreant cradle:
> Where they most breed and haunt, I have observ'd
> The air is delicate.

Is this just a bit of 'poetry' or something put in to 'illustrate character'? I think not. The passage creates an imaginative 'atmosphere' that is important because it is so different from the atmosphere that we have come to associate with Dunsinane. But more: the birds are evoked with delighted attention to their free movements; and they are evoked in terms that make their sanctioned seasonal activities into something with a bearing on human life itself. What we have here, in short, is an image of life delighting in life; and it powerfully reinforces our sense of the ideal presence of a life-bearing order in the human commonwealth— something that Macbeth describes, when he has lost it, as 'Honour, love, obedience, troops of friends.' This, the play makes us feel, is the reality where man finds himself: when he steps outside that order—as Macbeth in his pursuit of power does by the murder of Duncan and the increasingly pointless murders that follow—he loses himself in a world that in one sense is real enough, but that in another sense is mere unreality—'where nothing is, but what is not.'

There is of course far more than that to say about Shakespeare's exploration of the nature of power. But the example may suffice to illustrate the point that it is the main object of my paper to establish. Shakespeare's 'thought' is not something that can be extracted from the body of his work or discursively paraphrased. We can point to certain preoccupations and describe in a general way some of the main directions of his mind. But in any fundamental sense, his 'thought'— in all its depth, fullness, complexity, and energy—can be apprehended only as an imaginative activity evoked and directed by all the resources of his art. We can never 'know about' Shakespeare's thought: we can only know it as living power.

NOTES

1 Compare H. D. F. Kitto, *Form and Meaning in Drama*, p. 248.

2 University of Michigan, *Contributions in Modern Philology*, p. 17.

3 *The First Part of King Henry VI* (New Arden Shakespeare), edited by Andrew S. Cairncross, Introduction, p. liii.

4 This is brought out in James Smith's brilliant essay on the play: *Scrutiny* IX, 1, June 1940, now included in the posthumous *Shakespearian and Other Essays* (C.U.P., 1974).

5 See J. I. M. Stewart, *Character and Motive in Shakespeare*.

6 A. P. Rossiter, 'The Unity of Richard III' in *Angel with Horns*.

7 Discussed in my *Explorations 3*, p. 184.

8 E. W. Talbert writes interestingly on this in *The Problem of Order: Elizabethan Political Commonplaces and an Example of Shakespeare's Art* (Chapel Hill), Chapter VI.

9 See Erich Auerbach, *Mimesis: the Representation of Reality in Western Literature*, tr. Willard R. Trask (Princeton University Press), Chapter 13, 'The Weary Prince'.

10 Harold Goddard, *The Meaning of Shakespeare* (University of Chicago Paperbacks), Vol. I, pp. 28–29.

11 Martin Foss, *Symbol and Metaphor in Human Experience* (Bison Book edition: University of Nebraska Press). p. 33. See also pp. 112–13.

8
Shakespeare's Tragedies and the Question of Moral Judgment

WHEN I WAS invited to take part in this Symposium* it was suggested that I might be willing to accept the role of the 'Arnoldian' critic. This, I assumed, was not intended as a compliment, however undeserved, but was simply a suggestion that someone committed to a view of poetry as in some sense 'a criticism of life,' someone whose writings on Shakespeare are thought to have a moral slant, should try to define the nature of his approach to Shakespearian tragedy; should try, in particular, to throw some light on the part played by moral judgment in his response to those master-works that are not easily landed in the moralist's net. It is a task that I am glad to accept. And although at the end I may leave you with no more than some self-evident truths, there may be some profit in the journey.

It certainly has its difficulties. 'Moral,' says the Dictionary,

> Of or pertaining to character or disposition considered as good or bad, virtuous or vicious; of or pertaining to the distinction between right and wrong, or good and evil, in relation to the actions, volitions, or character of responsible beings.

A play is a moving image of life: it is concerned with men in action. If we are thinking about it at all, and not merely giving ourselves up to an interest in story—which is anyhow virtually impossible—we simply cannot help making moral distinctions between right and wrong. On the other hand, to describe a critic *tout court* as 'a moralist' is to suggest some kind of limitation or disability: he has not an adequately free or open mind; he sets off with preconceived, and perhaps narrow, moral standards and forces his material to conform, or finds fault if it does not; or his moral preoccupations lead him to substitute for the vivid particulars of the work before him some comparatively inert generalizations. Alternatively, of course, the objectors may be expressing a feeling that in the long run moral judgment has no place in the work of art or in criticism: in this view the business of the critic, like that of the artist, is

* 'Approaches to Shakespeare,' a symposium sponsored by the Glasgow Endowment Committee at Washington and Lee University, Winter 1968. The other speakers were C. L. Barber, Kenneth Burke, and Stanley Edgar Hyman.

simply to understand and to make intelligible. There is clearly a problem here for the critic who, while feeling the force of these objections, believes that criticism, like art though in a humbler way, is a contribution to the life of reason, and that 'he who thinks reasonably must'—in some sense—'think morally.' And the problem is not only a critical one: it reflects the very much wider question of how a man can be committed to values, and all that that implies by way of judgment, and yet believe (as I do) that moralizing is the devil.[1]

If we want testimony to the moral function of literature—and that from creative writers themselves—we shall find no lack of it. George Eliot, for example, for all her admirable 'passion for the special case,' and her 'repugnance to the men of maxims,' her insistence on the need for *treatment*, which alone determines the moral quality of art,' on the need *not* to lapse 'from the picture to the diagram,' willingly accepted, as novelist, 'the office of teacher or influencer of the public mind.' Conrad spoke of 'the moral discovery that lies at the heart of every tale.' And D. H. Lawrence:

> The essential function of art is moral. Not aesthetic, not decorative, not pastime and recreation. But moral. The essential function of art is moral.

Lawrence of course went on to make the point that the morality he was concerned with was 'passionate', not 'didactic', and in the 'Study of Thomas Hardy,' he offered another criterion for distinguishing the morality of really great works of art which I shall come back to later. But the point is that all three of these great novelists are agreed that the function of their art is in some sense moral. I cannot imagine that any of them would demur when a recent critic of Henry James, Miss Dorothea Krook, invoking standards that she clearly expects to be taken for granted, writes of 'the double purpose of every great dramatist: that of a radical criticism of society . . . on the one hand, and, on the other, of a "criticism of life" in Matthew Arnold's sense—a radical exposure, sometimes in its comic aspect, more often in its tragic aspect, of some of the fundamental and permanent predicaments of human life.'[2]

All this of course is very general. Important as testimony, it means little more than that our concern with literature cannot be divorced from our normal human concerns in which the distinction beween right and wrong, or good and evil, is so inevitably present and active; that, in the words of L. H. Myers,

> When a novelist displays an attitude of aesthetic detachment from the ordinary ethical and philosophical preoccupations of humanity something in us protests.

But to say that tells us nothing at all about the way in which our moral sense enters into—or, for that matter, emerges from—a reading of any literary work, more especially when the work is a Shakespearian tragedy, which so completely refuses to be nailed down to a moral scheme. Dryden could sum up his *All for Love* in a couplet,

> And fame to late posterity shall tell,
> No lovers lived so great, or died so well;

you cannot treat *Antony and Cleopatra* so, not even if you stand that judgment on its head. When an eighteenth-century writer tells us, of *Hamlet*,

> all the moral we can deduce is, that murder cannot lie hid, and that conscience ever makes a coward of guilt,

or another, more subtly,

> The instruction to be gathered from this delineation is, that persons formed like Hamlet, should retire, keep aloof, from situations of difficulty and contention: or endeavour, if they are forced to contend, to brace their minds, and acquire such vigour and determination of spirit as shall arm them against malignity,[3]

something in us protests. What, then, is the nature of the moral consciousness to which a Shakespeare tragedy may properly be said to appeal, and what is the nature of the interaction between the two? The only way of throwing some light on these matters is to question ourselves as to what happens when we are engaged with a particular tragedy as fully and responsibly as we can. And we should take care that we do not sidestep that naïve, delighted and partly 'uncritical' engagement that is at the root of all good criticism, and that, in our search for profundity, we sometimes ignore.

When we read or watch a Shakespeare play, we are, I take it, much engaged with the story, with the question, What happens, what can possibly happen, next? This interest, I think, never entirely deserts us, and when we see a good performance of *Hamlet*, even if it is for the tenth time, we still wait for the end with a kind of agonized expectation, half hoping—though we know the hope is futile—that it need not end in catastrophe. And with the interest in story and situation goes some kind of emotional engagement with the persons who perform the action, movements of sympathy and antipathy that shift and change as the play goes on. We need not find Hamlet, as one critic has done, 'the most adorable of heroes,' but we could hardly be said to know the play if his fate left us entirely unmoved. Liking and disliking, approval and disapproval, are at work long before we begin to grasp the total pattern that the characters—their words and actions—compose. I suspect that even Professor Heilman was exasperated by and sorry for King Lear long before it began to dawn on him that what was even more deeply affecting him was a complex and magical web of meanings having to do with seeing and blindness, madness and reason, and the ambiguities of Nature.

It is at this naïve and indispensable level of response that our moral judgment is first engaged. Unless we were shocked by the murders in *Macbeth* and *Othello* we should hardly be human, let alone good readers. And some kind of moral assessment goes on even when we contemplate quite minor characters: Kent, for all his stubbornness and hot temper, is trustworthy, Osric is a moral cipher, and so on. And the fact that some cases are dubious—such as Brutus's decision to join the conspiracy—doesn't alter the matter: it may be a long time before we can come to any sort of clarity about Brutus's action, but the play makes us ponder its rightness or wrongness. And this spontaneous moral pondering operates not only when we stand back, as it were, and see characters and situations in their totality, but when we dwell on the minute details out of which our more massive reactions will be formed. When Iago says of Othello and Desdemona,

> His soul is so enfetter'd to her love,
> That she may make, unmake, do what she list,
> Even as her appetite shall play the god
> With his weak function,

we reflect not only that it is characteristic of Iago to see love simply as appetite, but that there is a curious and limiting distortion in that 'enfetter'd.' If we go on to reflect that Othello himself had indicated a view of marriage as in some sense a confinement—

> But that I love the gentle Desdemona,
> I would not my unhoused free condition
> Put into circumscription and confine
> For the sea's worth—

we are surely not indulging in gratuitous moral arithmetic, but following the dramatist's own lead to the significance of his action. The plays in short take for granted our moral interest and engagement as much as they take for granted our ability to understand the words and construe the language, even though linguistic and moral literacy alike may be forced to undergo a discipline of change and development.

There is of course, as I have indicated, another side to this basic and necessary *naïveté*, even more important than the unavoidable—though often tentative—habit of moral assessment that I have been discussing. It is simply openness and receptivity, a willingness to give oneself up, at least provisionally, to what the play offers, without any over-anxious or premature need to make sense of it all, which usually means to fit it into some preconceived intellectual or moral pattern. It is this dual process, simultaneously passive and active, simply receiving and yet actively relating what is received to our own permanent but developing moral life, on which we found our 'criticism' of Shakespeare's tragedies —that is, the way in which we describe to ourselves and others the furthest reach of meaning that we have been able to take from them. If, then, our accepted moral notions cannot be allowed to stand in the way of our openness and receptivity, and that in turn cannot inhibit the working of our moral consciousness, the question remains of how these interact in the full development of a tragedy, fully attended to.

What happens when we read or watch *Hamlet*? We see a young man in a state of intense melancholy because of the death of a loved father and the hasty remarriage of his mother to his father's brother. The young man has it revealed to him by a ghost that the supplanter is in fact the murderer of his father, and he is commanded to take vengeance. That task occupies the remainder of the play, and is only completed at the expense of seven other lives including Hamlet's own. The exciting action, with stratagem and counter-stratagem, is indeed enough to hold the most unsophisticated theatre-goer, as is abundantly proved. But of course Shakespeare gives us more than that. Our minds are engaged with the nature of the corruption that surrounds Hamlet and with the particular brooding darting consciousness that confronts that corruption, and of course, since the play heavily insists on it, with the ambiguity of the Ghost—'spirit of health, or goblin damned?'. It is Hamlet's reaction to the Ghost, his testing of it, and—'I'll take the Ghost's word for a thousand pounds'—his final submission to it, that is the main interest into which the interest in what-happens-next? is absorbed. The nature of that central consciousness, and its development in the course of the action, is something that, above all, we find ourselves trying to understand. It is of course something that comes home to us in a peculiarly intimate way: so much is compressed into that consciousness that we can hardly help seeing Hamlet, with D. G. James, as 'an image of modernity' or, with C. S. Lewis, as a kind of archetypal figure of a man who has lost his way. But in our attempt to understand, to bring home, questioning plays an essential part; and it is—we cannot avoid the word—moral questioning. What I do *not* mean should be clear. I do not mean that we judge Hamlet in relation to 'the ethics of revenge,' either our own, or those that we impute to the Elizabethans, for that would be to take him right outside the context in which he has his proper existence, the one that Shakespeare has created for him.* In coming to terms with a great work of art there are

* I am grateful to Miss Eleanor Prosser's scholarly and acute *Hamlet and Revenge*, not only for its challenge to rethink the play in detail. But her demonstration that the original audience was not likely to assume without

no short cuts. We do not hold our moral consciousness in abeyance (as though we were in the kind of cloud-cuckoo-land Lamb saw in Restoration comedy), for that would be impossible. But we do need to abandon any rigid moral stance, and to allow free intercourse between our moral notions and the great surge of fresh experience which is the play. What we attend to, in short, are those revealing tones and implications in their minutely appropriate words, which are the dramatic representatives of different attitudes in that complex play of attitudes-in-action which is the tragedy: the suspicious unction of Claudius's first speech, or the crass moral obtuseness with which Polonius, like his son before him, tramples on young love—'Affection! Pooh!'. Where Hamlet is concerned we respond not only to what he says but to its implications— the tone, the timbre, the lifestyle, all those subtle indications of consciousness as *displayed* in the developing drama. I am under the necessity here of cutting a long story short and appearing more dogmatic than I could wish. What I would say, then, is that as we attend to Hamlet in his inward communings and his multifarious relations with others, we become aware not only of a man trapped and imprisoned but of an imprisoning state of mind. The extent to which 'Denmark' is 'a prison' is clear from any attentive reading[4] and I do not intend to speak of it here, except to remind you that Hamlet's predicament is real and painful: in that society of spying, subterfuge and treachery there is certainly enough to make any honest man regard it as an unweeded garden: 'things rank and gross in nature possess it merely.' Among all the characters it is only Hamlet who has the potentialities of a strong, free mind: you see it in his prose rhythms, his range of interest and reference, the spontaneous eagerness with which he greets anyone who is, or seems to be, outside the circle of corruption. But Hamlet is not the moral norm: he too is subject to judgment—and by this I mean judgment by criteria that the play itself provides, that Hamlet provides, in terms of vitality, freemoving life and a capacity for relationships. From this point of view, what we are compelled to notice, from the moment that Hamlet gives himself up to an exclusive preoccupation with the Ghost's command, wiping from his memory,

> all trivial fond records,
> All saws of books, all forms, all pressures past,
> That youth and observation copied there . . . ,

---

question that Hamlet had a duty to avenge his father (as an older generation of scholars tended to assume) and was indeed likely to be highly suspicious of a ghost who commanded murder, can by itself do no more than free us from misleading assumptions. What Shakespeare himself 'meant' when writing the play can only be approached by the normal methods of literary criticism—i.e. by attending to what he says.

is an increasing entanglement in a self-consuming preoccupation with the very evil that he is required to set himself against: it is as though the world in which he feels himself required to play the avenger had a kind of fifth column in Hamlet's own consciousness; and the fifth column, if it never takes entire control, pretty thoroughly disrupts the autonomous system that is—or, we feel, ought to be—Hamlet. I have argued this at some length in 'An Approach to *Hamlet*', and a recent thorough re-reading of the play has given me no reason to change my mind. Hamlet's capacity for life is diminished to the extent that an exclusive concentration on corruption awakens a corresponding corruption in himself. I am not referring simply to the crudities of action—such as the sending of Rosencrantz and Guildenstern to their deaths, 'not shriving time allowed'—though we cannot ignore these, but to the words of dialogue and soliloquy in which Shakespeare reveals states of mind and feeling that are only crudely defined by our moral and psychological labels: sexual obsession, an exaggerated sense of unworthiness, a nostalgic longing for an impossible simplification, death if need be, as an escape from life's complexities, self-dramatization, self-righteousness, and a cruelty that ranges from the obscenities directed at Ophelia to the reasons given for not killing the King at prayer. All these qualities co-exist with those finer qualities that go to make 'the other Hamlet', who is never entirely lost sight of. But not even the beautiful and touching lines that are given to Hamlet as his death draws near can obscure the fact that what we are concerned with is a study—one of the most profound studies in our literature—of a trapped and death-directed consciousness. And to say that is to commit ourselves to a moral judgment.

I am perfectly aware that what I have just said, with all the crudeness of brevity, does not command universal assent. It does represent an approximation to my own thoughts and feelings about *Hamlet*; but just now I have no desire to convince anyone of the rightness of my own views. For what I want to say is this. Supposing I am right, and that the tentative following through of qualities and attitudes embodied in words that the play calls on us to perform, issues in some such over-all or inclusive judgment as I have sketched, there is still an important sense in which we cannot moralize the play, or feel that we have done our duty as critics, let alone as human beings, when we have provisionally defined the flaw, indeed the evil, in the central consciousness. Moral judgment is like our knowledge of the dictionary meanings of words and their history; we cannot do without it, but no more than our construing of the sense is it adequate to our experience of a great tragedy such as *Hamlet*.

Hamlet, we may say—and by Hamlet I mean not a real-life figure we have extracted from the play, but the dramatic embodiment of a particular complex attitude to life who affects us, *within the conventions of Shakespeare's art*, as if he were a fellow human—Hamlet has followed a disastrously wrong path. But when we have *felt* the play, entered into it imaginatively, it seems worse than inadequate simply to say that: and this for three reasons. The first is contained in Yeats's saying that in great tragic drama 'it is always ourselves that we see upon the stage'— and this in a more profound sense than is contained in Coleridge's remark that he had 'a smack of Hamlet' in him. We are too deeply involved; for in following Hamlet's fortunes we are trying out our own attitudes to a world that is hardly as we would wish it to be, and that may indeed contain people who have done us some wrong. And when we are involved in this way our judgment, while sensitized beyond the normal, becomes something different from judgment in the usual sense, when we acquit, excuse or condemn in the light of an abstract code or previously defined standards. The second reason is suggested by Northrop Frye when he says that 'tragic heroes are wrapped in the mystery of their communion with that something beyond which we can see only through them, and which is the source of their strength and their fate alike.' 'As for the something beyond [he goes on], its names are variable, but the form in which it manifests itself is fairly constant. Whether the context is Greek, Christian, or un-defined, tragedy seems to lead up to an epiphany of law, of that which is and must be.'[5] In *Hamlet* I think we have an especially acute sense of the tragic hero as a person; but that sense is constantly taken up into the sense of law that Frye speaks of, the sense of *how things must be*, which tragedy gives us the courage to face. And this, we remark, is mediated through the 'flawed' hero himself—a tension that is recog-nized in all theories of tragedy from Aristotle onwards. And finally, of course, even when we condemn Hamlet, when, that is, our aroused sympathy recoils from what he offers or enacts, it is Hamlet himself who provides some of the norms against which we measure his swervings. And if one of the norms, and that the greatest of all—the 'rarer action' of Prospero's great speech in *The Tempest*—is absent from the play, except by implication, it remains true that almost all the positives against which we can define the evil of Denmark as a perversion of life, are mediated through him. To quote Professor Frye once more: 'The discovery or *anagnorisis* which comes at the end of the tragic plot is not simply the knowledge by the hero of what has happened to him . . . but the recognition of the determined shape of the life he has created for himself, with an implicit comparison with the uncreated potential he has forsaken.'[6] In *Hamlet* that uncreated potential, like the workings of Dîke or the law, is something we only know through the Prince him-self. It is partly a matter of what others—Ophelia, Horatio—say about him; partly of what he himself says when we feel that he is most free.

But it also has to do with something less easily defined—a way of speech, flexible, ranging, responsive, capable of infinite modulation, that contrasts not only with the way of speech given, say, to Polonius or to Claudius, but with the speech of Hamlet himself when he is given over to his obsessions with corrupted sex or with revenge. In other words it is Hamlet himself, or Shakespeare speaking through Hamlet, who clarifies whatever standards of judgment we may feel bound to apply. But the play doesn't merely ask us for judgment; it asks us to stretch our imaginations. And at the end what we feel is not the desire to judge, but simply pity and fear.

At this point we may perhaps pause on what Coleridge liked to call a landing-place and look back over the course of the argument. At the beginning of this paper, when I was anxious to insist that literature has a moral function, I supported myself with some quotations. It will have been noticed that these were taken from novelists, or referred to the novel. The suggestion will by now, I hope, have entered your minds that what, with due qualification, is right and adequate for the novel is not necessarily right or adequate for great poetic drama.* Miss Dorothea Krook, in her study of Henry James in which she rightly considers his novels as being in a fairly direct sense a 'criticism of life', makes a further observation. She is considering the question of why James's heroes and heroines are often so very rich, and she writes:

> James's millionaires and heiresses have in his novels exactly the same dramatic function as the kings, queens and princes in Shakespeare's plays. They are 'representative' of all humanity in the modern world in exactly the same sense as Shakespeare's kings, queens and princes are representative: in the sense that they are the acknowledged symbols of supreme power and prestige in their society. . . . They embody, in short, the dominant (though not necessarily the exclusive) ideal of human possibility in that society; consequently, what 'happens' to them—their vicissitudes, their 'rise and fall', their suffering and joy—is exemplary and instructive for the purpose of drama in exactly the way that Shakespeare conceived the fate of a Hamlet, a Macbeth, a Lear to be exemplary and instructive.[7]

We may readily agree that James's heroes and heroines are, for all their money, representative. But, leaving on one side the question of whether Shakespeare's heroes do in fact embody 'the dominant . . .

* Though this may also be said of novels that in some way approach poetic drama, e.g. *Moby Dick* or, perhaps, *Wuthering Heights*.

ideal of human possibility' in their society, we may well ask ourselves whether the comparison between the great novelist and the great tragic poet does not contain a quite misleading implication about the work of the latter. For the truth is, as I hope we have seen, that the fate of Hamlet isn't merely 'exemplary and instructive'. It may, perhaps, be that; but it is also very much more; and it is in the very much more that we find the defining qualities of great tragedy. Clearly you can't make too sharp a distinction between the varying modes of the novel and the varying modes of tragedy; but the fact remains that the attention we give to Hamlet is different in kind from the attention we give to Isabel Archer, or to Mr. Casaubon.

Perhaps we are now near the heart of the matter. At the level of human response, where we feel for the tragic hero *as though* he were a fellow human being—and even in the most patterned and stylized of tragedies, like the Greek, this is a necessary and unavoidable part of our total apprehension—at this level we admire, or sympathize with, the hero, for all his blindness, his faults and sins. Even with Macbeth, who is the most damnable of Shakespeare's heroes, even with Coriolanus, who is the least likeable, we assimilate some of 'their' energy, or the energy that is conveyed through them. Macbeth has made for us, so to speak, the terrible journey of fear, a journey backwards away from the 'good things of day' towards the meaningless dehumanized fragments of the Witches' cauldron; made it because the very thought that such things could be, inside him, fills him with a desperate panic which seems to demand actualization of the potential evil within. And in the very course of that journey he reveals for us qualities of courage and insight that, in the world of the play, we should not otherwise have known. And this counterbalancing energy does something to our unavoidable moral judgment. It is necessary that the 'butcher' should be removed; but we do not contemplate his end with any satisfaction, however grim.[8]

The fact remains, however, that in Shakespeare's tragedies what I have called the human response is only a part of our total engagement. Even in *Othello*, which everyone recognizes as the most domestic, in some ways one of the least metaphysical, of the tragedies, the human action engages with and reveals a psychological, indeed a metaphysical, pattern, that is part of the play (as Robert Heilman has shown in *Magic in the Web*), however much this may affect us in the theatre simply as suggestion and overtone. And it is at this more universal level that the normal mode of our moral judgment undergoes its most radical transformation. I have hinted at something of this in relation to *Hamlet*. Perhaps we may clarify the matter still further if we turn our attention, briefly, to the concluding movement of *King Lear*.

Nothing is more wonderful in Shakespeare's mature art than the assured and flexible technique that allows him to move without strain or apparent incongruity into quite different dramatic modes, whilst yet preserving the unity of the whole: to move, for example, from scenes where the focus is on the directly personal and individual (so that our immediate response is as though to this particular man in this particular situation) to the more or less overtly symbolic. And between these extremes are virtually infinite gradations, so that within our simply human response to *this* predicament wide-reaching overtones are evoked with different degrees of intensity, and even the most directly 'symbolic' situations and events (Prospero's storm, Hermione's statue) are firmly rooted in feelings and insights that belong to the common stuff of our humanity.

It would not be true to say that *King Lear* begins at the simply human and naturalistic level: from the start formalizing devices are at work that both concentrate and extend our attention. But it is true to say that we are aware of a powerful individual presence, Lear himself, whose behaviour as a man demands our judgment. King Lear, we say, made a wrong choice—a choice springing from the total personality that is revealed to us—and the rest of the play shows him learning the lesson of its consequences. This of course is an almost grotesque over-simplification: well before the central scenes on the heath we know that we are concerned not simply with the fate of one old man but with the nature and place of man in the world; our minds and imaginations are engaged, though always with a precise particular focus, with the relation of every man to the chaotic forces of 'nature', with the nature of reason and its relations to feeling and impulse, with in short the possibility of affirming any kind of humanity (what does that mean?) in the face of the forces that threaten it.

It is beyond any man's powers to describe briefly the massive meanings that are built up in the course of the play. My purpose is simply to remind you of those meanings that press on the play's final movement, on which I wish now to concentrate with an eye to the particular problem that is engaging us. The scene of Lear's reconciliation with Cordelia is directly and poignantly human in its appeal, the more effectively so not only because it follows Lear's greatest outbursts of despair but because in the preceding Edgar and Gloucester sequence the play had moved well in the direction of a kind of Morality sparseness.

> *Lear*   Do not laugh at me;
> For, as I am a man, I think this lady
> To be my child Cordelia.
> *Cor.*   And so I am, I am.

Lear Be your tears wet? Yes, faith. I pray, weep not;
     If you have poison for me, I will drink it.
     I know you do not love me; for your sisters
     Have, as I do remember, done me wrong:
     You have some cause, they have not.
Cor.   No cause, no cause.

Yet even here, in this most simply moving of scenes, there is some
interplay of the natural and the formal, of personal feeling in a direct
relationship and symbolic overtones; and before Lear wakes, Cordelia,
in a dozen lines, recalls all that he has been through. In other words,
Shakespeare wants us to hold in our imagination all that has happened
in the storm, all those powerful overtones of universal meaning, together with what is now going on. It is as though all the questions that
the play has forced on us—What is justice? what is madness? what is
true need? all subsumed under the great question, 'Who is it that can
tell me what I am?'—were here receiving an answer. The moral balance
has now come down against those who embodied the belief that man
is a merely natural force in a world of natural forces, and on the side of
those who hold to the belief that man is utterly different from this, that
what makes him man is his capacity to feel something other than his
own immediate needs and desires.

The play however does not end here, and we are forced, as we watch,
to continue our questionings. Cordelia's forces are defeated, and she
and the King are sent to prison, where Edmund arranges for them to
be killed. He in turn is killed in a judicial combat by Edgar, and
although he sends word for his order to be countermanded—'some
good I mean to do Despite of mine own nature'—it is too late. Cordelia
is murdered, and Lear dies desperately trying to reassure himself that
she still lives. What do we make of that sequence?

Perhaps we can obtain some hint of an answer if we call to mind the
opening of the final scene (V.iii), where there is the same kind of alternation that occurs elsewhere between formal qualities, a rather severe
stylization, and qualities that seem designed to express a human, personal response to the situation. Cordelia again uses the rhymed speech
she had used in the play's opening, and uses it to the same effect:

             We are not the first
     Who, with best meaning, have incurr'd the worst.
     For thee, oppressed King, I am cast down;
     Myself could else out-frown false Fortune's frown.

But these impersonal and choric lines are at once followed by Lear's
rapturous expression of his happiness at being reunited with his
daughter, an expression that has something of the touching oblivious-

ness of all else of a man who has recovered what is most dear to him after the most extreme hazards. Ignoring here the multiple ironies of these twenty-five lines, I suggest that in this blending of the formal and the intensely personal and individual you have an anticipation of the play's end, which is so hard to describe. For there you have the almost unbearable expression of personal agony framed by a ritual solemnity.

Lear	Lend me a looking-glass;
	If that her breath will mist or stain the stone,
	Why, then she lives.
Kent	Is this the promis'd end?
Edgar	Or image of that horror?
Albany	Fall and cease. . . .

The feeling that these interjections support is that we are not only watching a rending personal grief: it is a solemn ritual of mourning, as though a world were coming to an end: 'O ruin'd piece of Nature! This great world Shall so wear out to nought.' All the pettiness of ambition and intrigue seems infinitely far removed; and even when Edmund's death is reported, 'That's but a trifle here.' And this perhaps is why the play ends with those curiously hesitant and unemphatic lines of Edgar's,

> The weight of this sad time we must obey;
> Speak what we feel, not what we ought to say.
> The oldest hath borne most: we that are young
> Shall never see so much, nor live so long.

It is almost a confession of the inadequacy of words, as though words no longer matter.

At this culminating point, then, moral judgment steps down. Who are we to say that Lear was an egotist or a fool? That question contains its own answer. But what of those more universal insights, part psychological, concerning the nature of man, part moral, concerning what man ought to be, that, I have claimed, are released when we fully engage with the play? Certainly we do not disown these; but in relation to the imaginative world of the play we hold them in a different way from the propositions of the moralist. The point is well put by D. H. Lawrence in his 'Study of Thomas Hardy':

> Every work of art adheres to some system of morality. But if it be really a work of art, it must contain the essential criticism of the morality to which it adheres. And hence the antinomy, hence the conflict necessary to every tragic conception. The degree to which the system of morality, or the metaphysic of any work of art is submitted to criticism within the work of art makes the lasting value and satisfaction of that work.

That is, in reading *King Lear*, we are false to the experience that Shakespeare offers if we in any way ignore or tone down the image of almost unbearable suffering with which the play ends: 'All's cheerless, dark, and deadly.' The sense of *that*, clearly, is something that runs strongly through the whole play, and helps to account for the profound irony. The play as a whole, however, is neither pessimistic nor finally committed to the irony of the absurd; it is an affirmation of human values. But even our affirmations are forced to observe a certain reticence.[9]

I said at the beginning that the most you could hope for from my examination of this problem was a reaffirmation of some simple truths. Our criticism of Shakespeare's tragedies, of plays depicting men in tragic action, is unavoidably moral. When we have lived through the experience of *Hamlet* or of *Lear* we are not in some mysterious realm 'beyond good and evil'—that is to say beyond humanity—because without our capacity for sure and delicate discrimination of good and evil in terms of life or its denial we should not in any sense possess that energizing vision which is the tragic artist's gift to mankind. But vision, not judgment, vision in which judgment has been transformed into something different from its workaday self, is the word that we are compelled to use. Neither does this vision belong to some special realm of 'aesthetic' experience. For just as we encounter tragedy equipped with the ordinary interests of our lives, including what we call our ethical interests, so we go back from the work to 'life' not with 'what we have learned' (that would be the moralistic way of putting it) but certainly with our minds—our awareness, sympathies, insights— extended, enriched and capable of a sturdier working. Our experience, in short, re-enters the world of action and relationship, the world of moral choice and judgment; but the attitudes with which we confront that world have now a deeper hinterland. Which is simply to say that more of life is open to the transforming energies of the imagination.

NOTES

1 See John Wren-Lewis, 'Love's Coming of Age', in *Psycho-analysis Observed*, ed. Charles Rycroft (Constable, 1966).
2 Dorothea Krook, *The Ordeal of Consciousness in Henry James*, p. 10.
3 I have taken the first of these quotations from R. W. Babcock, *The Genesis of Shakespeare Idolatry*, p. 131. The second is from William Richardson, *Essays on Some of Shakespeare's Dramatic Characters* (1797 edition), p. 120.

4 It has been well brought out by H. D. F. Kitto in his chapter on the play in *Form and Meaning in Drama*.

5 *Anatomy of Criticism* (Atheneum, N.Y.), p. 208.

6 *Ibid.*, p. 212.

7 *The Ordeal of Consciousness in Henry James*, p. 13.

8 See Wilbur Sanders, *The Dramatist and the Received Idea: Studies in the Plays of Marlowe and Shakespeare* (C.U.P., 1968), Chapter 13—a valuable, if sometimes puzzling, account of the play's disturbing power that was much in my mind whilst writing parts of this paper.

9 I should like to refer here to three recent studies that, in very different ways, enforce the difficulty of 'judgment' in a tragedy as great as *King Lear*: Marvin Rosenberg, *The Masks of King Lear* (University of California Press, Berkeley and London, 1972), Stanley Cavell, 'The Avoidance of Love: a Reading of *King Lear*', in *Must We Mean What We Say?* (Scribners, N.Y., 1969), and S. L. Goldberg, *An Essay on 'King Lear'* (C.U.P., 1974).

9
The Question of Character in Shakespeare

LET me begin with an unashamed bit of autobiography. In 1932 I was asked to give a paper to the Shakespeare Association in London. I was a comparatively young man, dissatisfied with the prevailing academic approach to Shakespeare, excited by the glimpses I had obtained of new and, it seemed, more rewarding approaches, and I welcomed the opportunity of proclaiming the new principles in the very home of Shakespearean orthodoxy, whilst at the same time having some fun with familiar irrelevancies of the kind parodied in my title, *How Many Children had Lady Macbeth?* I gave my paper and waited expectantly for the lively discussion that would follow this rousing challenge to the pundits. So far as I remember, nothing happened, except that after a period of silence an elderly man got up at the back of the room and said that he was very glad to hear Mr Knights give this paper because it was what he had always thought. The revolution was over, and I went home. It was hardly a historic occasion, and the only reason for mentioning it is that when my paper was published as one of Gordon Fraser's Minority Pamphlets it obtained a certain mild notoriety that has never since entirely deserted it: only a few years ago a writer in *The Listener* called it 'the Communist Manifesto of the new critical movement'. Well of course it was nothing of the kind. *How Many Children had Lady Macbeth?* has earned its footnote in the history of modern criticism partly, I like to believe, because it says a few sensible things about *Macbeth*, partly because of its sprightly title (which was suggested to me by F. R. Leavis), and partly because it reflected the conviction of an increasing number of readers that the prevailing language of Shakespeare criticism didn't quite fit what seemed to them of

THE QUESTION OF CHARACTER IN SHAKESPEARE

deepest importance in the experience of Shakespeare's plays. In the last twenty-five or thirty years there has certainly been a movement away from the older type of 'character' criticism which had for so long held the field and which culminated in A. C. Bradley's *Shakespearean Tragedy*. But so far as any one book can be said to have heralded the new movement it was G. Wilson Knight's *The Wheel of Fire* (1930), shortly to be followed by *The Imperial Theme* (1931).

Now what I am here to do today is to try to get one aspect of that movement into perspective; more specifically I want to ask, after some twenty-five years of Shakespeare criticism that has not on the whole been on Bradleyean lines, what we now understand by the term 'character' when we use it in giving an account of Shakespeare's plays, to what extent—and within what limitations—'character' can be a useful critical term when we set out to define the meaning—the living and life-nourishing significance—of a Shakespeare play.

I don't want to burden you with a history of Shakespeare criticism, ancient or modern, but a few historical reminders are necessary. Since Shakespeare criticism began, people have praised Shakespeare for the lifelikeness of his characters. But it was not until the end of the eighteenth century that Shakespeare's remarkable power to make his men and women convincing led to a more and more exclusive concentration on those features of the *dramatis personae* that could be defined in terms appropriate to characters in real life. The *locus classicus* is of course Maurice Morgann's *Essay on the Dramatic Character of Sir John Falstaff* (1777). Twelve years before, in 1765, Dr Johnson, in his great Preface, had given the more traditional view:

Nothing can please many, and please long, but just representations of general nature. . . . Shakespeare is above all writers, at least above all modern writers, the poet of nature. . . . His persons act and speak by the influence of those general passions and prin-

202

ciples by which all minds are agitated, and the whole system of life is continued in motion. In the writings of other poets a character is too often an individual; in those of Shakespeare it is commonly a species.

It is from this wide extension of design that so much instruction is derived. . . .[1]

Morgann, on the contrary, is interested in what is uniquely individual in the character he describes, and these individual traits, he affirms, can be elicited from the stage characters in much the same way as one builds up the character of an acquaintance in real life: 'those characters in Shakespeare, which are seen only in part, are yet capable of being unfolded and understood in the whole'.

> If the characters of Shakespeare [he goes on] are thus *whole*, and as it were original, while those of almost all other writers are mere imitation, it may be fit to consider them rather as Historic than Dramatic beings; and, when occasion requires, to account for their conduct from the *whole* of character, from general principles, from latent motives, and from policies not avowed.

It is this principle that allows him to distinguish between 'the *real* character of Falstaff' and 'his *apparent* one'. What R. W. Babcock, in his useful book, *The Genesis of Shakespeare Idolatry, 1766–99*, calls 'the psychologizing of Shakespeare' was well established even before Coleridge gave his lectures; and Coleridge's influence, though of course more subtly, worked in the same direction. It seems true to say that in the nineteenth century Shakespeare's characters became 'real people', and—

---

[1] We may compare Johnson's characteristic comment on *Macbeth*: 'The play is deservedly celebrated for the propriety of its fictions, and solemnity, grandeur, and variety of its action; but it has no nice discriminations of character, the events are too great to admit the influence of particular dispositions, and the course of the action necessarily determines the conduct of the agents. The danger of ambition is well described. . . .' Johnson, it is true, also says of Shakespeare, 'Perhaps no poet ever kept his personages more distinct from each other.'

with varying degrees of relevance—the plays were discussed in terms of the interaction of real people for whom sympathy or antipathy was enlisted. Bradley's tremendously influential *Shakespearean Tragedy* was published in 1904, and for Bradley 'the centre of the tragedy ... may be said with equal truth to lie in action issuing from character, or in character issuing in action': 'action is the centre of the story', but 'this action is essentially the expression of character'.

Now Bradley had the great virtue of being thoroughly immersed in what he was talking about, and I am sure that his book has helped very many people to make Shakespeare a present fact in their lives. Also there is no need to make Bradley responsible for all the vagaries of the how-many-children-had-Lady-Macbeth? kind, which mostly lie on the fringes of criticism. But Bradley's book did endorse a particular kind of preoccupation with 'character', and once 'character'-criticism became the dominant mode of approach to Shakespeare, certain important matters were necessarily obscured, and people's experience of Shakespeare became in some ways less rich and satisfying than it might have been. For one thing genuine perceptions became entangled with irrelevant speculations—'How is it that Othello comes to be the companion of the one man in the world, who is at once able enough, brave enough, and vile enough to ensnare him?'; Macbeth's tendency to ambition 'must have been greatly strengthened by his marriage'. And if the critic who accepts too naïvely the character-in-action formula is liable to disappear down by-paths outside the play, he is almost equally likely to slight or ignore what is actually there if it does not minister to his particular preoccupation—witness the ease with which the old Arden edition of *Macbeth* dismissed as spurious scenes that do not contribute to the development of character or of a narrowly conceived dramatic action. Even at its best the focus is a narrow one. Shakespearean tragedy, says Bradley, 'is pre-eminently the story of one person, the "hero", or at most of two, the "hero" and "heroine" '; and the mark of the tragic hero, besides his greatness, is that there is a 'conflict of forces' in his soul. I suppose, if you look at matters in this way it doesn't necessarily mean that you idealize the hero as Bradley does Othello, missing the critical 'placing' determined by the play as a whole. But it does mean that you are likely to ignore some important matters, such as the structure of ideas in *Macbeth*. After all, in his greater plays, Shakespeare was doing more than merely holding a mirror up to nature, more even than representing conflict in the souls of mighty characters: he was exploring the world and defining the values by which men live. In short, Shakespearean tragedy, any Shakespearean tragedy, is saying so much more than can be expressed in Bradleyean terms. It was some such perceptions as these—combined with an increasing knowledge of Elizabethan dramatic usage and convention—that prompted exploration of Shakespeare, not necessarily in opposition to Bradley, but to a large extent outside the Bradleyean frame of reference.

Simplifying for the sake of clarity, I would say that as a result of critical work done in the last quarter of a century, the approach to Shakespeare of an intelligent and informed reader today is likely to differ in three important respects from that of the intelligent and informed reader of a generation ago. To start with, he is likely to take it for granted that any one of Shakespeare's greater plays is very much more than a dramatized story; that it is, rather, a vision of life—more or less complex and inclusive—whose meaning is nothing less than the *play as a whole*. This is what Wilson Knight meant when he sometimes referred to his work in terms of 'spatial analysis', as distinguished from the analysis of a series of steps in time. Ideally, we try to apprehend each play as though all its parts were simultaneously present: there is an obvious analogy with music, and criticism of this kind tends to describe Shakespeare's meanings in terms of 'themes' rather than in terms of motive, character-development, and so on. Wilson Knight speaks of cutting below 'the surface crust of plot and character', and remarks that in *Macbeth*, for example, 'the logic of imaginative correspondence is more significant and more exact than the logic of plot'. He also, of course, told us that 'we should not look for perfect verisimilitude to life, but rather see each play as an expanded metaphor, by means of which the original vision has been projected into forms roughly correspondent with actuality'; and the fact that this remark has been quoted in innumerable examination papers shouldn't obscure its crucial importance in determining the kind of approach to Shakespeare that I am trying to define.[1] In the second place, our contemporary reader is likely to take for granted that the essential structure of the plays is to be sought in the poetry rather than in the more easily extractable elements of 'plot' and 'character'. I think our age is more aware of the complex structure, of the depth of life, of Shakespeare's verse, than any of its predecessors. Critics have written at length about his imagery, his ambiguities and overlaying meanings, his wordplay, and so on; and there is no doubt that such studies have sharpened our sense not only of the tremendous activity of Shakespeare's verse—its generative power—but of the strong and subtle interconnexions of meaning within the imaginative structure of the plays. It is significant that 'interpretation' relies heavily on extensive quotation and detailed analysis.[2] Finally—abandoning my hypothetical intelligent reader—I should say that our whole conception of Shakespeare's relation to his work,

---

[1] 'And Shakespeare's was a mind that thought in images, so that metaphor packs into metaphor, producing the most surprising collocations of apparently diverse phenomena; he thought of time, and death, and eternity, in terms of a candle, a shadow, and an actor. Is it not likely that the large and composite image of the story as a whole would serve him as a metaphor or symbol for his attitudes to certain aspects of experience?'—S. L. Bethell, *Shakespeare and the Popular Dramatic Tradition*, p. 115.

[2] A method that has its dangers, for we sometimes seem to run the risk of having the play read for us.

of what he was trying to do as an artist whilst at the same time satisfying the demands of the Elizabethan theatre, has undergone a very great change indeed. The 'new' Shakespeare, I should say, is much less impersonal than the old. Whereas in the older view Shakespeare was the god-like creator of a peopled world, projecting—it is true—his own spirit into the inhabitants, but remaining essentially the analyst of 'their' passions, he is now felt as much more immediately engaged in the action he puts before us. I don't of course mean that we have returned to Frank Harris's Shakespeare, engaged in drawing a succession of full-length portraits of himself, but that we feel the plays (in Mr Eliot's words) 'to be united by one significant, consistent, and developing personality': we feel that the plays, even if 'in no obvious form', 'are somehow dramatizing . . . an action or struggle for harmony in the soul of the poet.'[1] We take it for granted that Shakespeare thought about the problems of life, and was at least as much interested in working towards an imaginative solution as he was in making a series of detached studies of different characters, their motives and their passions. Here again, specialist studies are indicative: we think it reasonable that a scholar should inquire what evidence there is that Shakespeare had read Hooker, and if so what effect it had on his plays; we inquire into Shakespeare's political ideas and their background; we are prepared to examine *Shakespeare's Philosophical Patterns* (which is the title of a book by the American scholar, W. C. Curry). In short, we take seriously Coleridge's remark that Shakespeare was 'a philosopher'; the vision of life that his plays express is, in a certain sense, a philosophic vision. But at the same time we remember—at least, I should like to be able to say we remember—that the plays are not dramatizations of abstract ideas, but imaginative constructions mediated through the poetry. If Shakespeare's verse has moved well into the centre of the picture, one reason is that linguistic vitality is

[1] See T. S. Eliot's essays on John Ford, *Selected Essays* (London, 1932).

now felt as the chief clue to the urgent personal themes that not only shape the poetic-dramatic structure of each play but form the figure in the carpet of the canon as a whole.[1]

This short and imperfect account may serve as an indication or reminder of the main lines of Shakespeare criticism since 1930, or thereabouts. Happily my job is not to award marks of merit to different critics, and I don't intend to offer a list of obligatory reading. We all have our own ideas about the recent critics who have helped us most in our understanding of Shakespeare, and I don't suppose that we should all agree about all of them. But I think we should agree that there have been some books offering genuinely new insights, and that where criticism has been most illuminating it has usually been on quite non-Bradleyan lines. At the same time let us recall certain facts. If 'plot' and 'character'—mere 'precipitates from the memory'—sometimes seem to be described in abstraction from the full living immediacy of our direct experience of the plays, and therefore to lead away from it, so too 'themes' and 'symbols' can be pursued mechanically and, as it were, abstractly. Whereas it is equally obvious that criticism in terms of 'character' can be genuinely revealing; John Palmer's *The Political Characters of Shakespeare* is an example. And of course you can't get away from the term. Not only does the ordinary theatregoer or reader need it to explain his enjoyment, but even critics least in sympathy with Bradley at times naturally and necessarily define their sense of significance in terms appropriate to living people. Clearly the critical field has not been given over to those whom J. I. M. Stewart calls 'the new Bowdlers, whom man delights not, no nor woman neither, and who would give us not merely *Hamlet* without the Prince but the Complete Works without their several *dramatis personae*'. The notion of 'character', in some sense, has not disappeared, and is not going to disappear, from Shakespeare

[1] A few sentences in this paragraph are borrowed from *Some Shakespearean Themes*.

criticism. What we need to do is simply to clear up our minds about it, to make our handling of the term both more flexible and more precise.

Before I give my own simple summing up of things as I see them I should like to mention two books that have a direct bearing on the matters we are pursuing. The first is J. I. M. Stewart's witty, entertaining and instructive *Character and Motive in Shakespeare*. Stewart not only has some shrewd knocks at those who over-play the element of Elizabethan dramatic convention in Shakespeare and those who would tailor the plays too closely to the pattern of their own proprieties, he has some illuminating comments on particular plays. But his main interest, in the present connexion, lies in the way he develops the conception of character-presentation beyond the bounds of naturalism. To the extent that Shakespeare is concerned with character and motive—and he does 'present "man" and reveal psychological truths'—he works not through realistic portrayal but through poetry—that is, through symbolism and suggestion as well as by more direct means; and in this way he makes us aware not—or not only—of what we normally understand by character but of its hidden recesses.

> The characters, then (but I mean chiefly those major characters with whom the imagination of the dramatist is deeply engaged), have often the superior reality of individuals exposing the deepest springs of their action. But this superior reality is manifested through the medium of situations which are sometimes essentially symbolical; and these may be extravagant or merely fantastic when not interpreted by the quickened imagination, for it is only during the prevalence of a special mode of consciousness, the poetic, that the underlying significance of these situations is perceived. (pp. 9–10)

> Of just what Shakespeare brings from beyond this portal [of the depths of the mind], and how, we often can achieve little con-

ceptual grasp; and often therefore the logical and unkindled mind finds difficulties which it labels as faults and attributes to the depravity of Shakespeare's audience or what it wills. But what the intellect finds arbitrary the imagination may accept and respond to, for when we read imaginatively or poetically we share the dramatist's penetration for a while and deep is calling to deep. (p. 30)[1]

The other book I want to refer to is *Character and Society in Shakespeare* by Professor Arthur Sewell. It is a small book but, I think, an important one. Briefly, Mr Sewell's contention is that the characters of a play only exist within the total vision that the play presents: 'in Shakespeare's plays the essential process of character-creation is a prismatic breaking-up of the comprehensive vision of the play' (p. 19). There is, therefore, an absolute

---

[1] This insistence on the imaginative—on the non-rational but not therefore irrational—portrayal of character, and on the need to respond to it imaginatively, is important, and, as I have said, Mr Stewart can be illuminating. But it also seems to me that his method, as he pursues it, can sometimes lead outside the play, as in his use of psycho-analytic concepts to define Leontes' jealousy. The main criticism of any psycho-analytic account of Shakespeare's characters is not simply that it is irrelevant—though it may be —but that it reduces the material it works on to a category that can be known and docketed. To accept it is to feel that you know about a character something of importance that has been simply handed over, and that can be received alike by every reader, whatever the degree of his concern, the extent of his actual engagement, with the plays. It obscures not only the uniqueness but the *activity* of the work of art; whereas any play only exists for you to the extent that *you* have grappled with its meanings. Thus Mr Stewart's account of Leontes' repressed homosexuality (reactivated by the presence of Polixenes, and then 'projected' on to Hermione) is relevant inasmuch as it points to the presence in what Leontes stands for of unconscious motivations, of motives beyond conscious control. But within the context of the play as a whole their exact nature is irrelevant: they are simply an *X* within the equation which is the play. What the play gives us is the awakening of new life that can enlist the same impulses which, in the first part, have been shown as the material of an unruly aberration. All we need to know of the aberration is that it is a representative manifestation: to pin it down exactly as Mr Stewart does, is to make Leontes' jealousy something that we *know about* instead of something we *respond to* as part of the total generative pattern of the play.

distinction between a dramatic character and a person in real life whose conduct can be accounted for 'from general principles, from latent motives, and from policies not avowed'. 'We can only understand Shakespeare's characters so long as we agree that we cannot know all about them and are not supposed to know all about them' (p. 12). What is relevant for us is not an assumed hinterland of motives but simply the particular 'address to the world' that is embodied, with different degrees of explicitness, in the different characters. In the comedies the characters tend to be static and, so to speak, socially conditioned: they represent attitudes and modes of judgment that serve for the presentation and critical inspection of our everyday world. In the great tragedies the characters speak from out of a deeper level of experience—'metaphysical' rather than social, though the distinction is not absolute; the vision they embody is transformed in the full working out of the attitudes to which they are committed; and their reality is established by our own active commitment to the drama's dialectical play. Of both comedy and tragedy it can be said that 'unless Shakespeare had set our minds busy—and not only our minds—on various kinds of evaluation, his characters could never have engaged us and would have lacked all vitality' (p. 18). And again, there is the suggestion 'that character and moral vision must be apprehended together, and that when character is understood separately from moral vision it is not in fact understood at all' (p. 59).

Where, then, at the end of all this, do we come out? Perhaps only among what many people will regard as a handful of commonplaces. Let me start with the most thumping platitude of all: in Shakespeare's plays *some* impression of character is constantly being made upon us. It is likely to begin as soon as a major character is introduced.

> Why, I, in this weak piping time of peace,
> Have no delight to pass away the time,

> Unless to see my shadow in the sun
> And descant on mine own deformity.
>
> Though yet of Hamlet our dear brother's death
> The memory be green, and that it us befitted
> To bear our hearts in grief and our whole kingdom
> To be contracted in one brow of woe,
> Yet so far hath discretion fought with nature. . . .
>
> I pray you, daughter, sing; or express yourself in a more comfortable sort.

Here, and in innumerable other instances, we have what Mr Sewell calls the 'distillation of personality into style'. We know these people by the way they speak; as Mr Stewart puts it, 'In drama the voice *is* the character'—though we also have to add that often Shakespeare speaks *through* the person with a meaning different from, or even contrary to, that apparently intended by the speaker.

At the same time we have to admit that our sense of character —of a complex, unified tissue of thought and feeling from which a particular voice issues—varies enormously not only as between different plays, but as between the different figures within a single play. *All's Well That Ends Well* is nearer to a morality play, and is less concerned with characterization, in any sense, than is *Othello*. In *Measure for Measure* 'analysis of character' may take us a long way with Angelo; it is utterly irrelevant as applied to the Duke.

Let me give another example—which will serve to illustrate Mr Sewell's remark about the characters embodying 'an address to the world', in case anyone should have been left uneasy with that phrase. Here is Don John introducing himself in conversation with Conrade in Act I of *Much Ado About Nothing*.

> I wonder that thou, being—as thou say'st thou art—born under Saturn, goest about to apply a moral medicine to a mortifying

mischief. I cannot hide what I am: I must be sad when I have cause, and smile at no man's jests; eat when I have stomach, and wait for no man's leisure; sleep when I am drowsy, and tend on no man's business; laugh when I am merry, and claw no man in his humour.

Conrade advises that he should apply himself to winning the good opinion of his brother the Duke, with whom he is lately reconciled, and Don John goes on:

I had rather be a canker in a hedge than a rose in his grace; and it better fits my blood to be disdained of all than to fashion a carriage to rob love from any: in this, though I cannot be said to be a flattering honest man, it must not be denied but I am a plain-dealing villain. I am trusted with a muzzle and enfranchised with a clog; therefore I have decreed not to sing in my cage. If I had my mouth, I would bite; if I had my liberty, I would do my liking: in the meantime, let me be that I am, and seek not to alter me.

A good many things are plain from this—Don John's exacer-bated sense of superiority ('I . . . I . . . I . . .'), his particular kind of 'melancholy', and his affectation of a blunt, no-nonsense manner. Clearly he is related to Richard of Gloucester and to Iago. Their common characteristic is an egotism that clenches itself hard against the claims of sympathy, and that is unwilling to change—'I cannot hide what I am; I must be sad when I have cause . . . let me be that I am, and seek not to alter me.' It is, in short, the opposite of a character 'open' to others and to the real demands of the present. That is all we know about Don John and all we are required to know: we are not asked to consider his bastardy or his other grievances. He is simply a perversely 'melancholy' man who serves as villain of the piece, the agent of an otherwise unmotivated evil.

What is true of a minor figure like Don John is true of all the characters of Shakespeare: we know about them only what the play requires us to know. Even to put the matter in this way is—as we shall see in a minute—over-simplified and misleading, but it serves to remind us that however we define for ourselves a character and his rôle, there is a strict criterion of relevance: he belongs to his play, and his play is an art-form, not a slice of life. The fact that this at least is now a commonplace is a guarantee that we shall never again have to waste our time on the complete irrelevance of some forms of character-analysis as applied to Shakespeare's *dramatis personae*.

But we still haven't got to the heart of the matter. What is the 'play as a whole', to which we say the characters are subordinate? To this question there is no simple answer, but we can at least attempt an answer that will help our reading.

Poetic drama offers a vision of life, more or less complex, more or less wide-embracing. Shakespeare's poetic drama as a whole is different from Jonson's or Racine's; and within Shakespeare's poetic drama as a whole there are many different kinds. Even at its simplest there is some degree of complexity, of dialectical play, as persons embodying different attitudes are set before us in action and interaction. Of course when we are watching them we don't think of them as them ebodiment of attitudes—of different addresses to the world: we say simply, Rosalind is in love with Orlando. Yet while we know that two addresses to the world can't fall in love, we also know —and this knowledge moves from the back of our minds and comes into action when, having seen or read the play several times, we try to bring it into sharper focus—that Shakespeare is doing something more significant with Rosalind and Orlando than showing us how interesting it is when boy meets girl. *As You Like It*, which is a fairly simple play, will help us here. *As You Like It* is of course a romantic comedy, with its own interest and entertainment as such. But the plot and the structure of the incidents point to an interest in the meaning of a life lived 'according to nature'. Duke Senior's idyllic picture ('Hath not

old custom made this life more sweet Than that of painted pomp?'
etc.) is an over-simplification, as the play makes plain; but it is
a possible attitude, put forward for inspection, and as the play
goes on it is clear that we are meant to take an intelligent interest
in the varying degrees of naturalness and sophistication—each
playing off against the other—that are put before us. *As You
Like It*, in short, rings the changes on the contrasting meanings
of 'natural' (either 'human' or 'close down to the life of nature')
and 'civilized' (either 'well nurtured' or 'artificial')—all especially pointed with reference to the passion of love. It is largely
an entertainment; but at the same time it is a serious comedy of
ideas—not abstract ideas to be debated, but ideas as embodied
in attitude and action. So that by playing off against each other
different attitudes to life, the play as a whole offers a criticism
of various forms of exaggeration and affectation—either 'romantic' or professedly realistic—with Rosalind as arbiter, although of course she is not above the action but involved in
it herself.[1]

What is true of *As You Like It* is also true of greater plays, such
as *Measure for Measure*, *King Lear*, or *Antony and Cleopatra*,
though in these of course the play of varied sympathies and anti-
pathies, of imaginative evaluation as different possibilities of
living are put before us, is more complex, and the experience
handled is more profound. But of all the greater plays it is true
to say that *all* the characters are necessary to express the vision—
the emergent 'idea' or controlling preoccupation—and they are
necessary only in so far as they do express it. Gloucester's part
in *King Lear* is not to give additional human interest, but to
enact and express a further aspect of the Lear experience; for
with Gloucester, as with Lear, confident acceptance of an
inadequate code gives place to humble acceptance of the human
condition, and there are glimpses of a new wisdom:

[1] See James Smith's excellent essay on *As You Like It* in his *Shakespearian
and other essays* (Cambridge University Press).

> I have no way, and therefore want no eyes;
> I stumbled when I saw.

The striking parallels between the two men are proof enough of deliberate artistic intention in this respect.

What *King Lear* also forces on us, even when we are prepared to see the different characters as contributing to a pattern, is the inadequacy of terms relating to 'character'. What character has Edgar in his successive transformations? In the storm scenes, where Lear's vision of horror is built to a climax, we are acted on directly by the poetry, by what is said, in some respects independently of our sense of a particular person saying it. So too in the play as a whole, and in the other greater plays, our sense of the characters—of what the characters stand for in their 'address to the world', their 'moral encounter with the universe' —is inseparable from the more direct ways in which, by poetry and symbolism, our imaginations are called into play. To take one simple example. When Macbeth, on his first appearance, says, 'So foul and fair a day I have not seen', he does far more than announce himself as a character—tired, collected, brooding; echoing the Witches' 'Fair is foul, and foul is fair', he takes his place in the pattern of moral evaluations which make the play so much more than the story of a tragic hero, which make it into a great vision of the unreality, the negative horror, that evil is. In reading Shakespeare our sense of 'character', defined and limited as I have tried to define and limit it, is important; but so is our responsiveness to symbolism (the storm in *Othello* and Othello's trance, Lear's bare heath and Gloucester's Dover Cliff, Hermione's moving statue), and so is our responsiveness to imagery (the imagery of darkness conveying spiritual blindness in *Macbeth*), to verse rhythm, and to all the inter-acting elements of the poetry: it is from these that there emerges a controlling direction of exploratory and committed interests—of interests involving the personality as a whole—that we indicate by some such word as 'themes'.

Mr John Holloway has recently objected to the use of 'theme' in Shakespeare criticism[1]: it is a sign that the work in question is to be reduced to a generalized moral reflection, whereas literature does not provide us with general truths, only with particular instances. 'What *Macbeth* does . . . is to depict for us, in great and remarkable detail, one imagined case and one only.' 'Narrative', he suggests, is 'the fundamental quality of the full-length work', the essential principle of imaginative order. Now both these conceptions of the work of art as 'one imagined case and one only', and of 'narrative' as the controlling principle, seem to me to be, in their turn, open to objection. But I think we are dealing with something far greater than the particular question —Is Shakespeare most profitably discussed in terms of 'character' or 'theme' or 'narrative'? What has come into sight, what we must take account of, is nothing less than the depth of life of any great work of art, its capacity to enter into our lives as power. What do we mean when we say that a great work of art has a universal appeal? Surely something more than that it tells a story likely to interest everybody. We mean that the special case (and I grant Mr Holloway the artist's 'passion for the special case') brings to a focus a whole range of awareness, that it generates an activity of imaginative apprehension that illumminates not only the 'case' in question but life as we know it in our own experience: it can modify, or even transform, our whole way of seeing life and responding to it. It is this capacity to generate meanings that is the 'universal' quality in the particular work of art. And it is the presence of the universal in the particular that compels the use of such generalizing terms as 'themes' or 'motifs'. Of course, like other critical terms, they can be used mechanically or ineptly, can harden into counters pushed about in a critical game. But as simple pointers their function is to indicate the *direction* of interest that a play compels when we

[1] 'The New "Establishment" in Criticism', *The Listener*, September 20 and 27, 1956; more recently developed in his book, *The Story of the Night*.

try to meet it with the whole of ourselves—to meet it, that is (using De Quincey's term), as literature of power.

To read Shakespeare, then (and in reading I include seeing his plays performed), we need to cultivate a complex skill. But there is no need to make heavy weather of this. That skill can be largely intuitive; we can obtain it in many ways, and there is no need (especially if we are teachers) to be too insistent on any one approach. In 'Demosius and Mystes', a dialogue appended to *Church and State*, Coleridge refers to a mighty conflict between two cats, 'where one tail alone is said to have survived the battle'. There is always a danger of critical squabbles becoming like that; and I for one would rather see among my pupils an honest and first-hand appreciation of what is offered by way of 'character' than a merely mechanical working out of recurrent imagery and symbolic situations. We should remember also that the life of the imagination runs deeper than our conscious formulations. T. S. Eliot (in his Introduction to S. L. Bethell's book on Shakespeare), says of the persons of the play of a modern verse dramatist,

> they must on your stage be able to perform the same actions, and lead the same lives, as in the real world. But they must somehow disclose (not necessarily be aware of) a deeper reality than that of the plane of most of our conscious living; and what they disclose must be, not the psychologist's intellectualization of this reality, but the reality itself.

They must 'somehow disclose (not necessarily be aware of) a deeper reality': I think that what Eliot says of the persons in verse plays like his own, applies—*mutatis mutandis*—to the spectators of poetic drama. To the extent that a Shakespeare tragedy truly enlists the imagination (and this means enlisting it for what is in the play, not for a display of virtuosity) it is precisely this deeper level of apprehension—the hidden potentialities, wishes, and fears of the individual spectator—that is being worked on, even though the spectator himself may not be conscious of it, and thinks that he is simply watching someone else's 'character issuing in action'.

All the same, even when this is admitted, there is no reason why the common reader should not be encouraged to see rather more. For it is in our imaginative response to *the whole play*—not simply to what can be extracted as 'character', nor indeed to what can be simply extracted as 'theme' or 'symbol' —that the meaning lies; and Shakespeare calls on us to be as fully conscious as we can, even if consciousness includes relaxed enjoyment and absorption as well as, sometimes, more deliberate attention to this or that aspect of the whole experience.

Historical Scholarship and the
Interpretation of Shakespeare

IN *English Poetry: a Critical Introduction*, F. W. Bateson wrote:

> The readers . . . that the poet is implicitly addressing *determine* to a considerable degree the kind of poem that he is writing. It follows that to understand a poem's meaning today we need to be able to identify ourselves as far as possible with its original readers, the poet's contemporaries, whose ideal response to the poem in fact constitutes its meaning.

A good deal of Shakespeare scholarship and Elizabethan scholarship generally has in recent years worked in the spirit of this remark. The results are impressive, and the critic or interpreter of Shakespeare cannot ignore them. Shakespeare wanted neither education nor art, and even the unscholarly reader will read with more profit if he knows something of the ideas with which Shakespeare was in contact, and even, perhaps, of the terms of art in which Elizabethan poetry and drama were conceived. Yet as one watches the successive waves of Shakespearean and Elizabethan scholarship, each changing place with that which went before, one feels uneasy. It is not that the attempt to interpret Shakespeare in contemporary (*sc.* Elizabethan) terms is intrinsically unprofitable—far from it: it is simply that the claims that are sometimes made for 'scholarship' as against 'criticism' are excessive, that there is a danger of substituting accumulated 'knowledge about' for a living responsiveness; and that the search for 'ideal' contemporary meanings and implications *tends* to obscure the essential nature of art, and so to make particular works of art, such as Shakespeare's plays, less potently available and fructifying than they ought to be. I may state here my own conviction, as against Mr Bateson, that the meanings of a poem are not exhausted by the meanings it may have had for its original readers (who, as Lascelles Abercrombie remarked, did not respond as one man), adding too that the meanings it had for the original audience cannot in any case be identified with the meanings of which they were fully conscious. I shall return to these points; but first I should like to suggest by example how the historical approach, pursued as a means of interpretation, tends, by the very nature of its undertaking, to obscure as well as to elucidate Shakespeare's plays.

Shakespeare's Use of Learning: an Inquiry into the Growth of his Mind and Art, by Virgil K. Whitaker, is a valuable contribution to Shakespeare scholarship. I am not here concerned with Dr Whitaker's estimate of the extent of Shakespeare's learning: he comes down judiciously in favour of a Shakespeare whose interests slowly broadened from popular learning to philosophic ideas, who possessed considerable knowledge of contemporary psychology and theology, but who never read widely. Nor would I wish to challenge Dr Whitaker's insistence of the formative influence on the greater plays of a body of traditional ideas, transmitted largely, it is suggested, by the first book of Hooker's *Of the Laws of Ecclesiastical Polity*; it is certainly a reasonable contention that 'Macbeth is a greater play than *Richard III* not so much because Shakespeare knew more about the theatre as because he had developed a new understanding of life in terms of traditional Christian thought' (p. vii). What I am concerned with is the terms in which Dr Whitaker develops this thesis, for they seem to me characteristic of the 'historical' school.

The following are representative quotations:

Finally, about the turn of the century, his interests shifted markedly to the philosophical and theological interpretation of life which Christianity had erected during the Middle Ages upon the basis of Plato, Aristotle, and the Stoics, the Scriptures, and St Augustine. Most of the tragedies are constructed to study the working out of these principles in human conduct. . . . (p. 11)

[In the earlier plays] the plot determined the characters. Beginning with *Hamlet* the exact opposite is true. In using *Plutarch*, who furnished biographies that are really character studies worked out in terms of an elaborate ethical theory, Shakespeare made relatively few changes. . . . But he reshaped his other sources drastically in order to make the action reveal characters that illustrate or conform to philosophic concepts, the best examples of this process being *Macbeth* and *Lear*. (p. 179)

The earlier plays merely adapt a source narrative to stage presentation. The problem comedies try to superimpose philosophic interpretation upon material developed by the same easygoing methods, and trouble results. The tragedies, on the other hand, reshape the plot to fit a predetermined character problem. (p. 179)

'The tragedies are constructed to study the working out of these principles . . .', 'characters that illustrate or conform to philosophic concepts', 'the tragedies reshape the plot to fit a predetermined character problem'—do not these phrases make the plays seem to be more schematic, more deliberately intellectual, less exploratory, imaginative, and creative, than they actually are? The imagination can use intellectual formulations, and Shakespeare's poetic thought was certainly nourished and clarified by the best of what he read (including perhaps Hooker)[1];

---

[1] Leone Vivante (*English Poetry*, pp. 122–3) has some suggestive remarks on the distinction between what T. S. Eliot in his Preface to the same volume calls 'poetic thinking' and 'the thought of the poet'. Signor Vivante's suggestion that we should 'consider (adopting Coleridge's words) "truth operative", truth "original—more accurately . . . ever-originating", as compared with a process of thought in which the author is sharply distinct from his subject-matter' is decidedly relevant to the present discussion. (As a matter of fact, Coleridge's 'truth operative' is part of a quotation from Davenant—'truth operative, and by effects continually alive'. See *Biographia Literaria*, ed. Shawcross, Vol. II, pp. 101–2).

but to see his imaginative exploration as though it were merely the application of already formed concepts is to miss the dimension of depth, the personal vibrancy, that prevents, or should prevent, us from speaking of *Lear* or *Macbeth* in terms of the application of 'a formula for tragedy of moral choice' (p. 248). T. S. Eliot, in his essay on John Ford, long ago gave us the necessary corrective when he wrote:

> It is suggested, then, that a dramatic poet cannot create characters of the greatest intensity of life unless his personages, in their reciprocal actions and behaviour in their story, are somehow dramatizing, but in no obvious form, an action or struggle for harmony in the soul of the poet.[1]

It is that central dynamic that Dr Whitaker's method, his very terminology, implicitly ignores.

And corresponding to the rather rigid externalizing assumptions about the nature of the poetic process is a complementary distortion of the nature of the work of art in relation to the reader, of what the act of appreciation means. Dr Whitaker writes interestingly about *Troilus and Cressida*, 'the keystone in the arch of Shakespeare's intellectual development' (p. 195)—and indeed it is always refreshing to have this play treated as an intellectual structure rather than as an uncontrolled outburst of cynicism. Certainly it is a play of 'ideas'. But how are the ideas treated? How does the play demand that we should take them? Dr Whitaker holds that in the consultation of the Greek generals (I, iii), containing Ulysses' speech on degree, and in the parallel council of the Trojan leaders (II, ii), containing Hector's exposition of 'the moral laws of nature and of nation', 'Shakespeare was more interested in the ideas themselves than in the movement of his plot' (p. 196), and he proceeds to expound the implications and background (Elyot, the Homilies, and Hooker)

---

[1] *Selected Essays* (London, 1932), p. 196. It is in the same essay that Mr Eliot puts forward the idea of the whole of Shakespeare's work as 'one poem ... united by one significant, consistent, and developing personality'.

of these ideas. The exposition is relevant and sound, but the play is, after all, something more than the dramatic presentation of philosophic ideas, and it is the play as a whole—the play as an imaginative structure, permeated and not simply as it were buttressed by thought—that determines how we shall take the ideas that it contains. And the play as a whole certainly does not endorse Ulysses, for all his classic exposition of the traditional conception of an ordered universe. Neither does it endorse Troilus, whose subjectivism is the complementary opposite of the rationalism of the Greeks. Two attitudes to life are put in dramatic contrast; but the point is that they *are* attitudes to life, each of them containing emotional as well as intellectual elements—for even Troilus can rationalize his feelings, and even Ulysses' speech on degree needs to be seen in the context of what he does, says, and implies elsewhere. The play, in short, makes complex demands and asks of us something more than the ability to pick out ideas, however significant in themselves.[1] I should say that it is only in the light of a full imaginative responsiveness to the play as a dramatic poem, in which Elizabethan ideas are assimilated and used, but never merely applied, that we can see the full significance of Hector's admirable defence of the law of nature, to which Dr Whitaker rightly gives so much attention.

Of the failure of imagination that seems almost inevitable when the critic works too persistently and exclusively in terms of clearly formulated ideas two further examples may be given.

2 *Henry IV*, despite its parallels of structure, contains statements of contemporary learning of a kind which is completely absent from Part 1, so that it seems to have been written from Shakespeare's intellect, whereas Part 1 came from his heart. . . . An important part of this learning is the concept of order and of natural law. For the first time the vague hints of the earlier plays give way to explicit statement. (p. 169)

[1] See my essay on the play in *Some Shakespearean Themes*.

Now *2 Henry IV*, is, I agree, different from the first Part, and
I am sure that Shakespeare's intellect was active in the making
of it. But so was his heart. And if we find Part 2 more 'philosophic' than Part 1, this is due not merely to any 'explicit
statement' of ideas of order but to Shakespeare's imaginative
vision (expressed in the whole play, which includes Shallow and
Wart and even old Double, as well as the politicals) of life subject to time and change. And surely the condition of our recognizing *Macbeth* as 'Shakespeare's greatest monument to the
ethical system that his age inherited from Western Christianity
and the classical world' (p. 299) is not that we should exclude
from our consciousness all that does not *explicitly* demonstrate
the identity of the unnatural, the irrational, and the immoral—
all, that is, that cannot be formulated and expounded in strictly
rational terms. Yet this is oddly implied by the qualification
that Dr Whitaker thinks it necessary to make to his praise of that
tragedy.

> There is . . . something a little too pat about the relationship
> between man's sins and the universal disorder as Shakespeare
> presents it. Macbeth violates the law of nature by murdering a
> man who is his king, his kinsman, and his guest. At once all
> nature behaves unnaturally. What the play gives us is at times
> closer to the pathetic fallacy than to a genuinely philosophic view
> of the interrelationship between man and the rest of creation.
> (p. 209)

The unnatural behaviour of nature in *Macbeth*—

> The night has been unruly; where we lay,
> Our chimneys were blown down. . . .

> Is't night's predominance, or the day's shame,
> That darkness does the face of earth entomb,
> When living light should kiss it?

—is obviously one of the ways in which the inner darkness and
disorder of sin is evoked and defined. Thus the two passages

just quoted are nearer to St John's 'He that loveth his brother abideth in the light. . . . But he that hateth his brother is in darkness and walketh in darkness', or to Milton's

> not only tears
> Rain'd at their eyes, but high winds worse within
> Began to rise, high passions, anger, hate,
> Mistrust, suspicion . . .

than they are to any form of the pathetic fallacy.

I have spent some time on this book, deliberately and unfairly ignoring much that is valuable in it, because it seems to me representative of a whole approach to Shakespeare, and because it offers an example of what is likely to happen if you set out to interpret a great writer of the past exclusively in the intellectual terms of his own day; if, instead of starting with Shakespeare's plays, your own direct experience of Shakespeare's plays, and working back to what most deeply nourished them in the thought, the mental habits and the tradition of the time, you invoke a conceptual framework which you proceed to show the plays as illustrating. The attraction of the historical or reconstructive procedure is of course that it seems to approach something like a guaranteed meaning—*the* meaning in the minds of an ideal audience contemporary with the plays—and thereby to offer an escape from the uncertainty of merely personal interpretation and criticism, which varies not only with the taste of the age but with the predilections of the individual: now that Elizabethan scholarship has come of age and stands so sturdily on its own feet, our major effort must be directed to re-creating an 'Elizabethan' Shakespeare. But there are, I think, other reasons besides those so far touched on why, in the face of such advice, we should maintain a certain reserve.

If we believe that the attempt to reconstruct the Elizabethan or Renaissance meanings of Shakespeare's plays is almost inevitably attended by the danger of obscuring their imaginative life, does this mean that we must simply accept the fact of different meanings for different generations, or indeed for different individuals living at the same time? I think it does—but with a qualification that is as important as it is obvious. No one who has made his own the idea of a critical discipline embodied in Matthew Arnold's formula, 'To see the object as in itself it really is', is likely to accept the spineless relativism of 'So many men, so many minds'. For the worth of any interpretation or judgment of literary value depends on the mind that makes it, its lucidity, discipline, and capacity for genuinely confronting its object.

In his classic lecture, 'A Plea for the Liberty of Interpreting',[1] Lascelles Abercrombie insisted, as it is insisted here, that a work of art can only be judged in the light of what we ourselves find there. 'To limit interpretation to what the play may have meant to Elizabethans is, frankly, to exclude the existence of the play as a work of art; for as a work of art it does not exist in what it may have meant to someone else, but in what it means to me: that is the only way it can exist.' Abercrombie is, however, quite clear about the reasonable limits of interpretation:

> By liberty of interpretation I do not mean liberty to read into a play of Shakespeare's whatever feeling or idea a modern reader may loosely and accidentally associate with its subject: associate it, that is, not because he found it in the play, but because some idiosyncrasy of his own suggested it and irresponsibly brought it in from his private world. But I do mean that anything which may be found in that art, even if it is only the modern reader who can

[1] Annual Shakespeare Lecture of the British Academy, 1930 (*Proceedings of the British Academy*, XVI); reprinted in *Aspects of Shakespeare*.

find it there, may legitimately be taken as its meaning. *Judge by results*, I say; not by the results of reverie, which the poem merely sets going, and in which attention may ramble anywhere it pleases, for that is not criticism at all; but certainly by any result that may come of living in the art of the play and attending to everything it consists of: and I say that, so long as it keeps within that boundary, there is no proper ground for objection if this attention seems to be modern in its nature.

And again,

When I say that a play exists in what it means to any one who will receive it, the implication is plain, that everything is excluded from that existence which is not given by the author's technique. The existence of a work of art is completed by the recipient's *attention* to what the author says to him; whatever may come in through *inattention* to that does not belong to the art at all.

What this admirable statement means is that when, in Shakespeare criticism, we have discounted everything that clearly results from indiscipline, from inattention, prejudice or whimsy, we are still confronted with interpretations of the same material that differ widely one from another. But instead of being disturbed by this, we should rather rejoice at the evidence it affords of the perennial quickening activity of all genuine art.

To examine all the criticism of one of Shakespeare's greater plays—all, that is, that bears the impress of a mind genuinely at work; to trace how some of the major changes in what intelligent people have found there have come about; to show how shifts of interest or emphasis have brought into view fresh sets of relationships within the play, relationships and significances that were 'there' all the time, yet not visible until a particular viewpoint had altered, as though the play were a many-faceted crystal refracting the light differently according to the way it is held; to see how even individual words and phrases can suddenly reveal a richness previously latent and unguessed at:—this would be one way of suggesting what is meant when we speak of the perpetually generative power of a great work of art. But even without such demonstration the fact is clear enough. 'The existence of a work of art'—to quote Lascelles Abercrombie once more—'is not material at all, but spiritual. It is a continually creative existence, for it exists by continually creating experience.'

That this power is operative even when the cast of mind, the prevailing assumptions, are quite alien to those of the Elizabethan period, is evident from the genuine praise of Shakespeare throughout the eighteenth century. It is of course true that prejudices regarding language and decorum (themselves deriving from wider prejudices and presuppositions) did then prevent anything like a full exposure to some vitally important (we may say central) aspects of Shakespeare's genius—as we see from the list of 'considerable imperfections' with which Joseph Warton concluded his *Adventurer* papers in praise of *King Lear*[1]:

> The plot of Edmund against his brother, which distracts the attention, and destroys the unity of the fable; the cruel and horrid extinction of Gloucester's eyes, which ought not to be exhibited on the stage; the utter improbability of Gloucester's imagining, though blind, that he had leapt down from Dover cliff; and some passages that are too turgid and full of strained metaphors; are faults which the warmest admirers of Shakespeare will find it difficult to excuse. I know not, also, whether the cruelty of the daughters is not painted with circumstances too savage and unnatural; for it is not sufficient to say, that this monstrous barbarity is founded on historical truth, if we recollect the just observation of Boileau,
>
> > *Le vray peut quelquefois n'être pas vraisemblable.*
> > Some truth may be too strong to be believed.

This well suggests the nature of the presuppositions, both general and specific, that obscured Shakespeare's tragic vision in the

---

[1] *The Adventurer* (1752–4), Nos. 113, 116, 122.

eighteenth century. The point is, however, that they could not completely obscure it. Dr Johnson approved—at least, he refused to condemn—Tate's ending for *King Lear*; but it is impossible to doubt that his mind derived substantial nourishment from 'this deservedly celebrated' drama: 'So powerful is the current of the poet's imagination, that the mind, which once ventures within it, is hurried irresistibly along.' Clearly the play *meant* a great deal to Johnson, even though what it meant—the precise ways in which his mind 'ventured within it'—was something very different from what it means to, say, Mr Robert Heilman.[1]

It may of course be claimed that what has since informed our consciousness—romantic inwardness (Lamb's 'While we read ..., we see not Lear, but we are Lear'), the accumulated insights of different critics regarding the powers of language, a vastly increased knowledge of Elizabethan dramatic conventions and intellectual background (the fruits of that very scholarship towards which I have hinted some reserve)—that all this has made more of the Shakespeare experience available, has indeed brought us closer to the Elizabethan Shakespeare. It may be so; but so far as the present argument is concerned there are other relevant considerations. One, already glanced at, is that even for the unhistorical eighteenth century Shakespeare was a genuine possession: indeed what the men of that century lost from their ignorance of the Elizabethan setting was at least partially compensated by the very fact that their approach was *not* that of the 'Elizabethan specialist' but that of the moralist, man of the world, or common reader. Another, more important, is that when we call to mind representative samples of twentieth-century criticism, by writers most of whom are in possession of the advantages of modern scholarship, we are still forced to the same conclusion regarding the nature of 'the object'. I don't for one moment mean that all writers on, say, *King Lear* are equally 'right': criticism recognizes degrees of sensitiveness and

[1] See *This Great Stage: Image and Structure in 'King Lear'*.

centrality. But we certainly cannot assume that if all our critics were equally sensitive, intelligent and informed they would present us with the same interpretation of the play. Clearly they would not. And even if by chance they did—if all their findings harmoniously agreed instead of sometimes tugging different ways—the '*Lear* experience' of each of them, and of each of their readers, would still be a unique, individual experience. The assimilation of a play into a particular individual context— a context of life experience, which includes the experience of other books—is a necessary part of its meaning, even though that meaning is so far from being a merely private possession that criticism is not only a possible but a profitable activity. We come out of course at a paradox, beautifully suggested in Wallace Stevens' address to the 'Supreme Fiction'—encountered, it will be remembered,

> In the uncertain light of single, certain truth,
> Equal in living changingness to the light
> In which I meet you. . . .

It is with these lines in mind that Marius Bewley comments[1]:

> From Stevens' work as a whole we know that one of the intrinsic elements of the imagination (as of life) is motion and change. . . . 'Single, certain truth' is in constant motion, is glimpsed and realized in moments of vital, vivid apprehension, and this act of apprehension itself may constitute ontologically a part, and perhaps a large part, of the truth.

Transposing this gloss into terms immediately relevant to the present discussion, we may say of Shakespeare, as of literature generally, that what is 'there' for intelligent discussion— something belonging to the more-than-individual world of shared experience—exists only in individual apprehensions which themselves, in some sense, contribute to its being.

[1] *The Complex Fate*, p. 182.

Now it seems to me that it is only on condition of our not forgetting this truth that we can hope to get into perspective the large amount of work that is being done in reconstructing the Elizabethan background, and to understand something of the relation of Shakespeare's plays to contemporary and traditional ideas. Shakespeare, we may now safely assume, was not un-learned; he had a naturally philosophic mind; he was in touch with the ideas of his age. But those ideas entered into his plays in so far as they met an intense inner need to find meanings in experience. They were tested and assimilated as part of the 'action or struggle for harmony in the soul of the poet' of which T. S. Eliot speaks. And encountered and assimilated in this way they ceased to be concepts to be applied or illustrated: they became elements of imaginative power, 'united by one signifi-cant, consistent, and developing personality'.

Now in this personal exploratory process there is no doubt that Shakespeare found his way to certain traditional ideas of great importance. Various critics have shown the significance of traditional ideas concerning the law of nature in *King Lear*, and W. C. Curry, in *Shakespeare's Philosophical Patterns*, has shown how *Macbeth* is saturated with moral and metaphysical concep-tions deriving from the Schoolmen. But the point is that these ideas are never merely accepted and applied; they are re-lived; their adequacy is tested in a full and personal exposure to life, and only then are they assimilated into a work of art with a life of its own. Thus *Macbeth*, as Professor Curry insists, certainly contains the idea of the negative quality of evil which was developed within the framework of Scholastic philosophy. But the idea is not stated as an idea to be illustrated. It is embodied in the unique combination of perceptions, insights, and feelings that is *Macbeth*; it is apprehended simultaneously in sensory, emotional, and intellectual terms; it is made vivid by the con-

trasting presence of images of life; and in the intense pressure of
the imaginative process the idea acquires a new dynamic. In
other words, however much Shakespeare may have profited
from conceptions sharpened and made viable by theologians
and philosophers (by whatever ways these reached him), there
is no question of the dramatic embodiment or illustration of
ideas that remain as it were external to the poet. The creative
insights of *Lear* and *Macbeth* and the later plays were won in a
direct encounter with life's problems, and there is the felt
pressure of life in the forms in which they are embodied. That
is why they can 'continually create experience'.

It is time to draw together the threads of this paper and to
attempt a direct answer to the question I began by raising concerning the value of historical scholarship in the study of literature. Can we now see how the scholarly exploration of the
sixteenth-century climate of opinion may meet fruitfully the
criticism of Shakespeare's plays as living works of the imagination, as something other than repositories of Elizabethan
doctrine? I think we can. Starting from our own direct experience of the plays (and without that we have nothing to start
from) we are interested, first, in anything that may make that
experience deeper and more vivid, and then, but only then, in
anything that may illuminate the relation between living art
and the civilization behind it, and so give us a firmer grasp of
the nature of a living tradition. With that starting point, and
with these interests, we have some means of distinguishing the
value of different kinds of 'background' study.

The common reader, bent on understanding Shakespeare's
plays to the best of his ability, will not of course take a superior

attitude to any kind of honest scholarship. There are many pre-
liminaries to criticism that only scholarship can provide: information about stage conditions, dramatic conventions, the basic
contemporary meanings of some words, and so on. And if
you are genuinely interested in Shakespeare almost any reliable
information about his age is likely to come in handy—so long,
that is, as you do not allow yourself to become cluttered up with
miscellaneous information as a substitute for the more exacting
task of reading poetry: remembering also that a little personal
reading of Shakespeare's greater contemporaries is more profitable than too much reading of 'background' books.

In the second place, even as common readers, we need to know
something about the reading and listening habits of the poet's
first audience. I have in mind such things as L. A. Cormican's
suggestive account of the habits of mind fostered by a familiarity
with the Liturgy.[1] We need to know these things, not so that
we can attempt to make ourselves into Elizabethans (we cannot
do that), but so that we can cultivate comparable skills, a comparable flexibility of mind, in our own approach to Shakespeare's
meanings.

Finally—and here we come to the crux of the matter—aware
of the 'philosophical' aspect of Shakespeare's work, we shall find
that we want to know something of the traditional moral philosophy which nourished, without confining, his imagination—
whilst yet avoiding the danger of substituting such knowledge
for the direct experience of the plays, or of supposing that these
can be reduced to anything like an illustration or demonstration
of past systems of thought.[2] What we want to know about, I

[1] L. A. Cormican, 'Medieval Idiom in Shakespeare': (1) 'Shakespeare and
the Liturgy', (2) 'Shakespeare and the Medieval Ethic'. *Scrutiny*, XVII, 3
and 4. See also S. L. Bethell, *Shakespeare and the Popular Dramatic Tradition*.
[2] 'To apply medieval ideas to our understanding of Shakespearean
tragedy is no mere matter of supplying footnotes to particular lines or
references; it is a matter of grasping a whole mentality which is implicit, and
often explicit, in the plays.'—L. A. Cormican, loc. cit.

suppose, are those major elements in the thought of the time that themselves have a perpetually generative power—that is, that are capable of nourishing the greatest diversity of minds, of illuminating ever fresh combinations of circumstances. And the condition of our fruitfully applying these ideas to our study of Shakespeare is that we should *not* approach them as Shakespearean scholars bent on reconstructing a merely historical background, but—paradoxically—that we should study them for themselves, responding to them as themselves actual and vivifying. Thus when Professor Curry describes for us the traditional background of the metaphysics of evil in *Macbeth*, we value his work because it puts us in touch with creative insights, developed by religious teachers and philosophers, that apply in any age, and so enables us to grasp more firmly what is essential to *Macbeth* as an ever-present work of imagination. When Miss Pope shows us how, in *Measure for Measure*, Shakespeare cuts through common confusions of his time regarding the relations of justice and mercy, going straight back to the inspiration of the Gospels,[1] we are faced with something quite different from a literary 'source', something that cannot possibly be relegated to 'history' but that directly impinges on the here and now: and the very condition of our seeing the play in relation to the Sermon on the Mount is that both play and Sermon should be imaginatively apprehended as present facts of experience. When, helped for example by Professor A. P. d'Entrèves' admirable little book on Natural Law, we try to bring traditional thinking on this subject into relation with our experience of *King Lear*— with what J. F. Danby calls 'Shakespeare's Doctrine of Nature' —it is the present, and not merely the historical, significance of the conceptions of Natural Law thinking that we need to have in mind. When we try to find the roots of what I should call

---

[1] Elizabeth Pope, 'The Renaissance Background of *Measure for Measure*', *Shakespeare Survey*, II, 66 ff. See also G. Wilson Knight, '*Measure for Measure* and the Gospels', in *The Wheel of Fire*.

Shakespeare's personalist approach to politics, it is with a sense of the present relevance of the medieval insistence on the moral foundations of politics. And so with all the life-bearing ideas of Shakespeare's age, whether we try to get in touch with them by the help of scholars or whether we confront them directly in the great books that nourished the Elizabethan mind and the work of original thinkers of the period such as Hooker. Like calls to like, and living art can best be studied in the light of living ideas. Such 'historical' study as we find necessary would not pre-suppose as its ultimate aim the restoration of Renaissance meanings. For the most part it would not be 'historical' at all in any limited sense: it would be predominantly the study of the varying forms—the varying apprehensions—of the great perennial truths. I suggest that if we guide our studies in the light of some such ideal as this we shall be better equipped to see Shakespeare's work for what it is: a unique creation, nourished by the complex of living thoughts that we call tradition, but with such depth of life that its essential meanings need to be elicited afresh in each generation—'so rammed with life', as Jonson said of Virgil's poetry,

—so rammed with life,
That it shall gather strength of life, with being.

11

King Lear as Metaphor

I HAD better begin by saying that I am not altogether happy about the title I have chosen for this paper. 'Metaphor', like 'myth' and 'archetype', is in danger of becoming an incantatory word; and I must confess that if anyone were to ask me for a short definition of 'a metaphor', I should find myself hard pressed for an answer. My purpose, however, is not incantation but inquiry, and it seems to me that to apply such knowledge as we have of metaphoric working to *King Lear* may throw light on a problem raised not only by *King Lear* but by all works of literary art.

The problem I have in mind concerns the perpetually renewed meaning of any poem (and the sense I intend would include many works in prose: *Wuthering Heights*, for example, and *The Castle*, and *A Passage to India*). The greater the poem the more obvious it is that the meaning—unlike, say, a theorem in geometry—is not given once and for all, but that it includes the capacity for change and renewal. Harold Goddard, in 'A Word to the Reader' which prefaces his fine book, *The Meaning of Shakespeare*, puts well what I have in mind:

> That Shakespeare is primarily a poet ought to be so obvious that even to put the thought in words would be banal. That it is not only not banal but is the thing most necessary to emphasize about him at the present time is a comment on the long ascendancy of the historical school of criticism in Shakespeare study. In stressing what Shakespeare meant to the Elizabethan age the historical critics have helped us forget what he might mean to ours. Like the materialists of the nineteenth century, in focusing attention on where things come from they tend to forget where they are going. They tend to forget that poetry means creation, and creation is something that still goes on.[1]

[1] Harold Goddard, *The Meaning of Shakespeare* (Phoenix Books, University of Chicago Press), Vol. I, pp. viii–ix.

'Poetry', as Goddard says later in the same book, 'forever makes itself over for each generation': and I think it is plain not only that *King Lear* meant something different to Dr Johnson from what it means to any twentieth-century reader, but that it must mean something different for each reader, even of the same generation, who has genuinely entered into the play and made it his own. That is one side of the problem. But it is also true that the meaning of *King Lear* is not simply subjective, a matter of individual taste or fancy. Confronted by the poem you are certainly not at liberty to read into it anything you choose. Indeed the whole business of criticism, of the intelligent discussion of literature, presupposes that there is sound sense in Matthew Arnold's statement of the function of criticism, 'To see the object as in itself it really is'. The only way to reconcile these apparently contradictory truths it seems to me, is through an examination of the nature of metaphor and the metaphoric process.

At this point I propose to invoke the help of Martin Foss in that difficult but far-reaching and seminal book, *Symbol and Metaphor in Human Experience*.[1] Foss is concerned not with literary criticism in any limited sense but with ways of representing life, and therefore of living it. His argument is based on the distinction between the pursuit of 'ends' determined by the will (and therefore conceived in terms of what is fixed and static) and the acceptance of a 'direction'; between the closed world of the consistent empiricist and the 'open' (but not lawless) world of creative living. It is to the former of these two worlds that Foss rather arbitrarily and contrary to most current usage, assigns the symbol. (That for Foss's 'symbol' most of us would prefer to use the word 'sign' is, for the moment, irrelevant.) The symbol is a fixed representation of the empirical world: 'clear, exact and useful' (p. 3), it belongs to the 'purposive, constructed environ-

[1] Martin Foss, *Symbol and Metaphor in Human Experience* (Bison Book edition, University of Nebraska Press).

ment of the ego with all its deeds and fulfilments' (p. 131). To the symbolic reduction (subsuming manifold variety under a fixed representation) Foss opposes the metaphoric process: 'metaphors break up instead of fixing, keep us on the move instead of letting us settle down' (p. 58). Over against the symbolic world of 'similarity, comparison and repetition' (p. 89) is 'metaphorical life with its seeming contradictions, tensions, and its transcendence' (p. 87). 'Metaphor is a process of tension and energy, manifested in the process of language, not in the single word' (p. 61).[1]

It is the idea of process that is important, for what we have to do with is something that goes far beyond the concept of metaphor as an isolated figure of speech in which, as the dictionary says, 'a term or phrase is applied to something to which it is not literally applicable in order to suggest a resemblance'. It is a process in which terms representing items of our knowledge are brought into relation to each other and to something unknown; and in a mutual interaction (for even the unknown is felt like the tug of a current or tide) fixed meanings are modified or destroyed, and a new apprehension—or (shall we say?) a new direction of awareness—takes place. What Foss is describing is of course *the* creative movement of all literary form, from the highest poetry to the humblest expression of an intuitive awareness such as the proverb. Indeed what Foss says of the proverb will serve as a convenient summary of his thinking about the metaphoric process in its widest manifestations:

> A proverb may appear as a simile, a comparison, but it is very different. The comparison connects one object with another in order to procure additional knowledge. But if we take a proverb like 'Among blind men the one-eyed is king', we may consider

[1] For the 'tensive' quality of creative metaphor and some criticism of Foss, see Philip Wheelwright, *The Burning Fountain: A Study in the Language of Symbolism* (Indiana University Press), Chapter VI, and *Metaphor and Reality* (Indiana University Press).

it as a comparison between two groups, the blind and the seeing. If we, however, learn only what the simile tells us: that the one-eyed can be compared to a king when he lives among blind men, then the result of our comparison is rather foolish. In fact, neither the one-eyed man nor the king is the real interest, neither of the two is supposed to profit by the comparison. The true significance of the proverb goes far beyond the blind, the one-eyed, and the king: it points to a wisdom in regard to which the terms of the comparison are only unimportant cases of reference. It teaches the relativity and deficiency of all wordly power, and this wisdom, without being expressly stated, rises above the transient analogy and its inadequate formula. It lifts us above these and other cases of an arbitrary selection to a lawful necessity. Although the form of the proverb is still very much like the simile, even like the riddle, witty and surprising, playfully enclosing a general rule into the nutshell of particular cases, nevertheless its transcending character points to the metaphoric sphere. For it may now be stated: the simile and the analogy link the unknown to the known, in an expedient and practical way, closing the problematic entity into a familiar pattern. The metaphorical process, on the contrary, raises the problem even there where we seemed at home and shatters the ground on which we had settled down in order to widen our view beyond any limit of a special practical use. (pp. 55–56)

The metaphoric process, thus defined, is therefore the central drive of all literary creation (the making of a living image of experience that goes beyond the immediate representation), but more marked and explicit as the work approaches great poetry. There are many works of literature (e.g. realistic novels) where the metaphoric element is comparatively slight. There are others where to ignore or misunderstand the metaphoric working is to be left with but a meagre skeleton of the living experience that is offered in, for example, poetic drama. In a work almost wholly metaphorical a mind unsympathetic to this mode of understanding will be completely baffled and will find, not reason in its most exalted mood, but plain nonsense. A German critic once dismissed *King Lear* as 'a nursery story, but of the more horrible sort'. But the most eminent representative of this way of mistaking things is Tolstoy, whose remarks on *King Lear*, in the essay, 'Shakespeare and the Drama',[1] may serve to close this introductory section and lead us into some consideration of the play itself.

Tolstoy's conception of the function of art led him to claim that the aim of drama is 'to elicit sympathy with what is represented' (p. 353). For this, illusion—'which constitutes the chief condition of art' (p. 336)—is essential, and the context makes plain that what Tolstoy meant by illusion was an imaginative sympathy or identification with the *dramatis personae* as though they were characters in a real-life situation.

> An artistic poetic work, especially a drama, should first of all evoke in reader or spectator the illusion that what the persons represented are living through and experiencing is being lived through and experienced by himself. . . . However eloquent and profound they may be, speeches put into the mouths of acting characters, if they are superfluous and do not accord with the situation and the characters, infringe the main condition of dramatic work—the illusion causing the reader or spectator to experience the feelings of the persons represented. One may without infringing the illusion leave much unsaid: the reader or spectator will himself supply what is needed . . .; but to say what is superfluous, is like jerking and scattering a statue made up of small pieces, or taking the lamp out of a magic lantern . . . the illusion is lost, and to recreate it is sometimes impossible. (p. 354)

We may leave on one side for the moment the question of what is or is not superfluous and who is the best judge of this (for to determine what is superfluous means that one already has a conception of what is proper): it is plain that what Tolstoy demands

---

[1] Included in the World's Classics volume, *Recollections and Essays*, translated with an Introduction by Aylmer Maude. Page references are to this volume.

is a straightforward verisimilitude to life. With such a criterion
he has no difficulty in showing (though he does it at some length)
that *King Lear* is arbitrary, unnatural, and ridiculous. Mr
Wilson Knight, in a valuable paper,[1] claims that Tolstoy's powerful mind was misled by the nineteenth-century commentators
on Shakespeare, with their excessive emphasis on 'character':
Tolstoy was perplexed because he expected, and did not find,
in Shakespeare 'the novelist's skill, tending more towards "observation" and "imitation" ' than towards those poetic and
symbolic forms through which Shakespeare bodies forth 'a
central dynamic idea'. Not finding what he had been led to
expect, he was baffled and angry and inclined to shout humbug
at those who admire. What also has to be said (I think it is implied
in Mr Wilson Knight's analysis) is that Tolstoy seems to think
that for the purpose of critical demonstration a prose paraphrase
and summary will do as well as the original poetry, which is
essentially metaphoric.

There is no need to do more than remind you of how far, in
King Lear, Shakespeare is from concerning himself with naturalistic illusion. Not only are there bold improbabilities (the parallel
plots, Edgar's disguises, Dover cliff, etc.), there is an almost
complete rejection of verisimilitude in the portrayal of the
characters and their setting, of anything that might seem to keep
us in close touch with a familiar—or at all events an actual—
world. This, as I say, is now commonplace, but a rather obvious
contrast may be useful here. The first chapter of Turgenev's
novel, *A King Lear of the Steppe*, opens with a long description of
the hero, Kharlov:

> Imagine a man of gigantic height. On his huge torso rested, a
> little aslant and without any sign of a neck, an enormous head; a
> whole shock of tangled yellow-gray hair rose up from it, starting
> practically from his ruffled eyebrows themselves. On the broad

[1] G. Wilson Knight, *Shakespeare and Tolstoy*, The English Association,
Pamphlet No. 88.

square of his dove-coloured face there stuck out a big, knobby nose; his tiny little light blue eyes puffed out arrogantly, and his mouth hung open—also tiny, but crooked, chapped, and the same colour as the rest of his face. The voice that came out of this mouth was, though husky, extremely strong and stentorian. Its sound reminded you of the clanking of flat iron bars in a cart on a rough pavement, and Kharlov would talk as if shouting to someone across a wide ravine in a strong wind.[1]

Solidity of specification is the keynote, and Turgenev took great pains to ensure that characters and setting alike should seem to have an historical existence in a particular bit of Russia in the first half of the nineteenth century. 'Technical information—for example, the procedures connected with the division of the estate between the two daughters, or the correct names of the beams and rafters in a roof—[he] asked of his friends, acquaintances, and the steward of his own estate.'[2] Much of the success of the story depends on what Mr Franklin Reeve calls the 'accuracy and actualness of the incidents [Turgenev] imagined his characters tied to'.

By contrast, what do we know of Lear's appearance, or of what the heath looked like? Lear is a powerful old man, 'four score and upward', and the crown of his head ('this thin helm') is covered by a few white hairs; the heath is a desolate place ('For many miles about there's scarce a bush'): that is all we know of the appearance of either. And just as specificness of person and setting is a main feature of Turgenev's novel, so the rejection of it is characteristic of Shakespeare's tragedy.[3] A. C.

[1] Turgenev, *Five Short Novels*, translated and with an Introduction by Franklin Reeve (New York: Bantam Books).

[2] Franklin Reeve, Preface to *A King Lear of the Steppe*. The following quotation is from the same source.

[3] On the stage of course the characters 'look like' the actors who play their roles, but Shakespeare has provided indications enough that these should be, so far as possible, depersonalized: individualizing gestures and mannerisms should be at all costs avoided.

Bradley rightly speaks of 'the vagueness of the scene where the action takes place, and of the movements of the figures which cross this scene; the strange atmosphere, cold and dark, which strikes on us as we enter this scene, enfolding these figures and magnifying their dim outlines like a winter mist.'[1] Granville-Barker speaks of 'a certain megalithic grandeur . . . that we associate with Greek tragedy.'[2]

What this means is that a certain simplification of effect is an essential part of Shakespeare's method in *King Lear*. Ignoring for the moment the important conversation between Gloucester and Kent with which the play opens, we see that the first scene turns on a situation reduced to its bare essentials. It is of course the love-test that puts before us the central conflict in Lear—an old man who wants the prerogatives of age, but combined with the privileged treatment appropriate to babyhood; a king who wants power, but without responsibility; a father who wants love, but seeks to treat it as though it were some kind of commodity that could be bought or enforced. Since this sort of thing happens every day, I do not see how anyone can speak of the scene as 'unnatural'. But obviously it is not presented naturalistically: Granville-Barker speaks of 'the almost ritual formality of the first scene', and the formal quality is enforced not only by the starkness with which the issues are presented but by such devices as the use of rhymed couplets (instead of the more 'natural' prose or blank verse) at crucial points. Now the 'stripping' of character and situation, aided by a certain formality in the presentation, has, as the play develops, a curious effect. Instead of a simple sparseness (as in a morality play like *Everyman*)

[1] *Shakespearean Tragedy*, p. 247. Bradley feels the effect of this, even though he curiously complains that it 'interferes with dramatic clearness even when the play is read'.

[2] H. Granville-Barker, *Prefaces to Shakespeare*, First Series, p. 146. Granville-Barker quotes the passage from Bradley when answering the latter's contention that *Lear*, although 'Shakespeare's greatest achievement', is '*not* his best play'.

there is an almost overwhelming richness. Boundaries are firmly drawn: certain interests are excluded, and there are questions we are not allowed to ask. But this simplification is the condition of the greatest possible compression and intensification: character and situation alike take on a symbolic quality and are made to point to a range of experience beyond themselves. And they do this because of the ways in which the reader or spectator is involved in the metaphoric process that constitutes the play.

From the start *King Lear* sets you asking questions, and not only obvious and inescapable ones such as, Why has Lear staged this curious love-test in conjunction with the division of his kingdom? or, Is Cordelia right or wrong in refusing to humour her father? The questions we are made to ask are of a particular kind. Tolstoy sometimes makes it a matter of complaint that Shakespeare leaves us without explanations even when it would be easy to provide them;[1] but that is just where Tolstoy mistakes the nature of Shakespearean drama. The questions raised by *King Lear* do not allow 'explanations' that you can complacently store in a pocket of the mind: they seem designed to cause the greatest possible uncertainty, or even bewilderment. Within the areas cleared by a formal simplification they centre on certain words and conceptions: in the first scene, 'love' and 'nothing' and 'unnatural' (shortly to be joined by 'Nature'), and then as the play proceeds, 'fool' and 'need'.

Now all of these words are profoundly ambiguous. Let us glance in passing at 'nothing', recalling as we do so the unexpectedly wise words of Richard II in his dungeon:

> Nor I, nor anyone that but man is,
> With nothing shall be pleased, till he be eased
> With being nothing.

What this says is that no man will be content with mere deprivation until he is dead and so past caring; but simultaneously it has

[1] See 'Shakespeare and the Drama', *Recollections and Essays*, p. 346.

the effect of suggesting that all men are pleased with vanities ('nothings') until they are either physically dead or in some sense dead to the world. There is a similar ambiguousness in the 'nothing' that plays between Lear and Cordelia.

> *Lear.*   Now, our joy,
> Although our last, not least; to whose young love
> The vines of France and milk of Burgundy
> Strive to be interess'd; what can you say to draw
> A third more opulent than your sisters? Speak.
> *Cordelia.* Nothing, my lord.
> *Lear.*   Nothing?
> *Cordelia.* Nothing.
> *Lear.*   Nothing will come of nothing: speak again.

'Nothing': on the one hand mere negation, the absence of what is desired ('Can you make no use of nothing, Nuncle?' 'Why, no, boy; nothing can be made out of nothing.'); on the other hand, the possession of the inestimable, which the world does not regard.

> Fairest Cordelia, that art most rich, being poor;
> Most choice, forsaken; and most lov'd despis'd!

With these lines Richmond Noble compares 2 Corinthians vi, 10: 'As poor, and yet making many rich: as having nothing, and yet possessing all things.'[1]

It is the same with all our key-words, and I should like for a moment to present you with a ridiculously abstract description of their working. (1) The key-words—words to which special attention is directed—are all ambiguous and cover a wide range of meaning. (2) Poetry and situation release and bring into relation and conflict the different meanings: the words, in

---

[1] Richmond Noble, *Shakespeare's Biblical Knowledge*, p. 229, quoted by Kenneth Muir in a note to the New Arden edition. The section on Lear's Fool in Miss Enid Welsford's *The Fool: his Social and Literary History* is very relevant at this point.

Empson's phrase, are 'complex words'.[1] (3) So great is the activation of these words, instance piled on instance in quick succession, that they vibrate in the reader's mind beyond the limits of the specific instances. When within a space easily encompassed by the mind in one act of apprehension we have fire and whirlpool, bog and quagmire, whirlwinds and star-blasting, the web and the pin (cataract), squint-eyes, hare-lip and mildewed wheat, then our sense of natural calamity stretches on and on: behind the whirlpool is all shipwreck, behind the mildewed wheat is all failure of harvest and starvation.[2] (4) Just as there is interplay and tension between the different senses of the key-words, so there is interplay and tension between the different key-words themselves and all the other elements of the drama.

As a way of drawing to a point these observations, let us follow the course of one such key-word, arbitrarily disengaging it from the others. It is not, as it happens, mentioned in the opening scenes where the situation to be elucidated is set forth.[3] But it lies behind both the first scene, where Lear makes his test and divides his kingdom, and the second, where the parallel and intensifying plot is got under way. The word is Justice. Both Lear and Edmund are concerned for some form—a perverted form—of distributive justice. Lear is concerned that reward should be proportioned to merit, that is, the merit of proclaimed love to him ('That we our largest bounty may extend/Where nature doth with merit challenge'); Edmund is concerned with the unfair social discrimination in favour of legitimate sons and

[1] William Empson, *The Structure of Complex Words*.

[2] The effect is analogous to the effect of the sub-plot as described in W. B. Yeats' essay, 'The Emotion of Multitude', in *Ideas of Good and Evil; Essays and Introductions*, pp. 215–16.

[3] 'The distinctive Shakespearean structure comes, not so much from the need to compress a series of events within the framework of a play, but rather from a powerful urge to elucidate, and even exhaust, the meaning of the opening situation.'—L. A. Cormican, 'Medieval Idiom in Shakespeare', *Scrutiny*, XVII, 3–4.

the hardships of primogeniture, for both of which he would substitute the criterion of a particular kind of desert: 'To each', he seems to say, 'according to his ability to get'—'All with me's meet that I can fashion fit'. Lear's perfomance has even something of the appearance of a formal trial, just as trial procedure will appear again when Lear arraigns Goneril and Regan before the Bedlam and the Fool, and when Cornwall acts as accuser, judge and executioner in a summary trial for 'treason'. Legal or quasi-legal procedure is in fact enacted or referred to a good many times in the play: Kent is put in the stocks, Poor Tom has been 'whipp'd from tithing to tithing, and stock-punished, and imprison'd', and Edgar and Edmund engage in judicial combat; there are references to unfee'd lawyers, summoners, cases in law, beadles, hanging and the rack. All this is sufficient to raise some question about the nature of justice, even without the play's explicit insistence at crucial points.

To the question, What is Justice? the play offers many answers, more or less adequate. The commonest assumption of the characters is that it is some kind of assignment of reward or punishment according to desert, and their human assumptions are often projected on to 'the gods'.

> Let the great Gods,
> That keep this dreadful pudder o'er our heads,
> Find out their enemies now. Tremble, thou wretch,
> That hast within thee undivulged crimes,
> Unwhipp'd of Justice; hide thee, thou bloody hand,
> Thou perjur'd, and thou simular of virtue
> That art incestuous; caitiff, to pieces shake,
> That under covert and convenient seeming
> Hast practis'd on man's life: close pent-up guilts
> Rive your concealing continents, and cry
> These dreadful summoners grace.

'Unwhipp'd of Justice'; beind that conception of justice lies Lear's own vindictive desire to 'punish home' for offences against

himself. Its inadequacy is underlined by the play's two references to legal whipping: the lunatic beggar is 'whipp'd from
tithing to tithing' simply because he is a vagabond; the prosti-
tute is lashed by the parish beadle whose cruelty is fed by his lust.

Distributive and retributive justice alike assume that man can
determine degrees of desert and merit on a calculated scale.
What the play tells you is that he can't. There is indeed a justice
in the grain of things—something like, I suppose, the Greek
dîke—in the sense that there is an inner logic of events whereby
evil consumes itself: Albany's

> This shows you are above,
> You justicers, that these our nether crimes
> So speedily can venge.

But the merely human assignment of guilt and punishment,
desert and reward (mixed as this assignment is with unacknowledged and distorting passions), is shown to have no ultimate
justification at all: in the play's total vision there seems little
difference between the claim of the lawless individualist to assert
his own version of nature's law and socially sanctioned legal
forms. The *reductio ad absurdum* of Lear's view of his own role
as dispenser of justice is of course the mock trial of Goneril
and Regan.

Lear.   I'll see their trial first. Bring in their evidence.
        [*To Edgar*] Thou robed man of justice, take thy place;
        [*To the Fool*] And thou, his yoke-fellow of equity,
        Bench by his side. [*To Kent*] You are o'th' commission,
        Sit you too.
Edgar. Let us deal justly. . . .
        Purr, the cat is grey.
Lear.   Arraign her first; 'tis Goneril. I here take my oath before
        this honourable assembly, she kick'd the poor King her
        father.
Fool.   Come hither, mistress. Is your name Goneril?
Lear.   She cannot deny it.

Fool. Cry you mercy, I took you for a joint-stool.

Lear. And here's another, whose warp'd looks proclaim
      What store her heart is made on. Stop her there!
      Arms, arms, sword, fire! Corruption in the place!
      False justicer, why hast thou let her 'scape?

If I may quote what I have said elsewhere, there is ' "corruption in the place" indeed. Lear's fantasy spins right when, by bringing the trial to an end in mad confusion, it tells him that reality cannot be reached in that way'.[1] This, and much else, lies behind Lear's great explicit denunciation—'reason in madness'—of human authority and its legalistic claims.

Lear. What! art mad? A man may see how this world goes with
      no eyes. Look with thine ears: see how yond justice rails
      upon yond simple thief. Hark, in thine ear: change places,
      and, handy-dandy, which is the justice, which is the thief?
      Thou hast seen a farmer's dog bark at a beggar?

Gloucester. Ay, Sir.

Lear. And the creature run from the cur? There thou might'st
      behold
      The great image of Authority:
      A dog's obey'd in office.
      Thou rascal beadle, hold thy bloody hand!
      Why dost thou lash that whore? Strip thine own back;
      Thou hotly lusts to use her in that kind
      For which thou whipp'st her. The usurer hangs the
      cozener.
      Through tatter'd clothes small vices do appear;
      Robes and furr'd gowns hide all. Plate sin with gold,
      And the strong lance of justice hurtless breaks;
      Arm it in rags, a pigmy's straw does pierce it.
      None does offend, none, I say, none; I'll able 'em.

'None does offend, none, I say, none; I'll able 'em.' That last line shares the ambiguity of so many of the pronouncements

---

[1] *Some Shakespearean Themes*, p. 105.

made in this play. 'None does offend' because we are all as bad as each other. That is one sense. But because at more than one point Lear has now admitted his own guilt and involvement, there is a bridge to the second sense: 'none does offend' because at the most fundamental level of all no one has a right to condemn. And what is held in tension is not only two senses but two basic attitudes—utter revulsion ('Give me an ounce of civet, good apothecary, To sweeten my imagination'), on the one hand: on the other an unconditional and unquestioning charity, of the kind that had allowed Cordelia to invoke the unpublished virtues of the earth as remedies for 'the good man's distress', the good man being of course the erring Lear. Naturally, as we watch or read, we do not debate these alternatives as an abstract issue: we are simply carried forward—alert and engaged—to the immediately succeeding scene where this and other issues are resolved in terms of the awakened imagination.

> *Lear.* Do not laugh at me;
> For as I am a man, I think this lady
> To be my child Cordelia.
> *Cordelia.* And so I am, I am.
> *Lear.* Be your tears wet? Yes, faith. I pray, weep not:
> If you have poison for me, I will drink it.
> I know you do not love me; for your sisters
> Have, as I do remember, done me wrong:
> You have some cause, they have not.
> *Cordelia.* No cause, no cause.

It is subtly done. Lear's thoughts, as he comes to himself in his daughter's presence, are still on punishment for his sins, on the weighing of retribution against offence. It is with four words that Cordelia brushes aside all forms of proportionate justice and reveals a justice of an utterly different kind. It is, I suppose, what Paul Tillich would call reconciling or transforming justice, which can help a man to become what he is and what his nature

most deeply craves.[1] Clearly this raises the whole question of
man's nature and the wider 'nature' with which he finds himself
involved: and indeed within the Lear world the line of thought
we have been following has been developed in the context of
these wider questions. Here we will simply notice that within that
context the question of Justice has been lifted to a plane transcending that of our everyday conceptions. Not of course that
we are left with a new concept. It is simply that in the upward
surge of the metaphoric process a new direction for imaginative
thought appears. Rooted in the given instance—in the highly
complex metaphor that King Lear is—it unfolds, and goes on
unfolding, in our own lives. In a sense we live the metaphors we
have assimilated.

In The Transformation of Nature in Art Ananda Coomaraswamy glosses the term yün as used by a Chinese writer on
aesthetics: 'The idea yün, of operation or reverberation, is
strictly comparable to what is meant by the dhvani of Indian
rhetoricians, it being only as it were by an echoing in the heart
of the hearer that the full meaning of a word (or any other
symbol) can be realized.' Dhvani, he adds, 'is literally "sound",
especially sound like that of thunder or a drum, hence "reson-
ance" or "overtone" of meaning'—i.e. the verbal noun 'sounding', rather than the noun 'sound'.[2] I am ignorant of Chinese and
Indian aesthetics, but it seems to me that this comment throws
light on the metaphoric process we have been considering.
Martin Foss, you will recall, speaks of this as 'a process of tension
and energy'. The tension, as we have seen in King Lear, is the
apprehension of meanings somehow held in relation to each
other, and to a central drive of interest, so that each meaning is
more clearly defined in relation to the others, and what I have
called the drive of interest is established in a certain direction.

[1] See Paul Tillich, Love, Power and Justice.
[2] Ananda Coomaraswamy, The Transformation of Nature in Art (New
York: Dover Publications), pp. 187, 198.

The energy is an energy of understanding. It is of course obvious that more than the conceptual understanding is involved; it is only through the reader's imagination responding to the imagination of the poet (bringing 'the whole soul of man into activity') that the work becomes alive. But the point I am making is that the imagination thus conceived is an instrument of knowledge—not 'knowledge of' something fixed and definite, but knowledge as a 'sounding', 'an echoing in the heart of the hearer'.

It is in the hope of elucidating this process that I have examined some small part of *King Lear*. The play is not just a symbolic form in which modes of feeling are held before us for contemplation. It is a moving image of life, in the sense not of course that it merely affects our feelings, but that it sets in motion those powers of apprehension through which we simultaneously become aware of, and make, our world.

12

Shakespeare and History

POETRY, we have been told on good authority, "begins in delight" but "ends in wisdom"; and although any critic or teacher of literature would hesitate to say that he is teaching wisdom, he may properly use literature as part of a varied inquiry into human life that struggles toward, if it rarely achieves, wisdom. One such use lies in a consideration of the relations of literature and history, of imaginative works and the pattern of more-than-individual attitudes and acts as the pattern changes in the process of time. I am of course gesturing toward a very large field, which in its entirety would include such important matters as the ways in which imaginative writers—simply because they are imaginative writers and not simplifying polemicists—catch the stirrings of new attitudes, the tone and timbre of new ways of thinking and feeling, long before these display themselves on the public stage. It is now a commonplace—though first formulated, I think, by Berdyaev (in *The Origin of Russian Communism*)—that to understand the triumph of the Bolsheviks in 1917 and much that followed thereon we must have some knowledge of Russian literature in the nineteenth century. Ivan Karamazov's fable of the Grand Inquisitor and many of the goings-on in *The Devils* help to make the point. And Isaiah Berlin, in his brilliant and timely Romanes lecture (1970) on *Fathers and Children*, remarks: "If the inner life, the ideas, the moral predicament of men matter at all in explaining the course of human history," then Turgenev's novels are a basic document for the understanding of the Russian past and of our present. To come nearer home (and with reference to lesser works), J. W. Lever, in *The Tragedy of State*, has considered the tragedies of some of Shakespeare's contemporaries in the Jacobean period as "a product

of the intellectual ferment and spiritual upheaval which preceded the first great European revolution . . . a sounding-
board for the ideas of a new age of protest," a preliminary
rumbling of the midcentury ferment. I do not think we can
use Shakespeare in this way; but such approaches to history
through literature are a legitimate extension of the primary
task of the critic.

In another part of the field—and here, sounding like a stage
direction in the more confused scenes of Elizabethan drama,
I draw nearer to my main subject—we may pursue an interest
in the way in which imaginative writers use their "sources"
when their ostensible purpose is to re-create a particular historical epoch. Clearly they use—or depart from—their sources
in very different ways. A comparison of *The Dynasts* and
War and Peace may perhaps suggest that permanent value is
in inverse proportion to the writer's attempt to *impose* a philosophy of history. Hardy was a great poet, and he wrote
some great novels, but *The Dynasts,* I think, fails because its
"philosophy" is so vague and unconvincing:

> This tale of Will
> And Life's impulsion by Incognizance. . . .
>
> The Immanent, that urgeth all,
> Rules what may or may not befall. . . .

And it fails because neither the philosophy nor Hardy's great
gift of direct and sensitive observation of human feelings in
any way vivifies the human drama, whether this is invented
or taken more or less directly from standard histories, parlia-
mentary reports, or the like. Tolstoy, who also read widely in
source material, also tries to domineer over history: he has
a theory to propound and to hammer home, and the pages
in which he expounds it are difficult and a little dull. At all
events I have to count myself among the "reasonably critical,
moderately sensitive" readers who, Isaiah Berlin says, are
likely to find the philosophy of history in the novel "arti-

ficial.["] *War and Peace,* however, succeeds—magnificently— in spite of this: Tolstoy's vitality and abundance swamp the theorizing. In obvious contrast to both these writers, Shakespeare, in his history plays, is innocent of theory: he does not so much impose as observe and explore—observing and exploring, in the great masters, being very much part of the one process of finding and creating—of finding by creating—meaning and significance.

What a writer observes is a very complicated matter. It includes his own feelings and motives, the attitudes and behavior of those about him, and what he reads. In writing his English history plays Shakespeare turned naturally to such sources as were available to an educated Elizabethan. Although I am far from being an expert on Elizabethan historiography I must now say something about these.

Shakespeare wrote ten plays on subjects taken from English history. Apart from *King John,* which is not altogether satisfactory, and *Henry VIII,* which is a late collaborative work, there are two tetralogies, each of which seems to have been planned as a more or less unified sequence; and between them they cover the historical period from the decline, abdication, and death of Richard II (d. 1400) to the battle of Bosworth, the death of Richard III, and the establishment of the House of Tudor in 1485. It is on the first tetralogy that I concentrate, for a variety of reasons.

There is a persistent notion among Englishmen with some slight knowledge of history that the fifteenth century in England was preeminently the century of the Wars of the Roses. The term is of course a misleading one for what S. B. Chrimes, reviewing J. R. Lander's *Crown and Nobility 1450–*

---

[1]Isaiah Berlin, *The Hedgehog and the Fox: An Essay on Tolstoy's View of History* (1953). This remarkable essay shows convincingly the drives that compelled Tolstoy to construct his vast edifice of theory, and it has some splendid pages on the unifying vision that Tolstoy desperately wanted to attain. But since Sir Isaiah says that Tolstoy's "sense of reality . . . served to explode all the large theories which ignore his findings, but proved insufficient by itself to provide the basis of a more satisfactory general account of the facts," it would seem that he too is among those whom, in the phrase quoted above, he gently dismisses.

1509, has referred to as "the series of battles that occurred
between 1455 and 1487, which . . . occupied only about
twelve or thirteen weeks in thirty-two years, and which had
no significant effect on the numbers or wealth of the English
landed classes" (*TLS,* 26 November 1976). It is a half century since C. L. Kingsford, in *Prejudice and Promise in XVth
Century England,* warned his readers against exaggerating
the effect of the dynastic battles on the social life of a century when there was such vigorous development in the
spheres of religion, language, literacy, and scholarship, as well
as "the vigorous growth of town life and the growing importance and enterprise of the mercantile class." Shakespeare was not concerned with all this, for the simple reason
that he didn't know it. What he knew was the facts, and the
interpretation of those facts, presented by the Tudor chroni-
clers. For all of these the main theme—apart from the
French wars of the early part of the century—was the rivalry
of the Houses of York and Lancaster subsequent to the "original sin" of the deposition and murder of Richard II. This
rivalry lay behind the violence and bloodshed of the middle
years of the century; and although some accommodation had
to be made for Henry V—after all, a popular hero—the curse
of fratricidal and mutually destructive strife was not lifted
until Henry Tudor (who had Lancastrian claims) destroyed
Richard III at Bosworth, and, as Henry VII, married Elizabeth
of York, thereby—as they began to say in the next century—
uniting the White Rose and the Red.

Clearly this is history with a Tudor monarchical slant,
emphasizing both the providential accession of Henry VII and
his line and the "establishment" insistence on the heinousness
of rebellion and the need for internal order and strong
government. Every undergraduate reading English knows at
least two passages—they are frequently quoted—in which
these views are expressed. One is Hall's introduction to *The
Union of the Two Noble and Illustrious Families of Lancaster
and York* (first published in 1548, and Shakespeare's principal, though not his only, "source" for his early history plays).

Here in his prolix way Hall enlarges on the theme of the "mischief [that] hath insurged in realms by intestine division": it is "clearer than the sun" that "as by discord great things decay and fall to ruin, so the same by concord be revived and erected." The other is the *Homily against Disobedience and Wilful Rebellion,* added to the Book of Homilies appointed to be read in churches in 1570 after the failure of the rebellion of the North. "How horrible a sin against God and man rebellion is cannot possibly be expressed according to the greatness thereof. For he that nameth rebellion nameth not a singular or one only sin . . . but he nameth the whole puddle and sink of all sins against God and man. . . . All sins, I say, against God and all men heaped together nameth he that nameth rebellion."

This simplified bit of pedantry has been necessary to indicate the prevailing Tudor view of recent English history, since Shakespeare knew not only the chronicles but such fictionalized (and moralized) "Histories" as the enormously popular *Mirror for Magistrates* (1559, and much amplified in subsequent editions), and it would be absurd to assume that Shakespeare was not touched by contemporary beliefs and attitudes. He read very widely and the plays contain innumerable echoes of Tudor doctrine. But although it would be wrong to take a cynical view of the Histories and Homilies as mere government propaganda (if you consider the alternatives Elizabeth's strong government really was something to be glad of), it would be equally mistaken to assume that Shakespeare swallowed whole the current political orthodoxies. For the essential insights, imaginatively apprehended and dramatically expressed, we must step outside the bounds of historiography.

E. M. W. Tillyard, in his pioneering study *Shakespeare's History Plays,* says of the first tetralogy: "The greatest bond uniting all four plays is the steady political theme: the theme of order and chaos, of proper political degree and civil war, of crime and punishment, of God's mercy finally tempering his justice, of the belief that such had been God's way with

England." I think that true, but not the whole truth, for, by making Shakespeare more "Tudor" than he was, it leaves out something of the greatest importance that, first showing itself in these early plays, is fundamental for our understanding of Shakespeare's work as a whole. What he did take from the available chronicles was the habit of seeing history in contemporary terms (inevitably so, of course, for modern history, with its attempt to capture the pastness of the past, was not yet born); and the belief that the public and political events of the past were neither random nor rigidly determined stages in a mere temporal succession, but formed a significant pattern of causes and effects. His purpose was neither to write dramatic "chronicles" nor to illustrate "the Tudor view of history," but to shape his material according to a creative "idea" or informing principle; and his exploration of political-social action went so deep that it is impossible to think of a time when his so-called Histories will not speak directly to men who inescapably live in a public as well as a private dimension. To the question why this should be so there are many answers. All I propose to do here is to pick out two characteristics that both illustrate Shakespeare's distinctive dealing with historical material and open up perspectives on later, and greater, plays.

It still seems to me, as it did many years ago, that one of the most pregnant comments on the early Shakespeare and the relation of the early plays to the whole canon is that made by Harold Goddard when, early in *The Meaning of Shakespeare*, he remarked that one fruitful way of looking at nearly all the plays was to see them as different and continually deepening attempts to answer the question "What is the cure for chaos?"—chaos being a subject that, so to speak, met Shakespeare head-on at the start of his career. In the three parts of *Henry VI* chaos is exemplified not only in the action—"this jarring discord of nobility"—but in the pervasive imagery. In the second and third parts this is not only of tumultuous natural forces—storms, winds, tempestuous seas—but of "the jungle, the chase and the slaughterhouse . . . symbolic of the cruelty and wild justice of civil war."⁷ In the second part, at the first battle of St. Albans, the son of Lord Clifford finds the body of his father, and his mind leaps at once from the individual to the universal.

> O! let the vile world end,
> And the premised flames of the last day
> Knit earth and heaven together;
> Now let the general trumpet blow his blast,
> Particularities and petty sounds
> To cease! Wast thou ordain'd, dear father,
> To lose thy youth in peace, and to achieve
> The silver livery of advised age,
> And, in thy reverence and thy chair-days, thus
> To die in ruffian battle? Even at this sight
> My heart is turn'd to stone: and while 'tis mine
> It shall be stony. York not our old men spares;
> No more will I their babes: tears virginal
> Shall be to me even as the dew to fire;
> And beauty, that the tyrant oft reclaims,
> Shall to my flaming wrath be oil and flax.
> Henceforth I will not have to do with pity:
> Meet I an infant of the house of York,
> Into as many gobbets will I cut it
> As wild Medea young Absyrtus did:
> In cruelty will I seek out my fame. . . .

He keeps this promise in the third part, when he kills the unarmed youngest son of York: "Thy father slew my father; therefore die"—thus giving one more instance of the apparently unending process of wrong and retribution that runs through these plays. In the speech I have just quoted Mr. Cairncross has a note on the dozen lines beginning

⁷I have run together quotations from A. S. Cairncross's introduction to the Arden editions of 2 *Henry VI* and 3 *Henry VI*.

> O! let the vile world end,
> And the premised flames of the last day
> Knit earth and heaven together;
> Now let the general trumpet blow his blast. . . .

He comments that we have here "a regular Shakespearean group of images, compounded from various sources, and centring on the Last Judgment, as presented in medieval art and thought. The situation is always one of horror aroused by the death of a dear friend or relative, and the effect on the bereaved that of chaos come again," and he gives examples from *Macbeth* and *King Lear*. There are in fact more anticipatory echoes of *Lear* than Cairncross notices, but he has made the essential point. From the start Shakespeare is aware that man's perverted energies can produce the kind of universal anarchy associated with the end of the world. The same note is sounded at the beginning of *2 Henry IV*, in the lament of Northumberland for his son, Harry Percy, killed at Shrewsbury:

> Now let not Nature's hand
> Keep the wild flood confin'd! Let order die!
> And let this world no longer be a stage
> To feed contention in a ling'ring act;
> But let one spirit of the first-born Cain
> Reign in all bosoms, that, each heart being set
> On bloody courses, the rude scene may end,
> And darkness be the burier of the dead!

And it recurs in *King Lear*, where we have one of the most powerful representations in all literature of men using their reason in the service of brute appetite and assertiveness—"hog in sloth, fox in stealth, wolf in greediness, dog in madness, lion in prey." As Albany says in a speech of crucial significance,

> If that the heavens do not their visible spirits
> Send quickly down to tame these vilde offences,
> It will come,
> Humanity must perforce prey on itself,
> Like monsters of the deep.

In all these envisagings of a general doom, not super-
naturally determined but brought on by man himself, there
is, it seems to me, a peculiar urgency. In *The Decline and
Fall of the Roman Empire* there are horrors enough, but they
do not disturb the assured decorum of Gibbon's prose: the
horrors belong to the past, and, Gibbon implies, we can in-
spect them from our civilized vantage-point. For Shakespeare
the menace is ever present and frightening.

Of course, as soon as one has said that, other complementary truths have to be recalled. Besides tragedies Shakespeare also wrote comedies. And if there is often—Dr. Johnson said always—"some melancholy in his mirth," he could
also be simply funny in a high-spirited life-enhancing way.
Recall, as just one example, Falstaff's self-commiserations in
The Merry Wives of Windsor as he recovers from the ducking
that rewarded his amorousness:

> Have I lived to be carried in a basket, like a barrow of
> butcher's offal, and to be thrown in the Thames? Well,
> if I be served such another trick, I'll have my brains ta'en
> out and buttered, and give them to a dog for a New
> Year's gift. The rogues slighted me into the river with as
> little remorse as they would have drowned a blind bitch's
> puppies, fifteen i'th' litter; and you may know by my size
> that I have a kind of alacrity in sinking.

I suppose I am not alone in finding that this always makes
me laugh, even in a silent reading. *The Merry Wives* was
produced not long after—perhaps even at much the same time
as—the somber part 2 of *Henry IV*, and not so very long be-

fore *Hamlet*. This continuing ability to produce belly-laughs (something quite different from Conrad's sardonic humor in *Heart of Darkness*, where we are also invited to a view of the depths) means that Shakespeare's sense of the fragility of civilized forms—"to ride on a bay trotting-horse over four-inch'd bridges"—had nothing obsessive about it: it was part—enormously important, but only a part—of a comprehensive vision that we need a lifetime to explore.

There is another qualification, too, to which I shall come presently. For the moment I am simply calling attention to the fact that in the early history plays we are presented with a picture of human life in which unrestrained power-seeking can split wide open the social fabric. This is not just a view of past history: it is a vision of the latent possibilities of the present, of all our presents. Harry Levin, in the title essay in *Shakespeare and the Revolution of the Times*, remarks that the Elizabethan proponents of tradition, hierarchy, and fixity "may have been protesting overmuch out of a distrust of innovation, alienation, and disruption." Shakespeare shared the "official" preoccupation with order—but with a difference. Like Plato he knew, and came to recognize more and more clearly, that a healthy social order was not merely analogous to, but was intimately connected with, an inner order, even though that is not easy to define. And unlike the majority of his contemporaries he had a profound and terrifying vision of what, then as now, lay not far below the surface. In Levin's words "behind the gorgeous pageantry and the official mythology looms an apparition of chaos." It is because Shakespeare from the start had what Henry James was to call "the imagination of disaster" that even his earliest "history" plays go so far beyond Tudor history, as they go beyond the merely political.

I am picking out two characteristics of Shakespeare's way of dealing with historical material. The first I have dwelt on at some length: it is what I think it is not too emotional to call an awareness of the abyss underlying the forms of civilization. The second, of at least equal importance, is harder to define. Perhaps I can help myself out by referring to two writers of our time whose concern for history is also a concern for the present. Henry Gifford, in his recent book on Pasternak, has an admirable chapter on that strange great novel *Doctor Zhivago*. Speaking of the episodes set in the postrevolutionary civil war, Gifford remarks: "There was abundant bestiality in either camp, as the book reveals. Pasternak's aim is to bring the whole age to judgment, and the verdict comes from Lara. She blames the World War for having destroyed the authority of individual conscience: 'It was then that falsehood came to the Russian land. . . . There began to grow the dominion of the phrase, at first monarchical, then revolutionary.'" That is why Yury Zhivago comes to set so high a value on poetry—because poetry is at the opposite pole from the bombastic, and therefore mendacious, rhetoric of politics.

"The dominion of the phrase": in his sense of the connection between perversions of language and social evil Pasternak is at one with Solzhenitsyn. In the latter's Nobel Prize speech (published in *Index on Censorship*, autumn/winter 1972) he wrote:

> They will say to us: what can literature do against the remorseless onslaught of open violence? Ah, but let us not forget that violence does not and cannot exist on its own, it is inextricably bound up with the *lie*. The link between them is fundamental and entirely natural and organic. Violence has nothing to cover itself with except the lie, and the lie has no way of maintaining itself except by violence. Anyone who proclaims violence as his *method* is inexorably bound to choose the lie as his principle.

And later in the same speech: "In the Russian language the

most popular proverbs are about *truth*. They emphatically express the not inconsiderable and hard experience of the people and sometimes do so with astonishing force: *One word of truth shall outweigh the whole world.*"

The relevance of this to my main theme is clear. Shakespeare, as poet, is committed to the language of truth—precise, firm, flexible, and subtle, a language that can "thoughts unveil in their dumb cradles"—whether in the realm of history and politics or elsewhere. The simple prescription "True poets must be truthful" (Wilfred Owen's phrase) is not so simple as it seems. I quote it here because in mastering the art of telling "the whole truth" (as much, at least, as human minds can comprehend) Shakespeare the dramatist learned to distinguish between saying what one means and saying what one would like other people to believe, what one would like to believe, and even what one thinks he means. In other words Shakespeare shows an increasing mastery of the language of deception, including self-deception. Recent critics have made much of Shakespeare's knowledge and use of the rhetorical skills with which his contemporaries were much concerned. One can compile from his works an impressive list of those technical devices described at length in the books of rhetoric. He was to make fun of them, but he certainly used them as expressive forms. What has not been noticed is that even in these early plays Shakespeare shows a distrust of rhetoric. Sometimes you take it "straight." But sometimes, I think, you are encouraged to ask *what lies behind* the arts of formal invective or persuasion —"the dominion of the phrase." To look forward a little, *Richard II* is not only the tragedy of a particular man: it is a political play (the materials drawn from Hall and Holinshed, but shaped and altered), and it centers on—two difficult but important words—justice, or the lack of it, in the state, and sincerity, or the lack of it, in the individual. In other words, as I have suggested elsewhere, the play incites us to make a connection between Richard's self-indulgent public rhetoric and his failure as a ruler. It is putting it mildly to say that almost all his public speeches, taken in their context, impel us to look rather critically at his assertion of the divine aid that anointed kings may unquestioningly expect. Harry Levin, in the essay from which I have quoted, speaks of Shakespeare's "unremitting quest for justice—not legal justice, which is constantly being challenged, nor poetic justice, which too neatly balances sufferings with rewards and villainies with punishment, but the problematic sanction of a higher morality, a tragic ethos, an insight into the *rerum natura*," and, we may add, a creative principle. That insight, that principle of growth, is inseparable from a respect for, and mastery of, the living language. Shakespeare reminds us that the poet's public role is to cure us of our speech-defects and their underlying consequences—cracks into chaos.

Although the second tetralogy of Shakespeare's English history plays is far more enjoyable and important than the first, I can give only a few sentences to it here. I have touched on *Richard II*. This, in the "historical" sequence, was followed by *Henry IV;* and although both parts of that play are about much more than history and politics, a strong political interest continues and deepens. Not only do the plays show the continuing tug of disruption: the nature of political order and authority, even though it is necessary, is now put in question. As before, Shakespeare does not tell us what to think: he merely asks us to do some thinking, as he himself had thought when pondering the chronicles. There is, for example, that typically Lancastrian figure—more fox than lion—Prince John, who disarms the leaders of the rebellious Northumberland faction by promising redress of their grievances and then, when their army is disbanded, executes them. Of this Dr. Johnson wrote: "It cannot but raise some indignation to find this horrible violation of faith passed over thus slightly by the poet, without any note of censure or detestation." And later in the eighteenth century, which liked its morals explicit, Maurice Morgann wished that Shakespeare, for his own credit, had marked the scene "with the blackest strokes of Infamy." But of course Shakespeare had no need to be explicit. Prince John's action, attributed by Holinshed to the Earl of Westmoreland, and noted in the margin as "politike dealing," is not only "politic" in the pejorative Elizabethan sense: it is an example of the dry light in which Shakespeare examines the nature of state power. And I think the same irony plays a large part in *Henry V*. I do not mean that we should in any simple-minded twentieth-century way stand on its head the view popular in Elizabethan times and later: that the play is a celebration of the patriot warrior-king. It is merely that even here there is a more complex attitude toward the realities of power than is sometimes supposed. We may briefly return to the question of rhetoric versus poetry. Henry's warlike speech to the troops before Harfleur is more forced, less *true,* than the Duke of Burgundy's long and splendid eulogy of peace (5.2): peace not as the mere absence of war, but as positive, energetic, and creative. But with *Henry V* Shakespeare had virtually exhausted what he could get from the English histories of his day. He was to write other political plays based on historical material (*Julius Caesar, Coriolanus*). But by 1599 he needed, so to speak, more elbow-room. His concern with political anarchy and the threat of chaos even more embracing than political disruption finds its supreme embodiment in *King Lear*.

I hope all this has been clear enough not to need a summarizing conclusion. But I should like to add a postscript. It is well known that Shakespeare often uses very comic scenes for very serious purposes. Thus in *2 Henry VI* there is the demagogue Cade addressing his followers.

> Be brave then: for your captain is brave, and vows reformation. There shall be in England seven half-penny loaves sold for a penny; the three-hoop'd pot shall have ten hoops; and I will make it felony to drink small beer. All the realm shall be in common, and in Cheapside shall

my palfrey go to grass. And when I am king, as king I
will be—
All. God save your Majesty!

And at the end of Shakespeare's career, in *The Tempest,* Caliban, dead-drunk, sings his song of liberty as he follows
Stephano and Trinculo into new servitude: "Freedom, high-
day! high-day, freedom!" In *Coriolanus,* perhaps the greatest
of the political tragedies, there is a rare touch of comedy
when the servants of Tullus Aufidius, learning that Coriolanus has been reconciled to their master in an alliance
against Rome, rejoice in the prospect of a new war.

> *Second Serv.* Why, then we shall have a stirring world
> again. This peace is nothing but to rust iron, increase
> tailors, and breed ballad-makers.
> *First Serv.* Let me have war, say I: it exceeds peace as
> far as day does night; it's sprightly, [waking], audible,
> and full of vent. Peace is a very apoplexy, lethargy;
> mulled, deaf, sleepy, insensible; a getter of more bastard
> children than war's a destroyer of men.
> *Second Serv.* 'Tis so: and as wars, in some sort, may be
> said to be a ravisher, so it cannot be denied but peace
> is a great maker of cuckolds.
> *First Serv.* Ay, and it makes men hate one another.
> *Third Serv.* Reason: because they then less need one
> another. The wars for my money.

Funny? Well, yes, of course; but not only funny. For what
we have here is not only a devastating parody of the values
that Volumnia had expressed with some force earlier in the
play, but sentiments that have played their part in our own
troubled century. The German historian Fritz Fischer, in *War
of Illusions: German Policies from 1911 to 1914,* has a section on "The Nation's Psychological Preparations for War."
I select what seem to be representative views from a variety
of "organs of opinion":

As late as 29th December 1912 the Editor-in-Chief of the *Deutsche Arbeitgeberzeitung*, Felix Kuh, . . . had come out *against* the argument that a "European world war" was inevitable. On 9th February 1913 faced with the new army bill, Kuh took a different line: war now appeared "sometimes" as "the only possible means of curing existing diseases", in short: "war as the saviour". . . . In December 1912 the leading Conservative paper in East Prussia . . . expressed itself in favour of a "brisk, merry [frisch, fröhlich] war". . . . On 25th January 1913 Otto von Gottberg wrote an article entitled "Der Krieg". . . . He acclaimed war as "the noblest and most sacred manifestation of human activity. . . ." Let us therefore make fun of old women in men's trousers who are afraid of war and complain that it is horrible or ugly. No, war is beautiful. Its noble grandeur raises man high above earthly, daily things.

And more to the same effect, including an extract from a Berlin newspaper which, on Christmas Eve 1912, praised war "as part of a divine world order" which ensured the preservation "of all that is good, beautiful, great and noble in nature and in true civilization." Shakespeare's Volscian serving-men are not, obviously, ancient Italians; nor are they simply Elizabethans; they are, one is tempted to say, timeless figures—though one hopes they are not quite that. But their few minutes on the stage—anticipating what one may properly call demonic views of historical development and destiny in a later age—serve to remind us that Shakespeare's dealings with history are part of an exploration of political attitudes and acts that are no more merely political than they are merely of historical interest. That is one reason why his history plays continue to be read and performed.

13
How Many Children Had Lady Macbeth?

FOR some years there have been signs of a re-orientation of Shake-speare criticism. The books that I have in mind have little in common with the majority of those that have been written on Shakespeare, but they are likely to have a decisive influence upon criticism in the future. The present, therefore, is a favourable time in which to take stock of the traditional methods, and to inquire why so few of the many books that have been written are relevant to our study of Shakespeare as a poet. The inquiry involves an examination of certain critical presuppositions, and of these the most fruitful of irrelevancies is the assumption that Shakespeare was pre-eminently a great 'creator of characters'. So extensive was his knowledge of the human heart (so runs the popular opinion) that he was able to project himself into the minds of an infinite variety of men and women and present them 'real as life' before us. Of course, he was a great poet as well, but the poetry is an added grace which gives to the atmosphere of the plays a touch of 'magic' and which provides us with the thrill of single memorable lines and lyric passages.

This assumption that it is the main business of a writer—other than the lyric poet—to create characters is not, of course, confined to criticism of Shakespeare, it long ago invaded criticism of the novel. 'Character creation', says Mr. Logan Pearsall Smith, 'is regarded as the very essence of English fiction, the *sine qua non* of novel writing.' And in a recent book of extracts from Scott, Mr. Hugh Walpole writes:

> The test of a character in any novel is that it should have existed before the book that reveals it to us began and should continue after the book is closed. . . . These are our friends for life—but it is the penalty of the more subconscious school of modern fiction that, when the book is closed, all that we have in our hands is a

boot-button, a fragment of tulle, or a cocktail shaker. We have dived, it seems, so very deep and come to the surface again with so little in our grasp.... But (he continues) however gay, malicious, brilliant and amusing they [modern novels] may be, this hard business of creating a world for us, a world filled with people in whom we may believe, whom we may know better than we know our friends, is the gift of the very few.[1]

It should be obvious that a criterion for the novel by which we should have to condemn *Wuthering Heights*, *Heart of Darkness*, *Ulysses*, *To the Lighthouse* and the bulk of the work of D. H. Lawrence does not need to be very seriously considered.

There is no need to search for examples in the field of Shakespeare criticism. In the latest book on Shakespeare that has come to hand, we read: 'His creations are not *ideas* but *characters*—real men and women, fellow humans with ourselves. We can follow their feelings and thoughts like those of our most intimate acquaintances.'[2] The case is even better illustrated by Ellen Terry's recently published *Lectures on Shakespeare*. To her the characters are all flesh and blood and she exercises her ingenuity on such questions as whether Portia or Bellario thought of the famous quibble, and whether it was justified.[3] And how did the Boy in *Henry V* learn to speak French? 'Robin's French is quite fluent. Did he learn to speak the lingo from Prince Hal, or from Falstaff in London, or did he pick it up during his few weeks in France with the army?'[4] Ellen Terry of course does not represent critical Authority; the point is not that she could write as she did, but that the book was popular. Most of the reviewers were enthusiastic. The *Times Literary Supplement* said that the book showed 'the insight of a genius', and the reviewer in the *Times*, speaking of her treatment of Falstaff's page, declared, 'To Ellen Terry, Robin was as alive and as real as could be; and we feel as if she had given us a new little friend to laugh with and be sorry for'.

And if we wish for higher authority we have only to turn to the book by Mr. Logan Pearsall Smith, *On Reading Shakespeare*. Mr. Smith demands respect as the author of *Words and Idioms*, in which he showed the kind of interest in language needed for the critical

---

[1] *The Waverley Pageant*, pp. 38–40.
[2] Ranjee G. Shahani, *Shakespeare Through Eastern Eyes*, p. 177.
[3] *Four Lectures on Shakespeare*, pp. 119–120.   [4] *Op. cit.*, p. 49.

approach to Shakespeare. But there is nothing of that interest in the present essay. Here Shakespeare is praised because he provides 'the illusion of reality', because he puts 'living people' upon the stage, because he creates characters who are 'independent of the work in which they appear . . . and when the curtain falls they go on living in our imaginations and remain as real to us as our familiar friends'.—'Those inhabitants of the world of poetry who, in our imagination, lead their immortal lives apart.' [1]

The most illustrious example is, of course, Dr. Bradley's *Shakespearean Tragedy*. The book is too well known to require much descriptive comment, but it should be observed that the Notes, in which the detective interest supersedes the critical, form a logical corollary to the main portions of the book. In the Lectures on *Macbeth* we learn that Macbeth was 'exceedingly ambitious. He must have been so by temper. The tendency must have been greatly strengthened by his marriage.' But 'it is difficult to be sure of his customary demeanour'. And Dr. Bradley seems surprised that 'This bold ambitious man of action has, within certain limits, the imagination of a poet'. These minor points are symptomatic. It is assumed throughout the book that the most profitable discussion of Shakespeare's tragedies is in terms of the characters of which they are composed.—'The centre of the tragedy may be said with equal truth to lie in action issuing from character, or in character issuing in action. . . . What we feel strongly, as a tragedy advances to its close, is that the calamities and catastrophe follow inevitably from the deeds of men, and that the main source of these deeds is character. The dictum that, with Shakespeare, "character is destiny" is no doubt an exaggeration . . . but it is the exaggeration of a vital truth.' It is this which leads Dr. Bradley to ask us to imagine Posthumus in the place of Othello, Othello in the place of Posthumus, and to conjecture upon Hamlet's whereabouts at the time of his father's death.

The influence of the assumption is pervasive. Not only are all the books of Shakespeare criticism (with a very few exceptions) based upon it, it invades scholarship (the notes to the indispens-

---

[1] Mr. Smith reminds us that, " There are other elements too in this draught of Shakespeare's brewing—in the potent wine that came to fill at last the great jewelled cup of words he fashioned, to drink from which is one of the most wonderful experiences life affords."

able Arden edition may be called in evidence), and in school children are taught to think they have 'appreciated' the poet if they are able to talk about the characters—aided no doubt by the neat summaries provided by Mr. Verity which they learn so assiduously before examinations.

In the mass of Shakespeare criticism there is not a hint that 'character'—like 'plot', 'rhythm', 'construction' and all our other critical counters—is merely an abstraction from the total response in the mind of the reader or spectator, brought into being by written or spoken words; that the critic therefore—however far he may ultimately range—begins with the words of which a play is composed. This applies equally to the novel or any other form of art that uses language as its medium. 'A Note on Fiction' by Mr. C. H. Rickword in *The Calendar of Modern Letters* expresses the point admirably with regard to the novel: 'The form of a novel only exists as a balance of response on the part of the reader. Hence schematic plot is a construction of the reader's that corresponds to an aspect of the response and stands in merely diagrammatic relation to the source. Only as precipitates from the memory are plot or character tangible; yet only in solution have either any emotive valency.'[1]

A Shakespeare play is a dramatic poem. It uses action, gesture, formal grouping and symbols, and it relies upon the general conventions governing Elizabethan plays. But, we cannot too often remind ourselves, its end is to communicate a rich and controlled experience by means of words—words used in a way to which, without some training, we are no longer accustomed to respond. To stress in the conventional way character or plot or any of the other abstractions that can be made, is to impoverish the total response. 'It is in the total situation rather than in the wrigglings of individual emotion that the tragedy lies.'[2] 'We should not look for perfect verisimilitude to life,' says Mr. Wilson Knight, 'but rather see each play as an expanded metaphor, by means of which the original vision has been projected into forms

[1] *The Calendar*, October 1926. In an earlier review, Mr. Rickword wrote: ' Mere degree of illusion provides no adequate test : novelists who can do nothing else are able to perform the trick with ease, since " nothing is easier than to create for oneself the idea of a human being, a figure and a character, from glimpses and anecdotes ".' (*The Calendar*, July 1926 ; both pieces are reprinted in *Towards Standards of Criticism*, Wishart.)

[2] M. C. Bradbrook, *Elizabethan Stage Conditions*, p. 102.

roughly correspondent with actuality, conforming thereto with greater or less exactitude according to the demands of its nature. . . . The persons, ultimately, are not human at all, but purely symbols of a poetic vision.' [1]

It would be easy to demonstrate that this approach is essential even when dealing with plays like *Hamlet* or *Macbeth* which can be made to yield something very impressive in the way of 'character'. And it is the only approach which will enable us to say anything at all relevant about plays like *Measure for Measure* or *Troilus and Cressida* which have consistently baffled the critics. And apart from Shakespeare, what are we to say of *Tamburlaine*, *Edward II*, *The Revenger's Tragedy* or *The Changeling* if we do not treat them primarily as poems?

Read with attention, the plays themselves will tell us how they should be read. But those who prefer another kind of evidence have only to consider the contemporary factors that conditioned the making of an Elizabethan play, namely the native tradition of English drama descending from the morality plays, the construction of the playhouse and the conventions depending, in part, upon that construction, and the tastes and expectations of the audience. I have not space to deal with any of these in detail. Schücking has shown how large a part was played in the Elizabethan drama by 'primitive technique', but the full force of the morality tradition remains to be investigated. It is, I think, impossible to appreciate *Troilus and Cressida* on the one hand, or the plays of Middleton (and even of Ben Jonson) on the other, without an understanding of the 'morality' elements that they contain. As for the second factor, the physical peculiarities of the stage and Elizabethan dramatic conventions, I can only refer to Miss Bradbrook's *Elizabethan Stage Conditions*. We can make a hasty summary by saying that each of these factors determined that Elizabethan drama should be non-realistic, conditioned by conventions that helped to govern the total response obtained by means of the language of each play. A consideration of Shakespeare's use of language demands a consideration of the reading and listening habits of his audience. Contrary to the accepted view that the majority of these were crude and unlettered, caring only for fighting and foolery, bombast and bawdry, but able to *stand* a great

---
[1] G. Wilson Knight, *The Wheel of Fire*, p. 16.

deal of poetry, I think there is evidence (other than the plays themselves) that very many of them had an educated interest in words, a passionate concern for the possibilities of language and the subtleties of poetry. At all events they were trained, by pamphlets, by sermons and by common conversation, to listen or to read with an athleticism which we, in the era of the *Daily Mail* and the Best Seller, have consciously to acquire or do our best to acquire. And all of them shared the speech idiom that is the basis of Shakespeare's poetry.[1]

We are faced with this conclusion: the only profitable approach to Shakespeare is a consideration of his plays as dramatic poems, of his use of language to obtain a total complex emotional response. Yet the bulk of Shakespeare criticism is concerned with his characters, his heroines, his love of Nature or his 'philosophy' —with everything, in short, except with the words on the page, which it is the main business of the critic to examine. I wish to consider as briefly as possible how this paradoxical state of affairs arose. To examine the historical development of the kind of criticism that is mainly concerned with 'character' is to strengthen the case against it.

A start must be made towards the end of the seventeenth century, and it is tempting to begin with Thomas Rymer. If Rymer is representative his remarks on *Othello* [2] show how completely the Elizabethan tradition had been lost. Of one of the storm speeches (II, i), important both as symbol and ironic commentary, he says, 'Once in a man's life, he might be content at *Bedlam* to hear such a rapture. In a Play one should speak like a man of business.' He had no conception of the function of rhetoric on the Elizabethan stage; of Othello's speech,

> O now, for ever
> Farewell the Tranquill minde; farewell Content;

he says, 'These lines are recited here, not for any thing Poetical in them, besides the sound, that pleases'. Combining a demand

[1] I have presented some of the evidence in an essay on 'Education and the Drama in the Age of Shakespeare,' *The Criterion*, July 1932.
[2] In *A Short View of Tragedy* (1693).

for realistic verisimilitude with an acceptance of the neo-classic canons he has no difficulty in ridiculing the play:

> The moral, sure, of this Fable is very instructive.
> First, This may be a caution to all Maidens of Quality how, without their Parents consent, they run away with Blackamoors.
> Secondly, This may be a warning to all good Wives that they look well to their Linnen.
> Thirdly, This may be a lesson to Husbands that before their Jealousie be Tragical the proofs may be Mathematical.

And so on to the triumphant conclusion:

> What can remain with the Audience to carry home with them from this sort of Poetry for their use and edification? how can it work, unless (instead of settling the mind and purging our passions) to delude our senses, disorder our thoughts, addle our brain, pervert our affections, hair our imaginations, corrupt our appetite, and fill our head with vanity, confusion, *Tintamarre*, and Jingle-jangle, beyond what all the Parish Clarks of *London* with their *Old Testament* farces and interludes, in *Richard* the second's time, could ever pretend to? . . . The tragical part is plainly none other than a Bloody Farce, without salt or savour.[1]

But perhaps Rymer is not sufficiently representative for his work to be called as evidence. He had a following which included such critics as Gildon and Dennis, and even Pope was influenced by him, but he was censured by Dryden, Addison and Rowe, amongst others, and the rules he stood for never gained anything like a complete ascendancy in the criticism of the eighteenth century. For evidence of the kind that we require we must turn to Dryden, who was not only 'a representative man' but also an enthusiastic admirer of Shakespeare, and if he was not 'the father of English criticism', he was at least a critic whose opinions must be reckoned with. When Rymer says of the Temptation scene in *Othello*, 'Here we see a known Language

---

[1] I cannot understand Mr. Eliot's remark that he has 'never seen a cogent refutation of Thomas Rymer's objections to *Othello*' (*Selected Essays*, p. 141). A narrow sensibility, a misunderstanding of the nature of dramatic conventions, and the command of a few debating tricks (e.g. the description of the play in terms of the external plot, which would make any tragedy look ridiculous) are sufficient to account for his objections. A point by point refutation is possible but hardly necessary.

does wofully encumber and clog the operation, as either forc'd, or heavy, or trifling, or incoherent, or improper, or most what improbable', it is permissible to disregard him; but when we find that Dryden makes similar remarks of other plays of Shakespeare, it is obvious not only that ways of thought and feeling have changed sufficiently since the Elizabethan period to demand a different idiom, but that the Shakespearean idiom is, for the time being, out of the reach of criticism. In the Preface to his version of *Troilus and Cressida* (1679) Dryden says: 'Yet it must be allowed to the present age, that the tongue in general is so much refined since Shakespeare's time that many of his words, and more of his phrases, are scarce intelligible. And of those which we understand, some are ungrammatical, others coarse; and his whole style is so pestered with figurative expressions, that it is as affected as it is obscure.' And of *Troilus and Cressida*: 'I undertook to remove that heap of rubbish under which many excellent thoughts lay wholly buried . . . I need not say that I have refined the language, which before was obsolete.' [1]

Not only the idiom but the Elizabethan conventions were now inaccessible. In the *Defence of the Epilogue* (1672) Dryden takes exception to *The Winter's Tale, Love's Labour's Lost* and *Measure for Measure*, 'which were either grounded on impossibilities, or at least so meanly written, that the comedy neither moved your mirth, nor the serious part your concernment'. And he proceeds to criticize Fletcher in the true spirit of William Archer.

The implications of Dryden's remarks became the commonplaces of criticism for the succeeding generations. It was permissible to speak of Shakespeare's 'Deference paid to the reigning Barbarism' (Theobald), and 'The vicious taste of the age' (Hanmer), and to write, 'The Audience was generally composed of the meaner sort of people' (Pope), and 'The publick was gross and dark. . . . Those to whom our author's labours were ex-

---

[1] Later he remarks: 'I will not say of so great a poet that he distinguished not the blown puffy style from true sublimity ; but I may venture to maintain that the fury of his fancy often transported him beyond the bounds of judgment, either in coining of new words and phrases, or racking words which were in use into the violence of a catachresis. It is not that I would explode the use of metaphors from passion, for Longinus thinks 'em necessary to raise it : but to use 'em at every word, to say nothing without a metaphor, a simile, an image, or description, is, I doubt, to smell a little too strongly of the buskin.'—The force of Elizabethan language springs from its metaphorical life.

hibited had more skill in pomps or processions than in poetical language' (Johnson). In his *Preface* (1747) Warburton writes:

> The Poet's hard and unnatural construction . . . was the effect of mistaken Art and Design. The Public Taste was in its Infancy; and delighted (as it always does during that state) in the high and turgid; which leads the writer to disguise a vulgar expression with hard and forced constructions, whereby the sentence frequently becomes cloudy and dark . . . an obscurity that ariseth, not from the licentious use of a single Term, but from the unnatural arrangement of a whole sentence. . . . Not but in his best works (he continues), we must allow, he is often so natural and flowing, so pure and correct, that he is even a model for style and language.

Of all the eighteenth-century critics only Johnson (an exception we have often to make) at times transcended the limitations of conventional Shakespeare criticism. He censures Hanmer, who in his edition of Shakespeare 'is solicitous to reduce to grammar what he could not be sure that his author intended to be grammatical', and he writes admirably of 'a style which never becomes obsolete. . . . This style is probably to be sought in the common intercourse of life, among those who speak only to be understood, without ambition of elegance.' But he stops short at that. This 'conversation above grossness and below refinement, where propriety resides' is where Shakespeare 'seems to have gathered his *comick* dialogue'. But it is in Shakespeare's tragedies that his style is most vividly idiomatic and full bodied, and Johnson was capable of writing, 'His comedy pleases by the thoughts and language, and his tragedy for the greater part by incident and action'. Johnson's great virtues as a critic did not include an understanding of Shakespeare's idiom. For him, 'The style of Shakespeare was in itself ungrammatical, perplexed and obscure', and many passages remained 'obscured by obsolete phraseology, or by the writer's unskilfulness and affectation'. We remember also how he could 'scarcely check his risibility' at the 'blanket of the dark' passage in *Macbeth*.

It should not be necessary to insist that I do not wish to deny the achievements of the Augustan age in poetry and criticism. But an age of which the commonplaces of criticism were that 'Well placing of words, for the sweetness of pronunciation, was not known till Mr. Waller introduced it',[1] and that Pope's *Homer* 'tuned the English tongue';[2] an age which produced the *Essay on Criticism* and the *Satires of Dr. Donne Versified,* and which consistently neglected the Metaphysical poets and the minor Elizabethans, such an age was incapable of fully understanding Shakespeare's use of words. Since the total response to a Shakespeare play can only be obtained by an exact and sensitive study of the quality of the verse, of the rhythm and imagery, of the controlled associations of the words and their emotional and intellectual force, in short by an exact and sensitive study of Shakespeare's handling of language, it is hardly reasonable to expect very much relevant criticism of Shakespeare in the eighteenth century. What can be expected is criticism at one remove from the plays, that is, of every aspect that can be extracted from a play and studied in comparative isolation; of this kind of criticism an examination of 'characters' is the most obvious example.

A significant passage occurs in Shaftesbury's *Advice to an Author,* published in 1710·

> Our old dramatick Poet, Shakespeare, may witness for our good Ear and manly Relish. Notwithstanding his natural Rudeness, his unpolish'd style, his antiquated Phrase and Wit, his want of Method and Coherence, and his Deficiency in almost all the Graces and Ornaments of this kind of Writings; yet by the Justness of his *Moral,* the Aptness of many of his *Descriptions,* and the plain and natural Turn of several of his *Characters,* he pleases his Audience, and often gains their Ear, without a single Bribe from Luxury or Vice.

We see here the beginning of that process of splitting up the indivisible unity of a Shakespeare play into various elements abstracted from the whole. If a play of Shakespeare's could not be appreciated as a whole, it was still possible to admire and to discuss his moral sentiments, his humour, his poetic descriptions and the life-likeness of his characters. Thus, Warburton mentions '. . . the Author's Beauties . . . whether in Style, Thought, Sentiment, Character, or Composition'.

The intensive study of Shakespeare's characters was not fully developed until the second half of the eighteenth century. Dryden had remarked that 'No man ever drew so many characters,

---

[1] Dryden, *Defence of the Epilogue.*   [2] Johnson, *Life of Pope.*

or generally distinguished 'em from one another, excepting only Jonson', and Pope observed, 'His *Characters* are so much Nature herself, that 'tis a sort of injury to call them by so distant a name as copies of her. . . . Every single character in Shakespeare is as much an Individual as those in Life itself; it is as impossible to find any two alike'; and Theobald echoed him in a lyrical passage, —'If we look into his Characters, and how they are furnished and proportion'd to the Employment he cuts out for them, how are we taken up with the Mastery of his Portraits! What draughts of Nature! What variety of Originals, and how differing each from the other!' [1] But in the second half of the century character study became one of the main objects of Shakespeare criticism. This is sufficiently indicated by the following titles: *A Philosophical Analysis and Illustration of some of Shakespeare's Remarkable Characters* (Richardson, 1774), *An Essay on the Character of Hamlet* (Pilon, 1777), *Essays on Shakespeare's Dramatic Characters* (Richardson, 1784), *Remarks on some of the Characters of Shakespeare* (Whately, 1785), *Shakespeare's Imitation of Female Characters* (Richardson, 1789), and so on.

Of the essays of this kind, the most famous is Maurice Morgann's *Essay on the Dramatic Character of Sir John Falstaff* (1777). The pivot of Morgann's method is to be found in one of his footnotes:

> The reader must be sensible of something in the composition of *Shakespeare's* characters, which renders them essentially different from those drawn by other writers. The characters of every Drama must indeed be grouped, but in the groups of other poets the parts which are not seen do not in fact exist. But there is a certain roundness and integrity in the forms of *Shakespeare*, which give them an independence as well as a relation, insomuch that we often meet with passages which, tho' perfectly felt, cannot be sufficiently explained in words, without unfolding the whole character of the speaker. . . . The reader will not now be surprised if I affirm that those characters in Shakespeare, which are seen only in part, are yet capable of being unfolded and understood in the whole; every part being in fact relative, and inferring all the rest. It is true that the point of action or sentiment, which we are most concerned in, is always held out for our special notice. But who

[1] Pope adds : 'Had all the speeches been printed without the very names of the Persons, I believe one might have apply'd them with certainty to every speaker.'

does not perceive that there is a peculiarity about it, which conveys a relish of the whole? And very frequently, when no particular point presses, he boldly makes a character act and speak from those parts of the composition which are *inferred* only, and not distinctly shown. This produces a wonderful effect; it seems to carry us beyond the poet to nature itself, and gives an integrity and truth to facts and character, which they could not otherwise obtain. And this is in reality that art in *Shakespeare* which, being withdrawn from our notice, we more emphatically call *nature*. A felt propriety and truth from causes unseen, I take to be the highest point of Poetic composition. If the characters of *Shakespeare* are thus *whole*, and as it were original, whilst those of almost all other writers are mere imitation, *it may be fit to consider them rather as Historic than Dramatic beings; and, when occasion requires, to account for their conduct from the* WHOLE *of character, from general principles, from latent motives, and from policies not avowed.*[1]

It is strange how narrowly Morgann misses the mark. He recognized what can be called the full-bodied quality of Shakespeare's work—it came to him as a feeling of 'roundness and integrity'. But instead of realizing that this quality sprang from Shakespeare's use of words, words which have 'a network of tentacular roots, reaching down to the deepest terrors and desires', he referred it to the characters' 'independence' of the work in which they appeared, and directed his exploration to 'latent motives and policies not avowed'. Falstaff's birth, his early life, his association with John of Gaunt, his possible position as head of his family, his military service and his pension are all examined in order to determine the grand question, 'Is Falstaff a constitutional coward?'[2]

In the Essay, of course, 'Falstaff is the word only. Shakespeare is the theme', and several admirable things are said incidentally. But more than any other man, it seems to me, Morgann has deflected Shakespeare criticism from the proper objects of attention by his preposterous references to those aspects of a 'character' that Shakespeare did not wish to show. He made explicit the assumption on which the other eighteenth-century critics based their work, and that assumption has been pervasive until our own

---

[1] These last italics are mine.

[2] I have discussed Falstaff's dramatic function—the way in which he helps to define Shakespeare's total attitude towards the matter in hand—in *Determinations*, edited by F. R. Leavis (Chatto and Windus).

time. In 1904 Dr. Bradley said of Morgann's essay, 'There is no better piece of Shakespeare criticism in the world'.[1]

I have already suggested the main reason for the eighteenth-century approach to Shakespeare via the characters, namely an inability to appreciate the Elizabethan idiom and a consequent inability to discuss Shakespeare's plays as poetry. And of course the Elizabethan dramatic tradition was lost, and the eighteenth-century critics in general were ignorant of the stage for which Shakespeare wrote.[2] But other factors should also be considered; for instance, the neo-classic insistence upon the moral function of art (before you can judge a person in a play he must have more or less human 'motives'), and the variations of meaning covered by the term 'nature' from the time of Pope to the time of Words-worth. Literary psychologizing also played a part; Kames and William Richardson [3] both found Shakespeare's persons useful illustrations of psychological theories, and Samuel Richardson fostered an interest in introspective analysis, so that Macbeth's soliloquies were assumed to have something in common with the introspections of Clarissa. Finally (and Richardson serves to re-mind us) 'the sentimental age set in early in the eighteenth cen-tury'. If we consider any of the Character writers of the seven-teenth century, Earle, Overbury or Hall, we find that they preserve a distance from their subjects which the eighteenth-century creators of characters do not. The early Characters have a frame round them, whereas the Vicar of Wakefield, Beau Tibbs, and even Sir Roger de Coverley make a more direct appeal to human sympathy and emotion. The 'human' appeal ('These are our friends for life . . .') which has made the fortune of Best Sellers, is an intrusion which vitiated, and can only vitiate, Shakespeare criticism.

One form of the charge against eighteenth-century Shakespeare criticism is that it made the approach too easy. In Pope's edition, 'Some of the most shining passages are distinguish'd by commas in the margin', and Warburton also marked what he considered particularly beautiful passages. From this it was but a step to

---

[1] *The Scottish Historical Review*, Vol. I, p. 291.
[2] 'Shakespeare's plays were to be acted in a paltry tavern, to an unlettered audience, just emerging from barbarity.'—Mrs. Montagu, *Essay on the Writings and Genius of Shakespeare* (Fifth Edition, 1785), p. 13.
[3] See Note p. 306.

collect such passages into anthologies. The numerous editions of the collections of *Beauties* show how popular this method of reading Shakespeare had become by the end of the century. This is an obvious method of simplification, but it is only part of the process whereby various partial (and therefore distorted) responses were substituted for the full complex response demanded by a Shakespeare play—a process that was fatal to criticism.[1]

There is no need, even if it were possible, to discuss nineteenth-century Shakespeare criticism in detail, partly because it is more familiar, partly because—as Mr. Nichol Smith and Mr. Babcock have helped us to realize—the foundations of modern Shakespeare criticism were laid in the eighteenth century. In the nineteenth century the word 'poetry' changed its significance, but preconceptions about 'the poetic' derived from reading Keats (or Tennyson) did not increase understanding of seventeenth-century poetry. And everything combined to foster that kind of interest in Shakespeare that is represented at certain levels by Mrs. Jameson's *Shakespeare's Heroines* and Mary Cowden Clarke's *Girlhood of Shakespeare's Heroines*. In so far as the word 'romantic' has other than an emotive use, it serves to distinguish individualist qualities as opposed to the social qualities covered by 'classical'. One of the main results of the Romantic Revival was the stressing of 'personality' in fiction. At the same time, the growth of the popular novel, from Sir Walter Scott and Charlotte Brontë to our own Best Sellers, encouraged an emotional identification of the reader with hero or heroine (we all 'have a smack of Hamlet' nowadays).[2] And towards the end of the century the influence of Ibsen was responsible for fresh distortions which can best be studied in Archer's *The Old Drama and the New*.

In Shakespeare criticism from Hazlitt to Dowden we find the same kind of irrelevance. Hazlitt says of Lady Macbeth:

> She is a great bad woman, whom we hate, but whom we fear more than we hate.

[1] For the collections of Shakespeare's *Beauties* see R. W. Babcock, *The Genesis of Shakespeare Idolatry*, pp. 115–118. The most famous of these anthologies, William Dodd's *Beauties of Shakespeare*, first published in 1752, not only went through many editions in the eighteenth century, but was frequently reprinted in the nineteenth.

[2] See the letters to popular novelists quoted on p. 58 of Q. D. Leavis's *Fiction and the Reading Public*: 'Your characters are so human that they live with me as friends', etc.

And of the Witches:

> They are hags of mischief, obscene panders to iniquity, malicious from their impotence of enjoyment, enamoured of destruction, because they are themselves unreal, abortive, half-existences—who become sublime from their exemption from all human sympathies and contempt for all human affairs, as Lady Macbeth does by the force of passion! Her fault seems to have been an excess of that strong principle of self-interest and family aggrandisement, not amenable to the common feelings of compassion and justice, which is so marked a feature in barbarous nations and times.

What has this to do with Shakespeare? And what the lyric outburst that Dowden quotes approvingly in his chapter on *Romeo and Juliet*?

> Who does not recall those lovely summer nights, in which the forces of nature seem eager for development, and constrained to remain in drowsy languor? . . . The nightingale sings in the depths of the woods. The flower-cups are half-closed.

And so on.

Wherever we look we find the same reluctance to master the words of the play, the same readiness to abstract a character and treat him (because he is more manageable that way) as a human being. When Gervinus says that the play *Hamlet* 'transports us to a rude and wild period from which Hamlet's whole nature recoils, and to which he falls a sacrifice because by habit, character and education he is alienated from it, and like the boundary stone of a changing civilization touches a world of finer feeling', he exhibits the common fault. In this instance Hamlet is wrenched from his setting and violently imported into the society described by Saxo Grammaticus. Criticism is not all so crass as Sir Herbert Tree's remark that 'We must interpret Macbeth, before and at the crisis, by his just and equitable character as a king that history gives him'.[1] But there are enough modern instances to show that the advice that Hartley Coleridge gave in *Blackwood's* needed no arguing. 'Let us', he said, 'for a moment, put Shakespeare out of the question, and consider Hamlet as a real person, a recently deceased acquaintance.'[2]

---

[1] *Illustrated London News*, September 9, 1911.
[2] *Blackwood's Magazine*, Vol. XXIV (1828), p. 585.

The habit of regarding Shakespeare's persons as 'friends for life' or, maybe, 'deceased acquaintances', is responsible for most of the vagaries that serve as Shakespeare criticism. It accounts for the artificial simplifications of the editors ('In a play one should speak like a man of business'). It accounts for the 'double time' theory for *Othello*. It accounts for Dr. Bradley's Notes. It is responsible for all the irrelevant moral and realistic canons that have been applied to Shakespeare's plays, for the sentimentalizing of his heroes (Coleridge and Goethe on Hamlet) and his heroines. And the loss is incalculable. Losing sight of the *whole* dramatic pattern of each play, we inhibit the development of that full complex response that makes our experience of a Shakespeare play so very much more than an appreciation of 'character'—that is, usually, of somebody else's 'character'. That more complete, more intimate possession can only be obtained by treating Shakespeare primarily as a poet.

SINCE everyone who has written about Shakespeare probably imagines that he has 'treated him primarily as a poet', some explanation is called for. How should we read Shakespeare?

We start with so many lines of verse on a printed page which we read as we should read any other poem. We have to elucidate the meaning (using Dr. Richards's fourfold definition [1]) and to unravel ambiguities; we have to estimate the kind and quality of the imagery and determine the precise degree of evocation of particular figures; we have to allow full weight to each word, exploring its 'tentacular roots', and to determine how it controls and is controlled by the rhythmic movement of the passage in which it occurs. In short, we have to decide exactly why the lines 'are so and not otherwise'.

As we read other factors come into play. The lines have a cumulative effect. 'Plot', aspects of 'character' and recurrent 'themes'—all 'precipitates from the memory'—help

---

[1] *Practical Criticism*, pp. 181–183.

to determine our reaction at a given point. There is a constant reference backwards and forwards. But the work of detailed analysis continues to the last line of the last act. If the razor-edge of sensibility is blunted at any point we cannot claim to have read what Shakespeare wrote, however often our eyes may have travelled over the page. A play of Shakespeare's is a precise particular experience, a poem—and precision and particularity are exactly what is lacking in the greater part of Shakespeare criticism, criticism that deals with *Hamlet* or *Othello* in terms of abstractions that have nothing to do with the unique arrangement of words that constitutes these plays.

Obviously what is wanted to reinforce the case against the traditional methods is a detailed examination of a particular play. Unfortunately anything approaching a complete analysis is precluded by the scope of the present essay. The following remarks on one play, *Macbeth*, are, therefore, not offered as a final criticism of the play; they merely point to factors that criticism must take into account if it is to have any degree of relevance, and emphasize the kind of effect that is necessarily overlooked when we discuss a Shakespeare play in terms of characters 'copied from life', or of 'Shakespeare's knowledge of the human heart'.

Even here there is a further reservation to be made. In all elucidation there is an element of crudity and distortion. 'The true generalization', Mr. Eliot reminds us, 'is not something superposed upon an accumulation of perceptions; the perceptions do not, in a really appreciative mind, accumulate as a mass, but form themselves as a structure; and criticism is the statement in language of this structure; it is a development of sensibility.' [1] Of course, the only *full* statement in language of this structure is in the exact words of the poem concerned; but what the critic can do is to aid 'the return to the work of art with improved perception and intensified, because more conscious, enjoyment'. He can help others to 'force the subject to expose itself', he cannot fully expose it in his own criticism. And in so far as he paraphrases or 'explains the meaning' he must distort. The main difference between good and bad critics is that the good critic points to something that is actually contained in the work of art,

[1] *The Sacred Wood* (Second Edition, 1928), p. 15. See also p. 11, *op. cit.*, and *Selected Essays*, p. 205.

whereas the bad critic points away from the work in question; he introduces extraneous elements into his appreciation—smudges the canvas with his own paint. With this reservation I should like to call the following pages an essay in elucidation.

Macbeth is a statement of evil. I use the word 'statement' (unsatisfactory as it is) in order to stress those qualities that are 'non-dramatic', if drama is defined according to the canons of William Archer or Dr. Bradley. It also happens to be poetry, which means that the apprehension of the whole can only be obtained from a lively attention to the parts, whether they have an immediate bearing on the main action or 'illustrate character', or not. Two main themes, which can only be separated for the purpose of analysis, are blended in the play—the themes of the reversal of values and of unnatural disorder. And closely related to each is a third theme, that of the deceitful appearance, and consequent doubt, uncertainty and confusion. All this is obscured by false assumptions about the category 'drama'; *Macbeth* has greater affinity with *The Waste Land* than with *The Doll's House*.[1]

Each theme is stated in the first act. The first scene, every word of which will bear the closest scrutiny, strikes one dominant chord:

> Faire is foule, and foule is faire,
> Hover through the fogge and filthie ayre.

It is worth remarking that 'Hurley-burley' implies more than 'the tumult of sedition or insurrection'. Both it and 'when the Battaile's lost, and wonne' suggest the kind of metaphysical pitch-and-toss that is about to be played with good and evil. At the same time we hear the undertone of uncertainty: the scene

---

[1] See the Arden Edition, p. xxii: ' The scenes (Act IV, scenes ii and iii) seem to have been composed with evident effort, as if Shakespeare felt the necessity of stretching out his material to the ordinary length of a five-act tragedy, and found lack of *dramatic* material, which was certainly wanting in his authority, Holinshed. *Hence* his introduction in Act V of the famous " sleep-walking scene " . . . and the magnificently *irrelevant* soliloquies of the great protagonist himself.' The italics are mine. There is something wrong with a conception of ' the dramatic ' that leads a critic to speak of Macbeth's final soliloquies as ' irrelevant ' even though ' magnificent '. I deal with the dramatic function of Act IV, scene ii and Act IV, scene iii below.

opens with a question, and the second line suggests a region where the elements are disintegrated as they never are in nature; thunder and lightning are disjoined, and offered as alternatives. We should notice also that the scene expresses the same movement as the play as a whole: the general crystallizes into the immediate particular ('Where the place?.'—'Upon the Heath.'—'There to meet with Macbeth.') and then dissolves again into general presentment of hideous gloom. All is done with the greatest speed, economy and precision.

The second scene is full of images of confusion. It is a general principle in the work of Shakespeare and many of his contemporaries that when A is made to describe X, a minor character or event, the description is not merely immediately applicable to X, it helps to determine the way in which our whole response shall develop. This is rather crudely recognized when we say that certain lines 'create the atmosphere' of the play. Shakespeare's power is seen in the way in which details of this kind develop, check, or provide a commentary upon the main interests that he has aroused.[1] In the present scene the description

> —Doubtfull it stood,
> As two spent Swimmers, that doe cling together,
> And choake their Art—

applies not only to the battle but to the ambiguity of Macbeth's future fortunes. The impression conveyed is not only one of violence but of unnatural violence ('to bathe in reeking wounds') and of a kind of nightmare gigantism—

> Where the Norweyan Banners flowt the Skie.
> And fanne our people cold.

(These lines alone should be sufficient answer to those who doubt the authenticity of the scene.) When Duncan says, 'What he hath lost, Noble *Macbeth* hath wonne', we hear the echo,

> So from that Spring, whence comfort seem'd to come,
> Discomfort swells,

[1] Cf. Coleridge, *Lectures on Shakespeare, etc.* (Bohn Edition), p. 406 : ' Massinger is like a Flemish painter, in whose delineations objects appear as they do in nature, have the same force and truth, and produce the same effect upon the spectator. But Shakespeare is beyond this ;—he always by metaphors and figures involves in the thing considered a universe of past and possible experiences.'

—and this is not the only time the Captain's words can be applied in the course of the play. Nor is it fantastic to suppose that in the account of Macdonwald Shakespeare consciously provided a parallel with the Macbeth of the later acts when 'The multiplying Villanies of Nature swarme upon him'. After all, everybody has noticed the later parallel between Macbeth and Cawdor ('He was a Gentleman, on whom I built an absolute Trust').

A poem works by calling into play, directing and integrating certain interests. If we really accept the suggestion, which then becomes revolutionary, that *Macbeth* is a poem, it is clear that the impulses aroused in Act I, scenes i and ii, are part of the whole response, even if they are not all immediately relevant to the fortunes of the protagonist. If these scenes are 'the botching work of an interpolator', he botched to pretty good effect.

In Act I, scene iii, confusion is succeeded by uncertainty. The Witches

> looke not like th' Inhabitants o' th' Earth,
> And yet are on't.

Banquo asks Macbeth,

> Why doe you start, and seeme to feare
> Things that doe sound so faire?

He addresses the Witches,

> You should be women,
> And yet your Beards forbid me to interprete
> That you are so. . . .
>   . . . i' th' name of truth
> Are yet fantasticall, or that indeed
> Which outwardly ye shew?

When they vanish, 'what seem'd corporall' melts 'as breath into the Winde'. The whole force of the uncertainty of the scene is gathered into Macbeth's soliloquy,

> This supernaturall solliciting
> Cannot be ill; cannot be good . . .

which with its sickening see-saw rhythm completes the impression

of 'a phantasma, or a hideous dream'.[1] Macbeth's echoing of the
Witches' 'Faire is foule' has often been commented upon.

In contrast to the preceding scenes, Act I, scene iv suggests the
natural order which is shortly to be violated. It stresses: natural
relationships—'children', 'servants', 'sons' and 'kinsmen'; hon-
ourable bonds and the political order—'liege', 'thanes', 'service',
'duty', 'loyalty', 'throne', 'state' and 'honour'; and the human
'love' is linked to the natural order of organic growth by images
of husbandry. Duncan says to Macbeth,

> I have begun to plant thee, and will labour
> To make thee full of growing.

When he holds Banquo to his heart Banquo replies,

> There if I grow,
> The Harvest is your owne.

Duncan's last speech is worth particular notice,

> . . . in his commendations, I am fed:
> It is a Banquet to me.

At this point something should be said of what is meant by
'the natural order'. In *Macbeth* this comprehends both 'wild
nature'—birds, beasts and reptiles—and humankind since 'humane statute purg'd the gentle Weale'. The specifically human
aspect is related to the concept of propriety and degree,—

> communities,
> Degrees in Schooles and Brother-hoods in Cities,
> Peacefull Commerce from dividable shores,
> The primogenitive, and due of byrth,
> Prerogative of Age, Crownes, Scepters, Lawrels.

In short, it represents society in harmony with nature, bound by
love and friendship, and ordered by law and duty. It is one of

---

[1] The parallel with *Julius Caesar*, Act II, scene i, 63–69, is worth notice :
> Between the acting of a dreadfull thing,
> And the first motion, all the Interim is
> Like a Phantasma, or a hideous Dreame . . .
Macbeth speaks of ' the Interim ', and his ' single state of Man ' echoes Brutus'
> The state of man,
> Like to a little Kingdome, suffers then
> The nature of an Insurrection.
The rhythm of Macbeth's speech is repeated in Lady Macbeth's
> What thou would'st highly,
> That would'st thou holily, etc.

the main axes of reference by which we take our emotional bearings in the play.

In the light of this the scene of Duncan's entry into the castle gains in significance. The critics have often remarked on the irony. What is not so frequently observed is that the key words of the scene are 'loved', 'wooingly', 'bed', 'procreant Cradle', 'breed, and haunt', all images of love and procreation, super-naturally sanctioned, for the associations of 'temple-haunting' colour the whole of the speeches of Banquo and Duncan.[1] We do violence to the play when we ignore Shakespeare's insistence on what may be called the 'holy supernatural' as opposed to the 'supernaturall solliciting' of the Witches. I shall return to this point. Meanwhile it is pertinent to remember that Duncan him-self is 'The Lords anoynted Temple' (Act II, scene iii, 70).[2]

The murder is explicitly presented as unnatural. After the greeting of Ross and Angus, Macbeth's heart knocks at his ribs 'against the use of Nature'. Lady Macbeth fears his 'humane kindnesse'; she wishes herself 'unsexed', that she may be troubled by 'no compunctious visitings of Nature', and invokes the 'murth'ring Ministers' who 'wait on Natures Mischiefe'. The murder is committed when

> Nature seemes dead, and wicked Dreames abuse
> The Curtain'd sleepe,

and it is accompanied by portents 'unnaturall, even like the deed that's done'. The sun remains obscured, and Duncan's horses 'Turn'd wilde in nature'. Besides these explicit references to the unnatural we notice the violence of the imagery—

> I have given Sucke, and know
> How tender 'tis to love the Babe that milkes me,
> I would, while it was smyling in my Face,
> Have pluckt my Nipple from his Bonelesse Gummes,
> And dasht the Braines out. . . .

Not only are the feelings presented unnatural in this sense, they are also strange—peculiar compounds which cannot be classified

---

[1] See F. R. Leavis, *How to Teach Reading* (now reprinted as an appendix to *Education and the University*), for a more detailed analysis of these lines.
[2] Later, Macduff says to Malcolm :
> Thy Royall Father
> Was a most Sainted King.
> (Act IV, scene iii, 108.)

by any of the usual labels—'fear', 'disgust', etc. Macbeth's words towards the end of Act II, scene i serve to illustrate this:

> Thou sowre [sure] and firme-set Earth
> Heare not my steps, which way they walke, for feare
> Thy very stones prate of my where-about,
> And take the present horror from the time,
> Which now sutes with it.

The first three lines imply a recognition of the enormity of the crime; Macbeth asks that the earth ('sure and firme-set' contrasted with the disembodied 'Murder' which 'moves like a Ghost') shall not hear his steps, for if it does so the very stones will speak and betray him—thereby breaking the silence and so lessening the horror. 'Take' combines two constructions. On the one hand, 'for fear they take the present horror from the time' expresses attraction, identification with the appropriate setting of his crime. But 'take' is also an imperative, expressing anguish and repulsion. 'Which now sutes with it' implies an acceptance of the horror, willing or reluctant according to the two meanings of the previous line. The unusual sliding construction (unusual in ordinary verse, there are other examples in Shakespeare, and in Donne) expresses the unusual emotion which is only crudely analysed if we call it a mixture of repulsion and attraction fusing into 'horror'.

'Confusion now hath made his Master-peece', and in the lull that follows the discovery of the murder, Ross and an Old Man, as chorus, echo the theme of unnatural disorder. The scene (and the Act) ends with a 'sentence' by the Old Man:

> Gods benyson go with you, and with those
> That would make good of bad, and Friends of Foes.

This, deliberately pronounced, has an odd ambiguous effect. The immediate reference is to Ross, who intends to make the best of a dubious business by accepting Macbeth as king. But Macduff also is destined to 'make good of bad' by destroying the evil. And an overtone of meaning takes our thoughts to Macbeth, whose attempt to make good of bad by restoring the natural order is the theme of the next movement; the tragedy lies in his inevitable failure.

A key is found in Macbeth's words spoken to the men hired to murder Banquo (Act III, scene i, 91–100). When Dr. Bradley is discussing the possibility that *Macbeth* has been abridged he remarks ('very aptly' according to the Arden editor), 'surely, anyone who wanted to cut the play down would have operated, say, on Macbeth's talk with Banquo's murderers, or on Act III, scene vi, or on the very long dialogue of Malcolm and Macduff, instead of reducing the most exciting part of the drama'.[1] No, the speech to the murderers is not very 'exciting'—but its function should be obvious to anyone who is not blinded by Dr. Bradley's preconceptions about 'drama'. By accepted canons it is an irrelevance; actually it stands as a symbol of the order that Macbeth wishes to restore. In the catalogue,

> Hounds, and Greyhounds, Mungrels, Spaniels, Curres,
> Showghes, Water-Rugs, and Demy-Wolves

are merely 'dogs', but Macbeth names each one individually; and

> the valued file
> Distinguishes the swift, the slow, the subtle,
> The House-keeper, the Hunter, every one
> According to the gift, which bounteous Nature
> Hath in him clos'd.

It is an image of order, each one in his degree. At the beginning of the scene, we remember, Macbeth had arranged 'a feast', 'a solemn supper', at which 'society' should be 'welcome'. And when alone he suggests the ancient harmonies by rejecting in idea the symbols of their contraries—'a fruitlesse Crowne', 'a barren Scepter', and an 'unlineall' succession. But this new 'health' is 'sickly' whilst Banquo lives, and can only be made 'perfect' by his death. In an attempt to re-create an order based on murder, disorder makes fresh inroads. This is made explicit in the next scene (Act III, scene ii). Here the snake, usually represented as the most venomous of creatures, stands for the natural order

---

[1] *Shakespearean Tragedy*, p. 469. *Macbeth*, Arden Edition, pp. xxi–xxii. I discuss the importance of Act III, scene vi, and of the Malcolm-Macduff dialogue later, pp. 296–300.

which Macbeth has 'scotched' but which will 'close, and be her selfe'.[1]

At this point in the play there is a characteristic confusion. At the end of Act III, scene ii, Macbeth says, 'Things bad begun, make strong themselves by ill', that is, all that he can do is to ensure his physical security by a second crime, although earlier (Act III, scene i, 106–107) he had aimed at complete 'health' by the death of Banquo and Fleance, and later he says that the murder of Fleance would have made him

> perfect,
> Whole as the Marble, founded as the Rocke.
> (Act III, scene iv, 21–22).

The truth is only gradually disentangled from this illusion.

The situation is magnificently presented in the banquet scene. Here speech, action and symbolism combine. The stage direction 'Banquet prepar'd' is the first pointer. In Shakespeare, as Mr. Wilson Knight has remarked, banquets are almost invariably symbols of rejoicing, friendship and concord. Significantly, the nobles sit in due order.

Macbeth. You know your owne degrees, sit downe:
At first and last, the hearty welcome.

Lords. Thankes to your Majesty.

Macbeth. Our selfe will mingle with Society,
And play the humble Host:
Our Hostesse keepes her State, but in best time
We will require her welcome.

Lady Macbeth. Pronounce it for me Sir, to all our Friends,
For my heart speakes, they are welcome.

Enter first Murderer.

---

[1] The murder of Banquo, like the murder of Duncan, is presented as a violation of natural continuity and natural order. Macbeth will 'cancell and teare to pieces that great Bond' which keeps him pale. 'Bond' has a more than general significance. The line is clearly associated with Lady Macbeth's 'But in them, Natures Coppie's not eterne', and the full force of the words is only brought out if we remember that when Shakespeare wrote them, copyholders formed numerically the largest land-holding class in England whose appeal was always to immemorial antiquity' and 'times beyond the memory of man'. The Macbeth-Banquo opposition is emphasized when we learn that Banquo's line will 'stretch out to the cracke of Doome' (Act IV, scene i, 117). Macbeth is cut off from the natural sequence, 'He has no children' (Act IV, scene iii, 217), he is a 'Monster' (Act V, scene vii, 54). Macbeth's isolation is fully brought out in the last Act.

There is no need for comment. In a sense the scene marks the climax of the play. One avenue has been explored; 'Society', 'Host', 'Hostess', 'Friends' and 'Welcome' repeat a theme which henceforward is heard only faintly until it is taken up in the final orchestration, when it appears as 'Honor, Love, Obedience, Troopes of Friends'. With the disappearance of the ghost, Macbeth may be 'a man againe', but he has, irretrievably,

> displac'd the mirth,
> Broke the good meeting, with most admir'd disorder.

The end of the scene is in direct contrast to its beginning.

> Stand not upon the order of your going,
> But go at once

echoes ironically, 'You know your owne degrees, sit downe'.

Before we attempt to disentangle the varied threads of the last Act, two more scenes call for particular comment. The first is the scene in Macduff's castle. Almost without exception the critics have stressed the pathos of young Macduff, his 'innocent prattle', his likeness to Arthur, and so on—reactions appropriate to the work of Sir James Barrie which obscure the complex dramatic function of the scene.[1] In the first place, it echoes in different keys the theme of the false appearance, of doubt and confusion. At its opening we are perplexed with questions:—Is Macduff a traitor? If so, to whom, to Macbeth or to his wife? Was his flight due to wisdom or to fear? Ross says,

> But cruell are the times, when we are Traitors
> And do not know our selves: when we hold Rumor
> From what we feare, yet know not what we feare.

Lady Macduff says of her son,

> Father'd he is,
> And yet hee's Father-lesse.[2]

She teases him with riddles, and he replies with questions.

---

[1] Dr. Bradley says of this and the following scene : 'They have a technical value in helping to give the last stage of the action the form of a conflict between Macbeth and Macduff. But their chief function is of another kind. It is to touch the heart with a sense of beauty and pathos, to open the springs of love and of tears.'—*Shakespearean Tragedy*, p. 391, see also p. 394.

[2] Compare the equivocation about Macduff's birth.

Secondly, the scene shows the spreading evil. As Fletcher has pointed out, Macduff and his wife are 'representatives of the interests of loyalty and domestic affection'.[1] There is much more in the death of young Macduff than 'pathos'; the violation of the natural order is completed by the murder. But there is even more than this. That the tide is about to turn against Macbeth is suggested both by the rhythm and imagery of Ross's speech:

> But cruell are the times, when we are Traitors
> And do not know our selves: when we hold Rumor
> From what we feare, yet know not what we feare,
> But floate upon a wilde and violent Sea
> Each way, and move——— [2]

The comma after 'way', the complete break after 'move', give the rhythm of a tide, pausing at the turn. And when Lady Macduff answers the Murderer's question, 'Where is your husband?'

> I hope in no place so unsanctified,
> Where such as thou may'st find him

we recall the associations set up in Act III, scene vi, a scene of choric commentary upon Macduff's flight to England, to the 'Pious Edward', 'the Holy King'.

Although the play moves swiftly, it does not move with a simple directness. Its complex subtleties include cross-currents, the ebb and flow of opposed thoughts and emotions. The scene in Macduff's castle, made up of doubts, riddles, paradoxes and uncertainties, ends with an affirmation, 'Thou ly'st thou shagge-ear'd Villaine'. But this is immediately followed, not by the downfall of Macbeth, but by a long scene which takes up once more the theme of mistrust, disorder and evil.

The conversation between Macduff and Malcolm has never been adequately explained. We have already seen Dr. Bradley's opinion of it. The Clarendon editors say, 'The poet no doubt

---

[1] Quoted by Furness, p. 218. The whole passage from Fletcher is worth attention.

[2] The substitution of a dash for the full stop after 'move' is the only alteration that seems necessary in the Folio text. The other emendations of various editors ruin both the rhythm and the idiom. Ross is in a hurry and breaks off; he begins the next line, 'Shall not be long', omitting 'I' or 'it'—which some editors needlessly restore. In the Folio a colon is used to indicate the breaking off of a sentence in Act V, scene iii, 20.

felt this scene was needed to supplement the meagre parts assigned to Malcolm and Macduff'. If this were all, it might be omitted. Actually the Malcolm-Macduff dialogue has at least three functions. Obviously Macduff's audience with Malcolm and the final determination to invade Scotland help on the story, but this is of subordinate importance. It is clear also that Malcolm's suspicion and the long testing of Macduff emphasize the mistrust that has spread from the central evil of the play.[1] But the main purpose of the scene is obscured unless we realize its function as choric commentary. In alternating speeches the evil that Macbeth has caused is explicitly stated, without extenuation. And it is stated impersonally.

> Each new Morne,
> New Widdowes howle, new Orphans cry, new sorowes
> Strike heaven on the face, that it resounds
> As if it felt with Scotland, and yell'd out
> Like Syllable of Dolour.

> Our Country sinkes beneath the yoake,
> It weepes, it bleeds, and each new day a gash
> Is added to her wounds.

> Not in the Legions
> Of horrid Hell, can come a Divell more damn'd
> In evils, to top *Macbeth*

> I grant him Bloody,
> Luxurious, Avaricious, False, Deceitfull,
> Sodaine, Malicious, smacking of every sinne
> That has a name.

With this approach we see the relevance of Malcolm's self-accusation. He has ceased to be a person. His lines repeat and magnify the evils that have already been attributed to Macbeth, acting as a mirror wherein the ills of Scotland are reflected. And the statement of evil is strengthened by contrast with the opposite virtues, 'As Justice, Verity, Temp'rance, Stablenesse'.

There is no other way in which the scene can be read. And if

---

[1] As an example of the slight strands that are gathered into the pattern of the play consider the function of the third Murderer in Act III, scene iii. It seems that Macbeth has sent him 'to make security doubly sure'. Only after some doubt do the first two decide that the third 'needs not our mistrust'.

dramatic fitness is not sufficient warrant for this approach, we can refer to the pointers that Shakespeare has provided. Macbeth is 'luxurious' and 'avaricious', and the first sins mentioned by Malcolm in an expanded statement are lust and avarice. When he declares,

> Nay, had I powre, I should
> Poure the sweet Milke of Concord, into Hell,
> Uprore the universall peace, confound
> All unity on earth,

we remember that this is what Macbeth has done.[1] Indeed Macduff is made to answer,

> These Evils thou repeat'st upon thy selfe,
> Hath banish'd me from Scotland.[2]

Up to this point at least the impersonal function of the speaker is predominant. And even when Malcolm, once more a person in a play, announces his innocence, it is impossible not to hear the impersonal overtone:

> For even now
> I put my selfe to thy Direction, and
> Unspeake mine owne detraction. Heere abjure
> The taints, and blames I laide upon my selfe,
> For strangers to my Nature.

He speaks for Scotland, and for the forces of order. The 'scotch'd Snake' will 'close, and be herselfe'.

There are only two alternatives; either Shakespeare was a bad dramatist, or his critics have been badly misled by mistaking the *dramatis personae* for real persons in this scene. Unless of course the ubiquitous Interpolator has been at work upon it.

I have called *Macbeth* a statement of evil; but it is a statement not of a philosophy but of ordered emotion. This ordering is of course a continuous process (hence the importance of the scrupu-

---

[1] For a more specific reference see Act IV, scene i, 50–61,—

> Though the treasure
> Of Natures Germaine tumble altogether,
> Even till destruction sicken . . .

[2] 'Hath' is third person plural. See Abbott, *Shakespearian Grammar*, § 334. I admit the lines are ambiguous but they certainly bear the interpretation I have given them. Indeed most editors print, 'upon thyself Have banished . . .'

lous analysis of each line), it is not merely something that happens in the last Act corresponding to the dénouement or unravelling of the plot. All the same, the interests aroused are heightened in the last Act before they are finally 'placed', and we are given a vantage point from which the whole course of the drama may be surveyed in retrospect. There is no formula that will describe this final effect. It is no use saying that we are 'quietened', 'purged' or 'exalted' at the end of *Macbeth* or of any other tragedy. It is no use taking one step nearer the play and saying we are purged, etc., because we see the downfall of a wicked man or because we realize the justice of Macbeth's doom whilst retaining enough sympathy for him or admiration of his potential qualities to be filled with a sense of 'waste'. It is no use discussing the effect in abstract terms at all; we can only discuss it in terms of the poet's concrete realization of certain emotions and attitudes.

At this point it is necessary to return to what I have already said (p. 22) about the importance of images of grace and of the holy supernatural in the play. For the last hundred years or so the critics have not only sentimentalized Macbeth—ignoring the completeness with which Shakespeare shows his final identification with evil—but they have slurred the passages in which the positive good is presented by means of religious symbols. In Act III the banquet scene is immediately [1] followed by a scene in which Lennox and another Lord (both completely impersonal) discuss the situation; the last half of their dialogue is of particular importance. The verse has none of the power of, say, Macbeth's soliloquies, but it would be a mistake to call it undistinguished; it is serenely harmonious, and its tranquillity contrasts with the turbulence of the scenes that immediately precede it and follow it, as its images of grace contrast with their 'toile and trouble'. Macduff has fled to 'the Pious Edward', 'the Holy King', who has received Malcolm 'with such grace'. Lennox prays for the aid of 'some holy Angell',

> that a swift blessing
> May soone returne to this our suffering Country,
> Under a hand accurs'd.

[1] If we omit Act III, scene v where for once the editors' 'spurious' may be allowed to stand. I thought at first that Shakespeare intended to portray the Witches at this point as rather shoddy creatures, thereby intensifying the general

And the 'other Lord' answers, 'Ile send my Prayers with him'. Many of the phrases are general and abstract—'grace', 'the male-volence of Fortune', 'his high respect'—but one passage has an individual particularity that gives it prominence:

> That by the helpe of these (with him above
> To ratifie the Worke) we may againe
> Give to our Tables meate, sleepe to our Nights:
> Free from our Feasts, and Banquets bloody knives;
> Do faithful Homage, and receive free Honors,
> All which we pine for now.

Food and sleep, society and the political order are here, as before, represented as supernaturally sanctioned. I have suggested that this passage is recalled for a moment in Lady Macduff's answer to the Murderer (Act IV, scene ii, 80), and it is certainly this theme which is taken up when the Doctor enters after the Malcolm-Macduff dialogue in Act IV, scene iii; the reference to the King's Evil may be a compliment to King James, but it is not merely that. We have only to remember that the unseen Edward stands for the powers that are to prove 'the Med'cine of the sickly Weale' of Scotland to see the double meaning in

> there are a crew of wretched Soules
> That stay his Cure. . . .

Their disease 'is called the Evill'. The 'myraculous worke', the 'holy Prayers', 'the healing Benediction', Edward's 'vertue', the 'sundry Blessings . . . that speake him full of Grace' are reminders not only of the evil against which Malcolm is seeking support, but of the positive qualities against which the evil and disorder must be measured. Scattered notes ('Gracious England', 'Chris-tendome', 'heaven', 'gentle Heavens') remind us of the theme until the end of the scene, when we know that Macbeth (the 'Hell-Kite', 'this Fiend of Scotland')

> Is ripe for shaking, and the Powers above
> Put on their Instruments.

irony. Certainly the rhythm of Hecate's speech is banal—but so is the obvious rhythm of *Sweeney Agonistes*, and it does provide a contrast with the harmony of the verse in the next scene. Certainly also Shakespeare did not intend to portray the Witches as in any way 'dignified' ('Dignified, impressive, sexless beings, ministers of fate and the supernatural powers . . . existing in the elemental poetry of wind and storm'—*Macbeth*, Arden Edition, p. xlii). But the verse is too crude to serve even this purpose.

The words quoted are not mere formalities; they have a positive function, and help to determine the way in which we shall respond to the final scenes.

The description of the King's Evil (Act IV, scene iii, 141–159) has a particular relevance; it is directly connected with the disease metaphors of the last Act; [1] and these are strengthened by combining within themselves the ideas of disorder and of the unnatural which run throughout the play. Lady Macbeth's sleepwalking is a 'slumbry agitation', and 'a great perturbation in Nature'. Some say Macbeth is 'mad'. We hear of his 'distemper'd cause', and of his 'pester'd senses' which

> recoyle and start,
> When all that is within him, do's condemne
> It selfe, for being there.

In the play general impressions are pointed by reference to the individual and particular (cf. Act IV, scene iii, where 'the general cause' is given precision by the 'Fee-griefe due to some single breast'); whilst at the same time particular impressions are reflected and magnified. Not only Macbeth and his wife but the whole land is sick. Caithness says,

> Meet we the Med'cine of the sickly Weale,
> And with him poure we in our Countries purge,
> Each drop of us.

And Lennox replies,

> Or so much as it needes,
> To dew the Soveraigne Flower, and drowne the Weeds
> (Act V, scene ii, 27–30).

—an admirable example, by the way, of the kind of fusion already referred to, since we have not only the weed-flower opposition, but a continuation of the medical metaphor in 'Soveraigne', which means both 'royal' and 'powerfully

---

[1] The original audience would be helped to make the connexion if, as is likely, the Doctor of Act IV, scene iii, and the Doctor of Act V were played by the same actor, probably without any change of dress. We are not meant to think of two Doctors in the play (Dr. A of Harley Street and Dr. B of Edinburgh) but simply, in each case, of ' a Doctor '.

remedial'.[1] And the images of health and disease are clearly related to moral good and evil. The Doctor says of Lady Macbeth,

> More needs she the Divine, than the Physitian:
> God, God forgive us all.

Macbeth asks him,

> Can'st thou not Minister to a minde diseas'd,
> Plucke from the Memory a rooted Sorrow,
> Raze out the written troubles of the Braine,
> And with some sweet Oblivious Antidote
> Cleanse the stufft bosome, of that perillous stuffe
> Which weighes upon the heart?

There is terrible irony in his reply to the Doctor's 'Therein the Patient must minister to himselfe': 'Throw Physicke to the Dogs, Ile none of it.'

We have already noticed the association of the ideas of disease and of the unnatural in these final scenes—

> unnatural deeds
> Do breed unnatural troubles,

and there is propriety in Macbeth's highly charged metaphor,

> My way of life
> Is falne into the Seare, the yellow Leafe.

But the unnatural has now another part to play, in the peculiar 'reversal' that takes place at the end of *Macbeth*. Hitherto the agent of the unnatural has been Macbeth. Now it is Malcolm who commands Birnam Wood to move, it is 'the good Macduff' who reveals his unnatural birth, and the opponents of Macbeth whose

---

[1] Macbeth himself says :

> If thou could'st Doctor, cast
> The Water of my Land, finde her Disease,
> And purge it to a sound and pristine Health,
> I would applaud thee to the very Eccho.

And he continues :

> What Rubarb, Senna, or what Purgative drugge
> Would scowre these English hence ?
> (Act V, scene iii, 50–56.)

The characteristic reversal (the English forces being represented as an impurity which has to be ' scoured ') need not surprise us since Macbeth is the speaker.

'deere causes' would 'excite the mortified man' Hitherto Macbeth has been the deceiver, 'mocking the time with fairest show'; now Malcolm orders,

> Let every Souldier hew him downe a Bough,
> And bear't before him, thereby shall we shadow
> The numbers of our Hoast, and make discovery
> Erre in report of us.

Our first reaction is to make some such remark as 'Nature becomes unnatural in order to rid itself of Macbeth'. But this is clearly inadequate; we have to translate it and define our impressions in terms of our response to the play at this point. By associating with the opponents of evil the ideas of deceit and of the unnatural, previously associated solely with Macbeth and the embodiments of evil, Shakespeare emphasizes the disorder and at the same time frees our minds from the burden of the horror. After all, the movement of Birnam Wood and Macduff's unnatural birth have a simple enough explanation.

There is a parallel here with the disorder of the last Act. It begins with Lady Macbeth sleep-walking—a 'slumbry agitation' —and the remaining scenes are concerned with marches, stratagems, fighting, suicide, and death in battle. If we merely read the play we are liable to overlook the importance of the sights and sounds which are obvious on the stage. The frequent stage directions should be observed—*Drum and Colours, Enter Malcolm . . . and Soldiers Marching, A Cry within of Women*—and there are continuous directions for *Alarums, Flourishes*, and fighting. Macduff orders,

> Make all our Trumpets speak, give them all breath,
> Those clamorous Harbingers of Blood, and Death,

and he traces Macbeth by the noise of fighting:

> That way the noise is: Tyrant shew thy face.
>   . . . There thou should'st be,
> By this great clatter, one of greatest note
> Seemes bruited.

There are other suggestions of disorder throughout the Act. Macbeth

> cannot buckle his distemper'd cause
> Within the belt of Rule.

He orders, 'Come, put mine Armour on', and almost in the same breath, 'Pull't off I say'. His 'Royal Preparation' is a noisy confusion. He wishes 'th' estate o' th' world were now undon', though the tone is changed now since he bade the Witches answer him,

> Though bladed Corne be lodg'd and Trees blown downe,
> Though Castles topple on their Warders heads:
> Though Pallaces, and Pyramids do slope
> Their heads to their Foundations.

But all this disorder has now a positive tendency, towards the good which Macbeth had attempted to destroy, and which he names as 'Honor, Love, Obedience, Troopes of Friends'. At the beginning of the battle Malcolm says,

> Cosins, I hope the dayes are neere at hand
> That Chambers will be safe,

and Menteith answers, 'We doubt it nothing'. Siward takes up the theme of certainty as opposed to doubt:

> Thoughts speculative, their unsure hopes relate,
> But certaine issue, stroakes must arbitrate,
> Towards which, advance the warre.

And doubt and illusion are finally dispelled:

> Now neere enough:
> Your leavy Skreenes throw downe,
> And shew like those you are.

By now there should be no danger of our misinterpreting the greatest of Macbeth's final speeches.

> To morrow, and to morrow, and to morrow,
> Creepes in this petty pace from day to day,
> To the last syllable of Recorded time.
> And all our yesterdays, have lighted Fooles
> The way to dusty death. Out, out, breefe Candle.
> Life's but a walking Shadow, a poore Player,
> That struts and frets his houre upon the Stage,
> And then is heard no more. It is a Tale
> Told by an Ideot, full of sound and fury
> Signifying nothing.

The theme of the false appearance is revived—with a difference.
It is not only that Macbeth sees life as deceitful, but the poetry is
so fine that we are almost bullied into accepting an essential
ambiguity in the final statement of the play, as though Shakespeare
were expressing his own 'philosophy' in the lines. But the lines
are 'placed' by the tendency of the last Act (order emerging
from disorder, truth emerging from behind deceit), culminating
in the recognition of the Witches' equivocation ('And be these
Jugling Fiends no more believ'd . . .'), the death of Macbeth, and
the last words of Siward, Macduff and Malcolm (Act V, scene vii,
64–105).

This tendency has behind it the whole weight of the positive
values which Shakespeare has already established, and which are
evoked in Macbeth's speech—

> My way of life
> Is falne into the Seare, the yellow Leafe,
> And that which should accompany Old-Age,
> As Honor, Love, Obedience, Troopes of Friends,
> I must not looke to have: but in their stead,
> Curses, not lowd but deepe, Mouth-honor, breath
> Which the poore heart would faine deny, and dare not.

Dr. Bradley claims, on the strength of this and the 'To-morrow,
and to-morrow' speech, that Macbeth's 'ruin is never complete.
To the end he never totally loses our sympathy. . . . In the very
depths a gleam of his native love of goodness, and with it a tinge
of tragic grandeur, rests upon him.' But to concentrate attention
thus on the *personal* implications of these lines is to obscure the
fact that they have an even more important function as the keystone of the system of values that gives emotional coherence to
the play. Certainly those values are likely to remain obscured if
we concentrate our attention upon 'the two great terrible figures,
who dwarf all the remaining characters of the drama', if we ignore
the 'unexciting' or 'undramatic' scenes, or if conventional
'sympathy for the hero' is allowed to distort the pattern of the
whole.

I must repeat that I have no illusions about the adequacy of
these remarks as criticism; they are merely pointers. But if we

follow them our criticism at least will not be deflected, by too great a stress upon 'personality', into inquiries into 'latent motives and policies not avowed', or into pseudo-critical investigations that are only slightly parodied by the title of this essay.

NOTE

William Richardson illustrates so well the main tendencies of later eighteenth-century criticism that a few quotations seem permissible. (The page references are to the fifth edition, 1797, of the *Essays on Some of Shakespeare's Dramatic Characters* which in corporated his Essays 'On Shakespeare's Imitation of Female Characters' and 'On the Faults of Shakespeare'):

'"The operations of the mind", as has been well observed by an anonymous writer . . . "are more complex than those of the body: its motions are progressive: its transitions abrupt and instantaneous: its attitude uncertain and momentary. . . . It would therefore be of great importance to philosophical scrutiny, if the position of the mind, in any given circumstances, could be fixed till it was deliberately surveyed: if the causes which alter its feelings and operations could be accurately shewn, and their effects ascertained with precision." To accomplish these ends, the dramatic writers, and particularly Shakespeare, may be of the greatest use. An attempt has accordingly been made . . . to employ the light which he affords us in illustrating some curious and interesting views of human nature.

'In Macbeth, misled by an overgrown and gradually perverted passion, "we trace the progress of that corruption, by which the virtues of the mind are made to contribute to the completion of its depravity" [He is quoting Burke]. In Hamlet we have a striking representation of the pain, of the dejection, and contention of spirit, produced in a person, not only of exquisite, but of moral, and correct sensibility, by the conviction of extreme enormity of conduct in those whom he loves, or wishes to love. . . . King Lear illustrates, that mere sensibility, uninfluenced by a sense of propriety, leads men to an extravagant expression both of social and unsocial feelings', and so on (pp. 395–397).

'In the faithful display of character, he has not hitherto been surpassed. . . . If we consider the sentiments and actions, attributed by the poet to his various characters, as so many facts; if we observe their agreement or disagreement, their aim or their origin; and if we class them according to their common qualities . . . we shall ascertain with some accuracy, the truth of the representation. . . . Thus the moralist becomes a critic: and the two sciences of ethics and criticism appear to be intimately and very naturally connected' (pp. 398–399).

The essay on the Character of Macbeth ends: 'Thus, by considering the rise and progress of a ruling passion, and the fatal consequences of its indulgence, we have shown how a beneficent mind may become inhuman: and how those who are naturally of an amiable temper, if they suffer themselves to be corrupted, will become more ferocious and more unhappy than men of a constitution originally hard and unfeeling. The formation of our characters depends considerably upon ourselves; for we may improve or vitiate every principle we receive from nature' (p. 68). Shakespeare indeed 'furnishes excellent illustrations of many passions and affections, and of many singular combinations of passion, affection and ability' (p. 397).

Mrs. Montagu places character delineation among 'the chief purposes of theatrical representation' (*An Essay on the Writings and Genius of Shakespeare*, fifth edition, 1785, pp. 19–20), and speaks of Shakespeare's 'invariable attention to consistency of character'.

On 'The Appreciation of Characters' and 'The Psychologizing of Shakespeare' in the later eighteenth century, see Chapters XI and XII of R. W. Babcock's *The Genesis of Shakespeare Idolatry, 1766–1799*, from which I extract some further illuminating quotations:

'We always behold the portrait of living nature [in Shakespeare] and find ourselves surrounded with our fellows'—*The Lady's Magazine*, 1784.

'Shakespeare's characters have that appearance of reality which always has the effect of actual life.'—William Jackson, *Thirty Letters*, 1782.

'. . . the historical dramas of Shakespeare. The wonder-working power of the poet's pen is there most eminently displayed. . . . His characters . . . are such genuine copies from life, that we must suppose the originals acted and spoke in the manner he represents them.'—Richard Hole ['T.O.'] in the Exeter Society *Essays*, 1796.

Shakespeare's characters 'are masterly copies from nature; differing each from the other, and animated as the originals though correct to a scrupulous precision'.—T. Whately, *Remarks on Some of the Characters of Shakespeare*, 1785.

I should like to acknowledge my indebtedness to Mr. Babcock's extremely thorough piece of research.